# THE ABRAMELIN DIARIES

# THE ABRAMELIN DIARIES

*Ramsey Dukes*

**AEON**

First published in 2019 by
Aeon Books Ltd
12 New College Parade
Finchley Road
London NW3 5EP

Copyright © 2019 by Ramsey Dukes

The right of Ramsey Dukes to be identified as the author of this work has been asserted in accordance with §§ 77 and 78 of the Copyright Design and Patents Act 1988.

All rights reserved. No part of this publication may be reproduced, stored in a retrieval system, or transmitted, in any form or by any means, electronic, mechanical, photocopying, recording, or otherwise, without the prior written permission of the publisher.

British Library Cataloguing in Publication Data

A C.I.P. for this book is available from the British Library

ISBN-13: 978-1-91159-719-3

Typeset by Medlar Publishing Solutions Pvt Ltd, India

www.aeonbooks.co.uk

*CONTENTS*

INTRODUCTION                                                                      vii

*CHAPTER ONE*
What is the Abramelin operation?                                          1

*CHAPTER TWO*
Background—why I attempted the Abramelin operation        7

*CHAPTER THREE*
What we should consider before undertaking this operation   9

*CHAPTER FOUR*
Notes towards a better understanding of my diary               17

*PHASE ONE*
The first two moons                                                               25

*PHASE TWO*
The second two moons                                                          73

*PHASE THREE*
Final two moons                                          111

*PHASE FOUR*
Consecration                                             169

*PHASE FIVE*
Culmination                                              173

*POSTSCRIPT ONE*
Introduction                                             189

*POSTSCRIPT TWO*
What happened after Abramelin                            193

*POSTSCRIPT THREE*
Is it now worth it?                                      211

*INTRODUCTION*

Why would anyone want to read—or even publish—the diary of a not very successful magical retirement by a relatively unknown occultist?

When I told David Evans[1] in the 1990s that I still possessed the hand-written magical diary of my 1977 Abramelin operation, he said that I must publish it. I asked him why. He replied that it was "history". (I pictured a gun to my head while a Schwarzenegger-like character snarls: "You're history!"). Both as someone who did magic, and as an academic engaged in the study of magic, he eventually convinced me that my diary might be worth publishing someday. He was also a good friend and I miss him.

Years later I was preparing *The Little Book of Demons* for Oliver Rathbone of Aeon Books, and we discussed the Abramelin project. So he arranged to have my hand-written diary transcribed in 2005, with a view to possible publication at some later date.

---

[1]The late David Evans later co-founded JSM—*The Journal for the Academic Study of Magic*—and his books included *The History of British Magic After Crowley*, published in 2007.

Ten years later I was persuaded to create a Ramsey Dukes YouTube channel to publish some videos of me discussing magical ideas. I have since been astonished to see the number of people who first discover these videos while searching the internet for "Abramelin". There is clearly a growing interest in the operation—maybe stimulated by the movie *A Dark Song*[2] in which the main protagonist undertakes a retirement with reference to Abramelin. So I contacted Aeon Books and suggested they send me the transcript so I could edit it and add some material to make a publishable book.

That is why it is being published. But why would anyone want to read this particular diary?

For a start, there are still very few people who have completed and written up the Abramelin retirement—even in the shorter, six-month format published by S.L. MacGregor Mathers. Compared with many more exotic, ancient grimoires, the Abramelin looks relatively simple and straightforward and yet, as I was to discover, a simple regular practice is very hard to maintain in today's world. The fact that even Aleister Crowley failed to complete it on his first attempt has added a lot to the book's mystique, and the operation it describes has acquired a formidable reputation.

When I was preparing for it in 1977, I came across only one published Abramelin diary: *The Sacred Magician* by George Chevalier (pen name of William Bloom), published the year before. With little else to help me (apart from Israel Regardie's chapter in *The Tree of Life*), I read it avidly and, even though the content seemed pretty boring, it did in several ways help me to prepare. I could see that publishing my diary might provide additional help for anyone seriously considering performing the operation themselves. So, in March 2017, I started correcting and editing the transcript.

As the diary is "sacred", I decided to edit as little as possible. I noticed that the 2005 transcriber of the original manuscript had already done a bit of editing to make some sentences flow better and I mostly accepted his changes, rather than go back through the text word by word. My main revision has been to replace people's names to preserve their anonymity, and to add some footnotes where extra explanation could be helpful.

---

[2] A 2016 Irish independent horror film, written and directed by Liam Gavin and starring Steve Oram and Catherine Walker.

I have also added four introductory chapters:

1. *What is the Abramelin operation?* explains the historic background of the operation. It is not the sort of academic study that Dave Evans could have provided, but just a very basic summary of what was known about the operation when I began, plus reference to material more recently discovered.
2. *Background. Why I attempted the operation* outlines my personal background to the operation: how I heard about and why I decided to try it.
3. *Preparing for the operation.* This is the most practical chapter, because it goes into some detail about the problems of performing an ancient ritual in a modern Western environment, and some of the challenges to be addressed.
4. *Notes towards an understanding of my diary* is added to outline some of the personal issues I had to face—like following instructions to pray to a God that I did not believe in, and what sort of meditative practices to choose. This chapter prepares the reader to make better sense of the diary, without my having to fill it with masses of extra explanatory footnotes.

Finally, I have added four *Postscript* chapters to address questions about the later impact of the operation on me and on my life. This does something to answer the inevitable question "was it all worth it?".

# CHAPTER ONE

# What is the Abramelin operation?

## The book as I knew it

*The Book of the Sacred Magic of Abramelin the Mage* is a fifteenth century grimoire, or book of magic, that includes instructions as to how an individual can make contact with their Holy Guardian Angel. It was translated into English by S.L. MacGregor Mathers in 1893 and his edition was published at the beginning of the twentieth century and has been reproduced in several editions since. I had a beautiful 1950s reprint of the original Watkins edition and—to be used as a working copy—a de Laurence 1929 edition that was ex libris *Order of the Cubic Stone*.

In the introduction Mathers explains that the manuscript was in French as part of the private collection of the Marquis of Paulny housed in the Biblioteque de l'Arsenal in Paris. It had been translated into French from the original Hebrew of "Abraham the Jew". Mathers had not found any other copy or replica of the book—not even in the British Museum's extensive occult collection. Ted Bryant (an ex-disciple of Aleister Crowley who helped me prepare for the Abramelin operation) said that was surprising. In his experience it was more usual for several copies of any grimoire manuscript, with variations, to be found in various collections across Europe, so the existence of just one unique copy was suspicious. George Dehn's later research (see below) confirmed Ted's doubts.

This version of the text is presented in three books. The first book is written as an epistle from Abraham the Jew to his son, outlining his story, his magical quest, how he discovered the true magic, and advising him on the one true path. The second book was the most important for my purposes, because it describes the main part of the operation: how to build an oratory, prepare the necessary materials, and conduct oneself for the six months of retirement. It concludes with a detailed description of what to do in the weeks after meeting one's Holy Guardian Angel. The third book is full of magical squares to be used to work wonders.

What the second book describes is a six-month preparatory retirement, beginning at Easter, and running through three phases of two months each. After that preparation, one should experience the knowledge and conversation of one's Holy Guardian Angel and, under its tutelage, one would subsequently be introduced to orders of spirits and would learn how to deal with them and be issued instructions on how to deploy the magical squares from the third book.

My main interest was in that initial six-month preparation. The concept was that no-one should attempt to work with these spirits unless they had first proven themselves by undergoing ritual purification and preparation—in this case for six months. This made sense to me, so I was more interested in this grimoire than others that put greater emphasis on conjuration and less on rigorous preparation (just as one might choose a university that actually required one to study for a degree, rather than simply pay for the certificate!).

I had read Israel Regardie's *Tree of Life*, and he too felt that the really powerful part of the operation was in the spiritual preparation it demanded, and the effect this could have on the candidate. One of the outstanding features of Abramelin is that it is a conjuration that does not require a protective "magic circle". Instead, the long preparation is expected to strengthen and seal the candidate and the oratory against evil.

It was not that I had no interest at all in conjuration, but I did have reservations. Firstly, I would not want to attempt it unless I had already proven my worth and ability to handle such stuff. Secondly, while I could accept the reality of a spiritual initiation over six months, I found it much harder to believe in magic squares that could, for example, make an army appear or enable one to fly through the air looking like an eagle.

So my attitude was that the retirement was something that I needed to do for my own progress; should I then find myself somehow transformed into a great sage or mighty spiritual warrior, I would be in a better position to judge the value of later magical operations and decide accordingly.

You could argue that, at this stage, my approach was more psychological than magical: more Regardie than Crowley.

## The book as it is now understood

In 2006 a totally new English language edition, called *The Book of Abramelin*, was published. It was translated from a German edition compiled by Georg Dehn. This new version was based on research into further copies of the manuscript that had since been discovered in Germany. These revealed that the French version used by Mathers was very incomplete, and the new edition could therefore be accepted as more accurate, and a better guide.

While recognisably similar to the Mathers version, it was different in several important respects. Most important from my point of view was the fact that the German version required eighteen instead of six months of retirement—divided into three phases of six months each, rather than three of two months each. The requirements for each phase were pretty much as in the Mathers version, except three times as long. Eighteen months would make a huge difference, but I was not altogether surprised, because I had felt at the end of my six months that the retirement was still far from complete—see Chapter Three.

Another difference that would have been extremely significant if I had attempted the ensuing spells, was that the magic squares provided in the Mathers version were found to be seriously incomplete. I may have intuited as much at the time, for I had my own doubts about attempting to use those squares.

A further big difference is that the German version has an additional book—making four parts in all. Between the biography and the instructional part was another book of folk-magic spells. This seems a bit odd, because the first book advises one against dabbling in magic, and suggests that nothing should be attempted without a thorough grounding in the true, holy magic as described in book three. Certainly I would not have been interested in this part, so its omission was relatively unimportant for me.

I will not go into any greater detail here, because I am not an historian or archivist. I have nothing to add to the account in *The Book of Abramelin* by Georg Dehn—so I recommend that edition to anyone needing to know more about the background. And I certainly recommend that version for anyone planning to perform the operation, because it is less ambiguous and more clearly written than the Mathers version.

On the other hand, I do value some of the comments added by Mathers in the footnotes. In a few respects—such as the outline of the morning oration—the Mathers version actually provides more detailed instruction than the German one. It may be that the person who copied it was adding their own refinements, as if they had personal experience of doing the operation. In that case the variations from the German original may have their own added value. I suggest that there is more to be gained by studying both versions, rather than simply dismissing the MacGregor version.[1]

### A brief outline of the operation

In this section I outline the main instructions about preparing for the operation, creating the necessary conditions, and how to conduct oneself for the required six or eighteen months.

This is not a detailed or complete description—for that, anyone planning to perform this operation must refer to the original books. Nor do I say much about the final stages after the knowledge and conversation of the Holy Guardian Angel. The purpose of this section is simply to outline my daily routine, in order that the following diary pages will make more sense to the reader.

**The place.** It is necessary to prepare an oratory for the operation. Two versions are described: an open one for deep countryside, and a room for use in town. Basically the space lines up with the cardinal points, has a door to the west, windows to the east and south, an altar in the middle, a lamp on high and, outside the door, a level space

---

[1] As this book goes to the press I have been in correspondence with Georg Dehn. He tells me that my 2006 edition of his book is out of date and that his latest edition has many more footnotes, incorporating Mathers' more useful notes, and other useful material that should make the Mathers edition redundant.

covered with river sand where the spirits will be invoked. My oratory was a self-constructed six by three foot pine shed lined up and fitted as described.

**The time.** The operation starts on the first morning after Easter or Passover, and ends at the Feast of Tabernacles, either six (or eighteen) "moons" later. In my diary I was never quite sure if a "moon" meant a lunar return or a full lunation.

**The clothes.** For most of the time I was simply instructed to dress in a "clean and moderate" manner "according to custom". I used a second-hand but apparently unused judo suit that conveniently turned up that month in a jumble sale—a good garment for sitting and extended kneeling. I also wore Helly Hansen thermal clothing when it got very cold. During the last two months I needed a white linen robe with short sleeves reaching to the knee and "mourning" clothes for the last days of the retirement and, for the following days, when commanding spirits, a red silk robe of similar proportions with a matching headband.

I made the white and red robes myself during the operation—quite a challenge for an inexperienced needleman when the operation demanded that no blood must be shed. I grew used to the specified "shorty" robe, finding it very comfortable and practical. In later years, when another magical order required me to make my own black cotton robe, I decided to stick with the Abramelin pattern. I became known for what they called my "baby doll" outfit, where everyone else looked like hooded monks.

**Other equipment.** A simple wand of almond wood—I decided to at least do this in style and I cut the branch with a single stroke at the equinox sunrise; a brazier and censor for incense; a lamp to hang above the altar; and an altar that was like a cupboard to hold all the other necessary kit. I made, or rather bodged, all these items.

**The first two months** required me to enter the oratory a quarter of an hour before sunrise, kneel before the altar and pray earnestly. This is repeated again after sunset each day. The outline requires one to praise God, confess one's unworthiness and implore him to grant success in this work. There are also recommendations about how to conduct oneself, not eating meat or sleeping during the day and suggestions for reading, etc.

One of the attractions of the Abramelin operation is that it does not insist on a parrot-like repetition of given prayers and incantations; instead, it invites you to speak from the heart and use your own preferred way of praying. This is appealing, but can present problems as you will see in the next chapter.

**The second two months** simply pile on the pressure—pray and study more earnestly and so on. By this time the candidate has a better idea of what they can endure.

**The third two months** require one to pray at noon as well as sunrise and sunset, with the addition of incense and wearing that white linen robe. It is necessary to fast once a week on "Sabbath eve". Again, a further intensification of effort.

**The finale.** The final phase is quite detailed but, as my experience was curtailed, I will not spell it out in full. Read the books for more about this. On the day after completing the six-month preparation there is an initial process of anointing the various implements and items of clothing, praying according to a given outline formula before praying in the normal manner. On the following day you do not wash as normally required before entering the oratory. Instead you dress in shabby mourning clothes and humiliate yourself before fervent prayer.

At this point the services of a young child are specified. In the next chapter I discuss this challenge and how I tried to get around it. With the help of the child's seership, one is then supposed to experience the presence of the angel and the later instructions begin.

## CHAPTER TWO

## Background—why I attempted the Abramelin operation

Like most children I was drawn to magic from an early age. Without any books to guide me I used to look up the word "magic" in big dictionaries or encyclopaedias and learn names for the many different types of magic—such as "black magic", "natural magic", "spirit magic" and so on. Then I discovered that the public library did have a few books on or around the subject, including books on Spiritism, from which I learned that it was mostly fraudulent.

The nearest available thing to an occult journal at that time was the astrology-based magazine *Prediction*, which had book reviews and adverts for weird stuff like dowsing pendulums and aura goggles. When I was about eleven I read its review of Watkins' reprint of *The Book of the Sacred Magic of Abramelin the Mage*. The reviewer suggested that, amongst all the available rubbish and nonsense, this book was the "real thing". So I got my brother to order a copy from the Gloucestershire Public Library and I took it to my prep school in Bristol to study. I was only twelve years old, and the book specified that one had to be older than twenty-five to perform the operation—so I decided I would do it "when I grew up".

Unfortunately growing up does not always lead to the sort of omnipotence that a child imagines that adults possess, so many years passed.

I had also come across many other magical and spiritual systems, including extensive study of the works of Aleister Crowley and Austin Osman Spare. I had even in the mid 1970s self-published my own book about magic—*SSOTBME an essay on Magic*—and sold a few copies in "alternative" bookshops. Some people wrote to me as a result.

In 1976 I was renting and sharing a small cottage with a large garden on the edge of the village green in Redbourn, Hertfordshire, when I received a letter from a woman who wanted to meet me as she had an intriguing matter to discuss. This woman lived nearby in Luton, Bedfordshire, so I arranged to visit her. She had a plan to perform the Abramelin operation and she wanted me to be her guide and advisor—on the strength of my reputation as someone who knew about magic. I confessed that I could not help her. I did not feel qualified because I had not performed the operation myself.

At the time I was unhappily working as a stressman for an ailing British aircraft industry and was pretty unhappy in my career. I wanted to do something better and it occurred to me that, if I did find a better job, I would hardly want to put it aside and spend six months invoking my Holy Guardian Angel. So this might be my last chance to chuck it all in and perform the operation myself.

I re-read the book in detail, we also shared a copy of Chevalier's book, and I gave in my notice. She would perform the operation in her town house in Luton and I would build an oratory in the shrubbery in Redbourn and we would keep in touch and compare notes as we performed the six-month ceremony in parallel.

So that is how I first learned about the magic of Abramelin, and why I decided many years later to perform the operation myself.

CHAPTER THREE

# What we should consider before undertaking this operation

Why does anyone consider performing this operation? The main attraction must be its reputation—both as a source of illumination but also, paradoxically, for the challenge presented by its real or imagined dangers.

Once the candidate has been drawn to it in some way, the second attraction is its relative realism. This grimoire does not make unreasonable demands for blood sacrifices, nor for grim paraphernalia (like the tongue of a hanged man or a stone from the skull of a toad), nor for extreme circumstances such as isolation in a mountain hideout. Instead it appears to accommodate itself to quite realistic urban as well as rural living conditions. These conditions accommodate a measure of religious freedom; one can live with a marriage partner; it even allows for the assistance of servants, and so on. In fact, it is tempting to skim through the book and decide that this operation will be an absolute doddle for anyone with six (or eighteen) months to spare.

Yes, it is relatively reasonable. It might even be undertaken by a complete sceptic who does not believe in religion or the spirit but can simply see the psychological value of acting "as if" and being subject to the discipline of a lengthy spiritual retreat.

However, my experience suggests to me that this operation is an example of "the devil being in the details": that the reputation for the difficulty in completing the operation could be due to people underestimating the real challenge of adapting a fifteenth-century practice to everyday life in the twentieth or twenty-first century.

In this chapter I draw attention to certain problems and decisions that the aspirant should consider carefully before deciding to perform the operation. These are based purely on my own experience, so take them merely as indicators, and then re-read the second book of Abramelin carefully to see how all the conditions might work out in your own reality.

## The vow

I had a surprise when, over thirty years later, I started to edit my Abramelin diary. On Wednesday 13 April 1977 at 9.30am I signed the following vow:

> I vow that, subject to conditions mentioned below, I will endeavour to keep to the Abramelin operation for six months starting on Easter Monday. As stated in the book, severe illness will be recognised as a God-sent hindrance. However, in the case of great danger to my immediate family, who have been such a support, I would also consider suspending the operation. Also, if I am the victim of bureaucratic intervention, and can find no way of delaying or buying time, then I will be forced to step down. In all such cases, or in any unforeseen mishap, I will consider very carefully and calmly and make my decision in the light of advice from the I Ching.
>
> I cannot see how I can obtain and use a child as instructed in the text, so I plan to do without—unless a suitable child conveniently makes himself known to me in time for training for the part.
>
> Signed,
> Lionel Snell

Something that I remembered clearly was not written in that vow: that was my assumption that, should overwhelming difficulties make it impossible to continue, I would understand this to be a message from my Holy Guardian Angel that I should not continue with the operation. Either I had remembered wrongly, or else there was a fuller version of the vow that I had left in my altar, or somewhere.

My point is that, in view of the overall reasonableness of the Abramelin operation, it might be tempting to simply vow to complete it, without thinking about possible changes in circumstance—yet the book insists that it is necessary to complete the operation where one began it.

First, consider someone performing this operation as Abraham the Jew did, in a remote desert location. What is the worst that might happen? One might fall ill—in which case this is treated as a "God-given" hindrance to completion (in fact the book gives instruction that one can continue to perform the daily orations while staying in bed and praying for recovery). Or the oratory and personal goods might be ransacked by robbers—in which case it might still be possible to struggle on with makeshift materials and still complete the operation in the same place where one had started, as insisted upon.

In today's western societies, however, it is far more difficult to operate incognito. However unlikely, it is too easy to find oneself in a Kafkaesque situation being dragged off by police and wrongly accused by suspicious neighbours of some heinous crime. Even if one were able to continue orating in a police cell, it would not be possible to "complete where you started". With modern communications, I could also imagine a situation where a close family member suffers an accident or emergency, and it would be impossible simply to say: "Sorry, I'm busy."

And how could anyone possibly recruit help from a young child for the final stages without risk of upsetting parents, being singled out as a paedophile, or falling victim to a tabloid campaign about evil Satanists corrupting innocent children?

That is why I added those clauses to my vow, as well as saying: "I will consider very carefully and calmly and make my decision in the light of advice from the *I Ching*."

What was missing from my remembered version was an additional comment that I would take such insurmountable difficulties as a message from my Angel. If, as the book admits, severe illness could be interpreted as a message from God, then in our times a police raid when one knows one is innocent could be interpreted as a message from the Angel.

This might seem a bit pussy-footed, but it reflects my views on magical vow-making. For several years I was an initiator for a formal magical order, and that required preparing the candidates for a secret ritual—i.e. one where they were not supposed to know what would happen to them during the ceremony. All these initiation rituals included a number of vows—for example a vow never to become addicted to drugs. According to tradition, the candidates do not know that they will be asked to make that vow, and it is sprung upon them. Unless they agree, they cannot be initiated further.

This seemed wrong to me, because I could not see how anyone could make a serious vow without carefully considering it in advance. If one were already a drug addict, the vow would require one to stop there and then—would that be possible without a rehabilitation programme? Does a fondness for wine or tobacco amount to addiction? Where does one draw the line?

I used to prepare my candidates by telling them that they would be required to take some vows, and then asking if they liked to know in advance what those vows would entail? Some were very grateful of my offer but, to my surprise, quite a few said they would rather not know in advance.

Initiation really is most potent when it puts you on the spot with something challenging and quite dangerous. The more apparently life-threatening, the more powerful the initiation. We all know instinctively the truth of this: witness all those movies where the hero does not change or become whole until a major crisis has been faced. But again: how can the initiator make this happen in today's safety conscious and litigious culture? I recall a media story about sadomasochistic pact in the UK where the police sought to convict the sadist for harm done, despite the consent of the masochist.

The idea that one should have vows sprung upon one without warning and be forced to make a commitment on the spot is quite sound magic. But is it realistic in view of the fringe nature of occult culture in our society? It is one thing to trust one's future to a long-established religious order but, when you are constantly being warned about "all those charlatans and perverts in occult circles", is it wise to place yourself totally in the hands of any initiatory order? In any case, most of the "secret initiatory rituals" have already been published by ardent transparentists, so it is quite possible for any candidate to read them up first if they really wanted to.

For me this is an open question. I have Sun in Aries, so my heart tells me that a true initiate should throw caution to the winds and plunge ahead—"a faint heart never won a fair lady", as my House Master used to insist when setting us a challenging geometry problem. But I also have Capricorn rising, so my head tells me that I should always look before I leap.

What, therefore, do I advise? Simply to bear in mind that one of the worst mistakes one can make with Abramelin is to break the vow and not complete the operation in the specified place and time. So consider carefully before you make the vow, and make sure it is a genuine promise about something that you really can keep to.

### *Location. Location. Location.*

The book says: "Although the best counsel that I can give is that a man should go into retirement in some desert or solitude ... as the Ancients used to do; nevertheless now this is hardly possible; and we must accommodate ourselves unto the era in which we live". What he says is even more true now.

Abraham the Jew performed his operation in a remote desert location, against the backdrop of a culture where it was understood that some people chose to be hermits on religious grounds and just wanted to be left alone. These conditions are even harder to replicate since the twentieth century. Remote deserts are now far-better mapped, and most land is "owned" by someone or some institution; surveillance is widespread; and choosing to be a hermit would now be considered "weird", and sufficient reason to be identified, filmed, and posted on social media.

There is also society's suspicion that anyone "lying low" might be doing so because they are up to no good, or on the run from authority. This suspicion has probably always existed, but in Abraham's time would be more likely to be sorted out directly by personal contact with the hermit, whereas now one would be more likely to be reported to the police, or the press, or security. The consequences could be highly invasive and demand a lot of explanation.

As a rural person born and bred, my instinct was to retire to deep country, find a lonely cottage and work in isolation—but I chose instead the relatively suburban setting of a cottage on a home counties village green. This was partly because I did not have time or money to find a perfect location, but also because I realised that in Britain nowadays it is easier to be anonymous in an urban setting. Redbourn in Hertfordshire was where I had been living for a few years, so people had seen me around and I would not stand out as a newcomer. Only a few close friends needed to know that I was doing something peculiar, otherwise I could get on with my vegetable garden and high street shopping apparently as normal.

The Book of Abramelin does give instructions for performing the operation in a country location, but it also advises on how to perform it in a city apartment. When I thought more about the social impact, I could see the sense of doing it in a city, but I still feel the magic would be more powerful when the aspirant is isolated. The downside of doing the operation in a familiar setting is that this has a definite normalising effect.

If I ever had the opportunity to perform the operation a second time, then I would choose somewhere isolated, because I believe that would lead to more dramatic—even scary—results. I discuss this matter more fully in my final chapter of commentary: the way that everyday normality tends to tame the paranormal.

This is actually a very profound question that the aspirant must ask when planning the operation. "Am I doing Abramelin in order to make weird things happen and so prove to myself that magic exists? Or do I already accept that magic can exist, and so am performing this operation to invoke such magic into my life?" Myself, I only saw the true significance of this dilemma many years later.

### The fourth dimension of location

There is another aspect of location that has not changed over all these centuries. It is the time of sunrise and sunset at a chosen place. Bearing in mind the instruction that the practitioner should not sleep during the day, it becomes necessary to ensure enough sleep during the night.

The location I chose meant that for a month at the heart of the operation the official time of sunrise was about 4:40 am and sunset was about 9:20 pm. If, as instructed, I was to enter the oratory at a quarter of an hour before sunrise, then I would need to get up around 4:15 am or earlier to allow time for the necessary washing, dressing and going from the chamber to the oratory. Even if I limited my oration to one hour in length, I would be lucky to get to sleep before 11 pm—leaving me no more than five and a quarter hours sleep. In my case that was not enough—as a consequence, my diary reads like a long record of failure.

It was a failure because I was being too strict in intention—using the astronomical definition of sunrise as the time when the sun appears over a level horizon. In Abraham's time that figure would not generally be available, and sunrise would more likely be judged by the actual appearance of the sun. I never recorded when that actually happened, because I was usually deep in my oration at that time.

So, this is a further consideration: are you someone who really needs seven or eight hours sleep, or are you one of those who can survive on much less? Bear in mind that most people who do sleep shorter hours can only do this because they are able to compensate with brief catnaps during the day. That is not permitted by Abramelin.

If you cannot find a location close enough to the equator to give you a reasonable schedule, then make a conscious decision to mark the rising and setting of the sun by its appearance at the location, and see whether that allows enough sleep. If not, you will need to work around this problem.

### *Something borrowed, something made ...*

There is a powerful magical tradition that everything used in a magical operation should be manufactured for the purpose by the practitioner. I seem to recall Crowley saying something along these lines: that the ideal would be to dig up the iron ore and smelt the iron, to grow the tree used for the wood, and so on. It is true that there is special power in a magical object that is consciously constructed from raw materials with the specific magical purpose constantly in mind.

But there is another magical tradition about the four magical implements that says something along the lines that the Cup should be *given to* the magician, the Dagger (or the Disk) should be *bought by* the magician, the Wand should be *found by* and the Disk (or the Dagger) *made by* the magician. This is also interesting, because it opens up the creative process to embrace many more valid forms of interaction. You could, for example, argue that it is impossible to mine that iron without first finding it, in which case it would be a gift from Mother Earth.

My recommendation when preparing for this, or any other magical operation, is not so much to be bound by a set of rules but, rather to expand one's awareness of the preparation to a more holistic appreciation of the provenance of everything that will be used. Buying a robe, instead of making it, need not be a passive act: for some people, buying things is a lazy option, for others it is a hunting activity that involves investigating, assessing, budgeting and many other skills.

In whatever manner you obtain your magical paraphernalia, do so consciously and all the time explore the symbolism of its provenance. If someone breaks one of the cardinal rules of magic and gives you their old robe to wear, should you refuse it? Or might it be more appropriate to first cleanse and deconsecrate it, and then use it in the spirit of a gift imbued with goodwill and kindness?

What I am implying is that each item in the ritual should not just be an object that fits certain specifications, but also something that has come into your life in a significant and appropriate manner.

CHAPTER FOUR

# Notes towards a better understanding of my diary

*A Thelemite's approach to a Judeo-Christian retirement*

One big attraction of the Abramelin operation is that the book allows one to adapt the practice according to one's own religious beliefs—Christian, Jewish or pagan. And when it comes to prayer the text advises: "let each one speak his own language", followed by some very sensible advice about not reading from a rigid script but rather praying from one's heart with conscious intention.

That looks pretty simple until one gets down to detail. There are plenty of instructions along the lines: "place yourself upon your knees before the altar". These present some difficulty for Thelemites, who are exhorted never to bend their knees in supplication!

A more profound difficulty for me was that my religious inclinations at the time did not embrace any personal deity—I was closest to Taoism and a sense of a universal "way" that directed the course of nature. So, however freely I was permitted to adapt my prayers to my "God", I was effectively praying towards nothingness. For some people that might present an insurmountable difficulty.

About a year later, however, I was writing the first chapter of *Thundersqueak* in which Lemuel Johnstone says: "what some people call hypocrisy, I call freedom of spirit". The decision I finally made was not an easy one; I wrestled with it for weeks, but eventually decided to perform the operation in the thoroughly magical spirit of acting "as if"—as described by Austin Spare—or what is popularly advocated as "fake it till you make it".

It will help you to understand what is happening on the following pages if you bear that in mind. During my oration, and at times through the day, I was adopting the attitude of one who believed in a personal God and prayed earnestly and with the greatest sincerity from that perspective. As you will see, that imagined deity did take on certain characteristics and behaviour during the course of six months, even if it did not take on visible manifestation.

## The meditations

It was one thing to ritually throw myself into a state of theistic "energised enthusiasm" two or three times a day for the duration of an oration, but it was quite another thing to orient my whole life in that direction for six months. I also needed to adapt the operation to accommodate my True Will as best I could.

My inclination at the time was towards a sort of quietist Taoism that saw everything in terms of flowing states along the lines of yin and yang, with the paradoxical feature that each of these opposing qualities contained the seed of the other, and that kept them locked in the eternal dance of existence. My intention was to extend my "religious" Abramelin practice along the lines of Taoist meditation, circulating the light within the framework of the body, and so on. I took *The Secret of the Golden Flower* as my guide, together with books on Taoist meditation by John Blofield and others.

I think there are far more practical instructions available nowadays, but what was available at the time were mostly translations using teasingly far-eastern terminology that gave my western mind nothing very solid to chew on. Therefore, I was strongly influenced by the clear and sternly ascetic instructions provided by Crowley in his *Eight Lectures on Yoga*—summarised by Regardie (or someone) as: "Sit down. Shut up. Get out."

Typically, I would sit in meditation, and control my breathing while circulating from the base chakra up the spine and down the front of my body, in a pretty standard fashion. I could not physically sustain a cross-legged posture, so I adopted the thunderbolt kneeling position. This lead to screaming pain in my legs as I arose after what was often an hour and a half of stillness three times a day. (Amazingly, I did get used to the pain, but it left me with varicose veins.) On the days when I write that the meditation was "good" or "successful", it typically means that I reached and sustained a sense of utter stillness, mental silence, and often a feeling of being detached from my body as if floating far above it.

Strictly speaking, that state of still detachment was all that I should have aspired to, and any more complex or interesting phenomena should have been dismissed as mere distractions along the way. But I was not that accomplished. Instead I was often aware of things happening and "energy" shifts taking place inside me that seemed impossible to express in words. For these my guide was certain texts of western alchemy, especially those such as *The Book of Lambspring* that had illustrations that spoke to me.

I cannot explain all of this in a short introduction, but I will give one simple example. At the beginning of *The Book of Lambspring* there is a figure with the heading: "BE WARNED AND UNDERSTAND TRULY THAT TWO FISHES ARE SWIMMING IN OUR SEA". Under the picture it says: "The Sea is the Body, the two Fishes are Soul and Spirit".

It goes on to say paradoxical things about the two fishes being only one and yet two, and gives advice to cook all three together. What was the relevance of this?

As I sat circulating my breath in my body, at times I became aware of a duality within me that might be called yin and yang, or soul and spirit, and that there was value in simply holding awareness of these two, gently "cooking" them in the body rather than trying hard to analyse or differentiate further. And so on, with other alchemical images and books: I was reaching a state where words failed, but I could still find meaning and some measure of guidance in images such as these. At one point late in the operation, I describe God splitting into two: a very vivid experience at the time, but hard to communicate in words.

Resorting to alchemical terminology means that my original handwritten diary included a number of traditional alchemical symbols for the elements, planets and qualities, and in this edition I have replaced these symbols with their written names—not so mystical looking, but easier to typeset!

I cannot say whether these explanations will convey much to the reader—they do not always mean much to me now forty years later—but at least this explanation might give the reader some idea of what was happening to me. If it does, then it will add value to what might otherwise be a boring description of one man's struggle with everyday routine.

## Watching the watcher

One other expression that turns up from time to time is "watch the watcher". I thought I got this idea from reading *The Kybalion*, but do not see it there. It is said somewhere that Hermetic teaching tells us to "Watch the watcher. Judge the judge. Examine the examiner." I have often found this principle very helpful when meditating.

When I first tried to meditate in my earlier years the usual thing happened: I tried to quieten my mind but soon found it was buzzing with ideas and that I simply had no success in controlling this fountain of thought. It was Gerald Yorke who taught me that the trick was not to try to block thoughts, but simply to observe them arising in a detached manner. When you do that the stream does start to dry up.

"Watch the watcher" suggests something similar. When you sit in meditation you become aware of all that is going on inside you—it is apparently uncontrollable. But then you ask yourself how is it possible to be aware of all this? How can one single consciousness be simultaneously busy and aware that it is busy? Then you realise that there is another "higher" part of you that is watching this flow. Thus you discover "two fish in the sea": a consciousness and a watcher or over-seer.

How do you become aware of this "higher" part and the division between the two? It is because there is an even higher part of you that is watching and observing that there are these two parts within you … And so the meditation can lead one gently up a ladder of awareness to ever purer, simpler forms of consciousness.

This is what I am referring to when I use terms like "watching the watcher".

To sum up: even when there is very little to report in my diary, I was throughout most days attempting to cultivate an ongoing state of detached awareness. This state came to a sharper focus during my twice or thrice daily orations and, not having an adequate language to describe the effects, I could sometimes only refer to them in this semi-alchemical language.

## "Obsessions incarnating"

I was undecided whether it was better to edit out some passages where I use my diary as a sort of therapy exorcism—because these were too personal to be of interest to the reader—or whether I should leave them in, simply as examples of how psychological issues come up during the months of preparation. I asked the advice of my editor, and decided to leave them in, here are some explanations of the background to the most obvious obsessions.

### Snobbery

Reading this diary again after forty years, I was at first puzzled by the early references to my "snobbery". What was that about? Snobbery is not something that I identify with, but when I thought back to that time it came back to me.

This was the 1970s when the hippy era I had grown up in was evolving towards the decay that was Thatcherism. In the 60s and early 70s there was a rebellion against "the system" that most people were trapped in, and a move for some to "drop out". Although I was not a dedicated drop-out, I had difficulty finding work that really suited me, and had extended periods "on the dole", claiming state unemployment payments. At those times, I met many people who were no longer contributing to society in the accepted economic sense but were, in my opinion, contributing a lot in other ways. These included people following a mystical path; or those spending time in groups discussing society's norms and considering alternatives (a sort of informal version of academia that sometimes developed into "free schooling"). And there were those who, being free of nine-to-five work restrictions, were able to be more active and valuable citizens at a local level. There are examples of this in my diary, when I was at home all day instead of using the village as a dormitory between days working in London: I was able to offer coffee and conversation to an elderly and recently widowed neighbour—one example of how I became a better citizen, more engaged in our neighbourhood.

When the media began to push the Thatcherite division of society into "decent hard-working citizens" versus "layabout drop-out scroungers", I was angry. I would never claim that no-one has ever dropped out simply to become a parasite, but I rebelled against the prejudice that being out of work labelled one as a worthless human being. I felt a temptation to go around telling everyone that, yes, I had dropped out of regular employment, but that I was doing it for superior spiritual reasons, etc., etc., and this was not to be confused with good-for-nothing parasitism.

This was, of course, just the sort of subtle temptation that one can meet as one begins such an operation—a desire to boast and draw attention just when one ought to be retiring and becoming invisible. It emerged initially in a form that I labelled "snobbery" and, although I resisted it during the operation, it returned in a purer form afterwards and had to be more properly dealt with, as I will explain in the postscript.

*Lust*

This was a much more lovable demon—it was, after all, the 1970s when fewer lovers would be taken as a sign of weakness rather than restraint. I was relieved that Abramelin only demanded absolute celibacy for the last two months, and I think I managed that, even if I could not control my dreams.

The resulting sex dreams were wonderful, and a real insight into the succubi torments experienced by mediaeval monks. At first I saw them as a bonus rather than a distraction, but when my dream lovers began to suggest that there was really no need to rise and meditate at sunrise—and far better to linger in bed and enjoy more sex—then I realised what was going on!

What about the general mystic's requirement not to indulge in sinful behaviour? Well, from a 1970s perspective sex was anything but sinful, it was a celebration of life, a near religious act and, if we had once been exhorted to pray continuously, then surely it was only the limits of bodily existence that prevented us from fucking continuously? I had no problem with the occasional sexual adventure during the first four months.

*Physical deterioration*

Re-reading my concerns about weight loss was much more of a shock to me, because this was, and still remains in a lesser degree, a very deeply ingrained concern.

I can now trace it back to the classic astrological observation that Sun in Aries and an excess of the fire element in the chart tends to accompany a split between body and spirit, and illusions about one's appearance that may be similar to the delusions driving anorexia and other eating disorders. In my case I have always seen myself as much smaller and frailer than others' image of me.

For those who spend a lot of time trying to reduce weight, this might seem a positive blessing. But I was born in 1945 and so have very early memories of news about what was discovered in post-war Germany with horrific images of skeletal corpses and survivors from Nazi death camps. I cannot describe what that meant, I was too young to process the information, but it left me with a very profound sense of evil. When, many years later, I went with a friend to visit her mother in hospital and saw how terminal cancer can reduce a healthy body to a gaunt and tremulous skeleton, I felt utter physical revulsion and a rebellion of my spirit against the flesh and its privations. Most people would be moved to compassion, and I was too, but my compassion was overwhelmed by a panicky desire to run away and never visit again.

That was all past and forgotten when I started the operation. But early on I was reading about certain Christian mystics and a description of "God's athletes" whose bodies were reduced to skeletons by their spiritual discipline and devotion to the spiritual path, and I felt a similar surge of horror. Of course, I would never allow that to happen … but the idea must have remained in my unconscious mind until later when I began to notice myself growing thinner with all the fasting and a vegetarian diet. Around that time, I joined a local gym and an instructor showed me weight-training exercises that would soon restore my losses, but a few weeks later I discovered that I was losing weight even faster and I felt an irrational panic that was very hard to shake off.

As demons go, this one was relatively harmless, and yet it was extremely persistent. Whereas the worst of my demons were manifested and tamed during the seven years following the operation, this one persisted into my early seventies and still surprises me at times. It has taken me many years to grasp the fact that I am actually much taller than my in-laws: when I visualise them I still see myself looking straight into their eyes, as if they were just as tall as I am. And I have at last grasped the fact that the reason that I need to push the car seat right back before driving is because I am actually a large person, and not simply because I have a funny driving position.

## "Mother's boy" lament

On 30 August 1977, I filled pages of diary with an absolutely classic and embarrassing lament about the way that girls favour "bad boys" over "goody goodies". On an immediate level, it was probably a backlash from a spiritual path that was requiring celibacy in an era when such abstinence was seen more as a failure than a victory, but it also had deeper personal roots.

In the postscript pages I discuss the way that Sun in Aries, versus Capricorn rising, created a demonic split between my wild and potentially dangerous martial nature and a more cautious and conscientious capricornian self, and how I tended to identify with the latter and project out the former onto other people. This was another of many demons that I began to meet and came to terms with in the years that followed my Abramelin operation.

*PHASE ONE*

# The first two moons

I had built my oratory: a six-foot by three-foot pine shed concealed in the shrubbery. It had the specified windows to east and south and a door opening onto a level space for a sandy forecourt, as required. It was about thirty yards from the cottage where I had arranged my sleeping chamber. The cottage was shared by an old college friend.

The instructions begin thus:

> Having carefully washed one's whole body and having put on fresh clothing: precisely a quarter of an hour before Sunrise ye shall enter into your Oratory, open the window, and place yourselves upon your knees before the Altar, turning your faces towards the window; and devoutly and with boldness ye shall invoke the Name of the Lord, thanking Him for all the grace which He hath given and granted unto you from your infancy until now; then with humility shall ye humble yourselves unto Him, and confess unto Him entirely all your sins; supplicating Him to be willing to pardon you and remit them. Ye shall also supplicate Him that in the time to come He may be willing and pleased to regard you with pity and grant you His grace and goodness to send unto you His Holy Angel, who shall serve unto you as a Guide, and lead you ever in

His Holy Way and Will; so that ye fall not into sin through inadvertence, through ignorance, or through human frailty. In this manner shall ye commence your Oration, and continue thus every morning during the first two Moons or Months …

When ye shall have performed your orations, close the window, and go forth from the Oratory; so that no one may be able therein to enter; and ye shall not yourselves enter again until the evening when the Sun shall be set. Then shall ye enter therein afresh, and shall perform your prayers in the same manner as in the morning …

You shall set apart two hours each day after having dined, during the which you shall read with care the Holy Scripture and other Holy Books, because they will teach you to be good at praying, and how to fear the Lord; and thus day by day shall ye better know your Creator.

A fuller account of the final form of my oration is given on 13 August. I followed it with an extended meditation as described under "The meditations" in Chapter Four.

### Easter Monday, 11 April 1977

Desperate rising, alarm went off 4.30, not 5.30. Felt a wreck. All seemed like a dream. Half hour or so, saw sun rising a few degrees. Breath rose in steam. Sweated after penitence. Used T's collect.[1]

Returned about 6.40 am to tea, washing up, tidying. Breakfast 8.30. Huge sweep out and cushion/carpet beating for dining room and kitchen to clear my sawdust, etc. 10 am I offered instant coffee to Mrs Smith—cocoa for me—and had welcome rest for half an hour plus. Then started on spare room [to be my "Chamber"]. Cleaning and leaving heaps of stuff elsewhere. Swept tons of dust and rubbish. Took out mattress into lovely sun (with cold North Wind). I had washed my pillow too. 12 pm I too reclined in sun and rested and read Hymn of Jesus before going to 1 pm lunch at Biker J's. Delicious vegetarian meal. Chatted. Clouds came. Back via SA to say I'd made altar myself.[2] Home

---

[1] The previous week T had sent me a lovely postcard of Tobias and the Angel, with the official collect for the Feast of the Guardian Angels (2 October).
[2] I had asked a craftsman friend to help me design and build an altar, but ran out of time and knocked up something for myself.

3-ish. Dusting and washing room. Made bed, set incense to consecrate room. Tea 6-ish and writing this diary since Friday. Dilemma: should I change for evening ceremony? Decide to try not to, but will shake clothes to save me from laziness. Beans are cooking; I've started soya sprouts too. Must put on some alfalfa to grow.

Aware of noisy traffic in evening, roar of motorway. Scared of dark after.[3] Lateish bed as I ate after evening session.

## *Tuesday 12 April*

Much fresher. A warmer morning. Washed up and had toast for breakfast (no eggs or cheese in house). Read chapter on circulation of the light in *Taoism and Creativity* and dozed slightly. Actually the dreaded drop-off[4]—on my second day! Oh help! Just for a flash, but I did feel different for it. Shopping on the High Street 10–11.30, about. Took along lots of dry cleaning and bought tons of food. My case had come and gone at antique shop. Looked at books. Some loss of awareness but I remained alert right across Redbourn Common on way back (slipping, bulging shopping bags probably helped). Noon I had scrambled eggs and Swiss chard. Read *Secret of the Golden Flower*. Put lime on garden, moved cloche to the peas. Re-planted onions and helped Mrs Smith with her boiler and clock. Read magazine after tea and somehow day seems short of achievement though I have done some necessary clearing jobs and now have a table in my "chamber". 9 pm, cloudy day, no sun.

MUST: make altar floor, lamp. Write up official diary.

## *Wednesday 13 April*

Damp, dark morning. Dream of Dobro player visiting me and me having a go. Later, dream of telling N about dream of Dobro player. Dream of returning to Eton: I'd asked to go back and was told to apply in normal way for the job. Another dream of [my recent work boss] coming round for a drink—he seemed to come in a sort of pleading way. My dwelling

---

[3]See Chapter Three concerning my fears in the first days of the operation.
[4]One of the strictures of the operation was not to sleep during the day, and I had erred on only my second day—if only for a few seconds. A sign of troubles to come.

was very grand and he was impressed and honoured. Another dream of C giving birth to a third child.

Morning operation: traffic loud, although morning. Better concentration, sat in meditation and withdrew through choice and not because of getting fidgety. Scratching on roof surprised me, but I was unshaken. 6.40 am.

Brek after washing up. 7.50. I read till N got up. 8.30 sat to write my Abramelin Diary. Wrote till 10.

Late lunch (1.45) as I spent morning making a lamp. Simple, but the result is surprisingly attractive. I hangs beside me in my chamber. Tonight I will fix a hook for it, but not take it in.

Large lunch: ersatz [soya mince] bolognese with nettles. Tasted grapefruity. Sun had appeared and after lunch it was sunny enough to lie out to read. Removed my jeans. It would have been good sunbathing except for cold when occasional clouds came. Cut wood for altar floor, planted out rest of potatoes. Made pea soup. Was washing up at 5.45 when N returned. Chatted over tea. Now 6.45 and writing up as sun sinks low. This room [my chamber] is good as a study. I like the view.

9.15 to bed after large welsh rarebit.

MUST: Wash some clothes, shorts. Take down floor. Get cream. Put in beans?

## Start of dedicated Abramelin diary

### Wednesday 13 April, 8.30 am

This morning I rose at 5.50, washed and put on my thermal underwear and judo suit and went to my oratory about a quarter of an hour before an invisible sunrise. It was a warmer morning than of late, but completely overcast and about to drizzle.

Kneeling before my altar I prayed as directed and also sat in silence, as in the Taoist meditation, to be receptive. I made use of the prayer that T had provided. All this will be the normal routine from now on. Half hour.

Today it was better, in that I stopped because I felt enough had been said, not because I felt ashamed of my deteriorating concentration. A sudden scratching on the roof surprised me, but did not shake me. Seeing the young green buds through my window, I made a special reference to nature and my country upbringing.

This is the first morning I have not been alone. N returned last night. The need to avoid clashing with him helped to structure my morning—I still need such props—so I have come up to write after a short reading about Taoist meditation after breakfast. Alas, two days have already gone without my writing up.

The idea of attempting this operation arose before Christmas. It might not have arisen at all but for K, who had contacted me out of the blue last autumn to ask my advice about doing the operation herself.

This left me with insufficient time for preparation, and I did not hurry even then! Lateness has been the hallmark so far: I did not read the book thoroughly until late, letting myself in for some shocks. The silver censer I ordered will not be ready till May or June. The order I'd placed with SA for an altar was too late to give him enough warning, so I had to bodge mine own at the last minute. The oratory is unfinished in detail. My wand is uncut. My lamp has yet to be made. No talismans are drawn and my robes are unfinished.

All this adequately mirrors my soul!

Why then am I doing it? Especially as Redbourn is anything but my ideal site, being suburban, rather noisy and overlooked.

My thought was this: I am old enough to look for a really satisfying career, and once set on that career it will not be easy to spare six months. So it should be soon.

At Christmas I decided to investigate the omens, and my heart. I struggled with the astrological *I Ching*.[5] So wearisome was the process that I said to myself: "If it makes out that 1976 was a good year I'll read no further". As it turned out, the previous years were adequately described.

1977 is "the well". The yearly hexagram interpretation revealed that it was not time to teach until I had learnt myself, "the well needs relining". This seemed very relevant to my present situation; *SSOTBME* has produced a few questions from interested readers. It was also a good year to "sink a well or dig a mine"; a reasonable metaphorical description.

By way of contrast, 1978 will be a year of dreams coming true—and of success. Should I not therefore wait until next year? No, because my present dreams are worldly and their coming true would hinder such an operation. The operation itself should refine my wishes.

---

[5]*The Astrology of I Ching: Translated from the "Ho Map Lo Map Rational Number" Manuscript*, edited by W.A. Sherrill.

In January, T came to supper and we discussed the operation. In subsequent letters, long and helpful, he showed considerable understanding and gave me much support. He raised doubts about the authenticity of the book, about its lack of connection with existing traditions. We discussed *I Ching* readings. But just before Easter he sent me a card, a picture of Tobias and the Angel. On the back was a collect for the Feast of the Guardian Angels (2 October).

Was this his own invention? Or is it indeed a part of the church ritual? If so, it is thrilling! It gives a direct link with tradition, for I finish on the week before.

I did not commit myself till very late—indeed I have yet to write my vow! I wanted to avoid the stupidity of making a vow before I had fully explored its practicability. Giving notice was a wrench, and required two rushed *I Ching* questions. Here I witnessed the general law that it is not good to consult oracles when too involved and worried about a question.

Only on Good Friday were my parents told I'd left work! B found out earlier, as she had stayed overnight the weekend before.

M was amused, but a bit upset about my life as a hermit. She sees introspection as "unhealthy". She does not realise that solitude charges me up so that I can discharge in company. (I think it is company that charges her up so she can discharge in solitude.) My worst fear was that the admirable and hard-working RM, whose cottage this is, would misunderstand and feel that his idle, spoilt, dilettante stepson had grown bored with work and had suddenly decided on a holiday. But as I left, he said that he "admired my courage", wished me luck and warned that "the devil would be after me". This was evidence of such understanding that I left weeping with joy. He even offered to withdraw rent, but I resisted for, after all, I had planned my spending around paying the rent in advance.

### *Wednesday 13 April, 9.30 am*

I vow that, subject to conditions mentioned below, I will endeavour to keep to the Abramelin operation for six months starting on Easter Monday. As stated in the book, severe illness will be recognised as a God-sent hindrance. However, in the case of great danger to my immediate family, who have been such a support, I would also consider suspending the operation. Also, if I am the victim of bureaucratic intervention, and can find no way of delaying or buying time, then I will be forced to step down. In all such cases, or in any unforeseen mishap, I will consider very carefully and calmly and make my decision in the light of advice from the *I Ching*.

I cannot see how I can obtain and use a child as instructed in the text, so I plan to do without—unless a suitable child conveniently makes himself known to me in time for training for the part.

Signed,
Lionel Snell April 24th '77

One of my early dilemmas was the extent to which I should make my own stuff. To an outsider the answer is obvious; all magicians should make their own stuff. To me it was less clear; I wanted to *do my best*, and I knew, being a poor handyman, that everything I made would be shoddy. On the other hand I am a good buyer. I know that sounds funny, but it is not meant as a joke. When I buy it is not a matter of convenience, it is quite an art—and an effort. I look long and hard to buy the best. Accordingly, I studied sheds.[6] I asked SA, the organ maker, to make an oaken altar. I searched long and hard for a silversmith with whom I could discuss the design of a censer. I bought silk for K to make robes (I had planned for Turnbull and Asser[7] to do my robes, for Abramelin does specify "properly made sleeves"! However, their minimum order increased from three to six shirts). I bought the extra three shirts and had already bought the oil—for Crowley says you cannot make it just by mixing the raw ingredients. I bought an almond tree, rather than steal a branch! Had my Canary Isle money come, I might have been more lavish, but it did not. So I ordered wood and, with help from K, built an oratory. This is my most positive work so far. It fits snugly into the shrubbery and is in no-one's way. It is rough, but a joy to me. My first big adventure in carpentry! The altar is even rougher, a last-minute panic. The censer is still being made and should be beautiful. Today I must try to make a lamp. K is making the robes. I think I get the point of making things, but still it took some convincing.

---

[6]Meaning that I looked at catalogues of garden buildings that could be adapted to an oratory.
[7]The famous Jermyn Street shirt maker.

7 pm. Less convinced now! Before lunch I made a very simple lamp from some aluminium I found in the garage. I must request permission to be proud of it, it does look really nice and I long to see it in situ. The only pity is that the lamp is seldom lit. Shame.

I have also prepared a floor for the altar. I hope it fits.

After the last-minute, late-night altar-building panic on Sunday I was bleary on Monday morning. It was very cold, so I was thankful for my Norwegian underwear suit. I noticed the steam of my breath ascending to the window as I prayed. Tried some cross-legged meditation but since then I have remained kneeling.

There is a sense of unreality about the operation. The oratory looks like a sauna inside—only freezing. Until today I always stopped when the fidgeting started.

Dilemma: should I consecrate the oratory with only the best-quality prayers, or should I try to improve myself with the struggle to lengthen them? As the book stipulates that they should be extended in the second two months, I have decided on the former. I must not go too fast only to deteriorate later, it is quite enough to instil regularity. Half an hour seems to be about right; in fact, I really should consider an *upper* limit if I find I can do much more.

Trying too hard at this stage could curdle my routine into a cycle of supreme efforts surrounded by collapsing relief. Actually, I feel that I should extend my prayer gradually to fill the whole day, with the time in the oratory as merely a focus of the prayer.

Accordingly, I have been "watching the watcher".[8]

As I lunched with Biker J on Monday, I saw quite a bit of the world. I was aware of my desire to impress strangers: "I say, I'm no ordinary drop-out; I'm really quite a posh mystic, you know". This idea is embarrassingly persistent. Even more persistent is the "teacher" habit; as I do things I mentally give directions to imaginary pupils, or compose essays on the subject. Perhaps writing this down will exhaust that one.

I ate after evening prayer—after finding that I was too agonisingly hungry during prayer—and it made for a late night. I'm ashamed to say I was slightly afraid of the dark.

---

[8] A reference to either *The Occult Way* by P.G. Bowen or *The Kybalion: A Study of The Hermetic Philosophy of Ancient Egypt and Greece*, by Three Initiates.

On Tuesday it was a dull morning, but much warmer. As I was not bleary, things went much better.

After breakfast I read about Taoist meditation and, horror of horrors, I dropped off! It's only my second day and I've broken a basic law, even if only for a second. I must get a bed of nails.

I did some shopping in the High Street, and wasted time looking at books. On my way back across the common I remembered myself non-stop! The awkward, slipping and about-to-burst shopping bag helped me to maintain awareness; I must remember that arcanum. However, come evening prayer, I felt disappointed in myself for lack of achievement or work done—hence my vow to start writing today and to make the lamps, etc.

Ate before evening prayer. This caused my gut to bulge with chilli bean soup and it was not satisfactory. I must work on that one. I must take either a *very* early supper or a quick snack straight after.

I have not yet adjusted to vegetarian food; the fish stall looked like a mirage of the holy grail, and at Hall's butchers I jokingly ordered a whole fillet for October. My farts ascend like incense smoke.

Today I pulled myself together a bit. Having to avoid clashing with N helped. I made a lovely lamp and prepared the altar floor. After (or *between*) the rain it was a sunny day and I managed to sunbathe as I read my *Gnostic Anthology*. Must confess I was very attracted by the antinomianist heretics.

My bible reading kicked off with *John's Gospel* and, I must say, I was stunned to find it so readable and so packed full of gags. It looks as though the Bible might prove to be my light relief to dilute the *Zohar*, etc. rather than vice versa.

Tunes run unnecessarily through my head—I wonder whether I can replace them with mantra?

Saw N as he returned this evening. Chatted over tea.

Now the shadows lengthen—but I wish the busy world would hush—and I must get ready for evening prayer. Not much red in the sky. 7.40 pm.

9.15 pm. I felt very detached and pure as I meditated, and probably could have continued for a much longer time, but found that I had left early!

N and I coincided as I ate after prayer. Sorry to see my old ridiculous irritation at his kitchen methods, but I was glad to note that a greater distance from them enabled me to avoid clinging to them so much.

This is important as it is my first clear sign of a change. I showed him my lamp; pride diluted with sociability.

Alas, my altar floor did not fit, so I'll have to take it down a bit.

### Thursday 14 April

Exciting dream: my house was large, I lived in one half and in the other half there was someone else. The basement was large and stuffed with rubbish—old wood, etc. (A woman came seeking her lost hamsters in it.) Part of my side were the offices of some sinister firm. They planned to kill the neighbour—a doctor (played by Jack Nicholson). In time, he infiltrated them disguised as a Rolling Stone—Charlie Watts (the corpse-like one)—but he failed to kill the two ringleaders and the alarm was raised. The firm was something a bit showbizzy.

Did this symbolize my conscious soul? There is half a house, littered with junk below and corrupted with the evil firm's office above, then there is the Saviour disguising himself as a corpse to gain admittance and then transforming into a young woman for victory. Oh well, it was great entertainment.

Lovely clear cold morning that later turned to cloud and irritating high wind. Hung my lamp this morning. Making an early and efficient start enabled me to sow beans and carrots before cycling to St. Albans. The return was a real test, which saw me slaving against high wind and cold. How will it compare with later tests? It nearly broke me.

Rather rushed and ungrateful today. Did some washing and small chores. Irritation at N's kitchen habits tried to get me again. After evening meditation I was being efficient when a lengthy phone call from PF ruined it and put me on edge. It is now 10.20. Oh dear.

### Friday 15 April

Dream of two conjurors. Before the show they took great care to make the stage symmetrical—for instance, they were worried that one had fewer Chinese rings than the other, and so on—but the act itself was quite asymmetrical. The right-hand one (who was known for his thesis on the psychology of cookery) left the stage and then came back on wearing long underwear. Unfortunately, his tool was hanging out. This produced a mixture of amusement and shock in the audience, but it turned to outrage when he made it clear that it was deliberate. M and G thought him rather offensive as the whole of the first half of their act consisted of a radical sociological diatribe. I was backstage and went round to the front to watch. By the time I'd got there the second half had begun. The right-hand conjuror was now looking very smart in a suit and they were both doing tricks, which seemed to consist entirely of them producing cakes. Everyone (including M) was impressed. I tried one of the cakes and it was delicious.

This seems like a parody of my operation. I would have liked to see the left-hand conjuror play an equal part. In yesterday's dream it was the left-hand side of the house that was not mine, and did not feature in the story.

Naughty untaxed ride on Bloaters to Harpenden—this was due to having prepared the seeds for sowing and then finding that Redbourn had sold out of peat pots. It felt unusual, even after only four days abstention.

Clumsiness was in evidence today: doing things in a rush without concentration and … crash!

I was aware of two demonic pacts: sitting, lazing, over lunch, I began to think wrathfully about the civil service. As my anger mounted I leapt to my feet and busied myself—i.e. I used the anger to combat my inertia. Similarly, in the evening I was working at seed-sowing too late—when I should have been making supper—but the desire to show off how well I was eating to N (and to shame his efforts) reminded me to start supper before he went out.

In a way it was clever to play off demons but, a) will I become enslaved by the process, and, b) does the fact that there are low-grade demons encouraging me in my work augur well for its effect on me?

I fitted a padlock on the oratory door and am preparing beeswax for polish.

### Saturday 16 April

Saw no significance in forgotten dream.

The wretched alarm woke me at about 4, so I was late and bleary for the sunrise. Very sharp frost—coldest morning yet. Lovely and clear till 11, when it clouded over.

After break, I read the chapter on Abramelin in *The Tree of Life*. It was very good, and reminded me of some important psychological points. I'm concentrating more on finding a routine than on putting a lot of pressure on, which could be all right provided I monitor my prayers carefully.

K rang a.m. She is okay, but she's had more trouble rising than me.

I'd been chatting with N immediately before "evenmed" and so kicked off with a silent meditation to cool valves.

Did some gardening (hoeing), cleaning of sitting room, fixing up warm electric propagator, and work in the oratory. It's been a good day, but not a great day.

At time of solar return I was hoeing garden.

Horror of horrors! On going to bed I glanced at Abramelin and saw that I'd misunderstood the cleaning and perfuming bit: I'd taken it for Sunday instead of Saturday. Of course, I can see now that the oratory must be cleaned *before* the holy day. This is so obvious that it led me to seek for the meaning of my absurd oversight. Yes, it typifies what has been wrong in much of my work: while I'm spending my time daydreaming and planning the wonderful completion of the work, I forget the most elementary beginning steps.

Late last night I hastily swept and perfumed the chamber, changed the linen and then had bath. Oh dear, what a hell of a lot of laundry! I resolved on an early start tomorrow morning so I can sweep the oratory *before* sunrise.

## *Sunday 17 April*

Interesting dream: I was at some sort of gathering or conference. I can't remember much about the early incidents except that they relate to my pride and snobbery. Amongst the names of those attending was an extraordinary one: *"Therese" (as it were) d'LionelSnell of ...* I was intrigued to find my name within another, and tried to locate her.

When she was pointed out to me I saw a rather black-haired, dusky-skinned (i.e. Spanish or Southern Italian) girl standing with another. I introduced myself and commented on our names, but she did not seem impressed. "What was that about your name?" her friend asked. (They both had nice foreign accents.) "Oh, it's just that it's made from an English name," she replied. They were a bit giggly, like girls together. She said something polite, like: "How interesting, nice to have met you," and they went back to their seats. I had been told they were from a nunnery (convent school).

Although I was a bit disappointed, I forgot about it, but was then surprised when she came up to me again and greeted me. In view of her background and earlier behaviour, even this modest greeting struck me as very forward. Interested, I suggested we meet again, to which she agreed and said we could have a chat. By now I was feeling a bit shy myself, so I said, "Perhaps I can buy you a meal". She laughed and said, "I hope we have more than a meal together!"

This parting remark embarrassed me and awoke old fears of inadequacy; she did seem a bit hot to handle! But very sweet about it.

Then she came for me. "Quickly," she said. "Follow me! We must not be seen together too much, because we are a party of schoolgirls and the rest will be jealous and spiteful."

I recall assuming that, being from a convent, she would not be on the pill; fortunately I had a (blue) contraceptive left over. Surprised at my confidence, I got under her clothes and we had a great time.

It struck me as all too good to be true; a sort of temptation for the Abramelin operation.

After that I became divided into the "observer" and "Lionel Snell" who became more glamorous and dashing. We had a happy time together and LS made some toast, holding the bread with his bare hands and deftly tossing it over. She laughed in admiration, saying, "You can do anything! I bet you can't interpret dreams though!"

LS said he could, but was a little uncertain. She described a dream of an old abbey in Nailsworth. "Nailsworth?" asked LS. "Write it," said she. "Ah yes, that was it, 'Nailsworth'." In this abbey's graveyard was a tomb with a *de LionelSnell* inscription.

Excited at the hope of solving the mystery of her name, LS and she went to "Nailsworth". She led him into a vast mausoleum, of the "these of our fellows who died in the Great War" type, with rows and rows of little plaques.

We searched in vain, though there were some near-misses. She tried to recall where.

An amusing sideline was provided by two smartly dressed men—lawyer types—who were also in the mausoleum and were evidently freemasons for, with exaggerated secrecy, they whispered together in urgent tones, "I say, did you notice the names on that row added up to ninety-nine?" "Yes, I bet there are ninety-nine of them too."

Suddenly she became excited and said, "Follow me." We dashed up some marble stairs and into a sort of library, where she rushed over to a bench and sat beside some young boys. "Look!" she said, and smiled at them while they, in turn, looked up and smiled back. There was a strong resemblance; I can't think how, for the boys were blond.

They were called "Snell-Thompson". The oldest had to leave to be beaten, and as we followed them the girl, excited to be on the trail, turned and said, "They went to Eton!"

As we waited outside the room, we heard the swish of cane. What had he done wrong? He'd carved some Latin nonsense on a form, which had included the word "Snell". She got excited and asked LS to write in my own writing, "Lionel Snell cometh" (or something like that). We compared it with the boy's crude carving and realised that it could be read as that.

This was the clue we needed for the rest of the truth to come out! Near the old abbey was an old pool with a notice saying that in times of invasion the bell would summon all the young men, and any who did not come at once would be denounced as traitors.

Years ago, one "Lionel Snell" had received this summons, and he had been supposedly slain in battle. The bodies were put on a great tip and burnt with chemicals—quicklime presumably. These chemicals would kill anything, so Lionel Snell could not have survived.

Here, young Snell-Thompson spoke up: "See that dog?"—it was a wretched, maimed and limping white mongrel amongst the debris—"a short while ago that dog was as stiff as a board. I kicked him there."

So that was it! Lionel Snell had not died, but had revived and got away.

The lad pointed to a tree that was supposed to be a silver birch, but was hideously deformed by the chemicals. One branch struggled off sideways like a pointing arm. "You see that tree? They say that when there is just one deformed tree like that it is Jesus Christ pointing the way for the dead souls to depart." The tree pointed downstream to the sea. So Lionel Snell of old had risen from the dead and struggled downstream to the ocean and, presumably, across it to another land where he had founded the family de LionelSnell ...

I recall thinking that the last section was bad cinema: the part about the dog was a bit overdone and, although the tree was grotesquely hideous, it was by no means the only tree that was deformed. But LS and Therese were happy that they were able to solve the enigma, and they left in a lover's state of bliss.

"Will you marry me then?" said she.

"You really are *very* forward for a nun!" laughed he. "Of course I will!"

I wondered how she would stand up to the test. After all, marrying a girl like this is all very well, but it would not help Abramelin. I went up to her, but to my surprise she cringed.

"You say you went to a nunnery," said I. "In that case you'll have no trouble reciting the Lord's Prayer with me, will you?"

She cringed and struggled as I recited it, and under her cloak she seemed to shrivel.

"Show me your face!" I cried repeatedly, though I half regretted it, expecting some awful Alfred Hitchcock type revelation! Eventually the hooded head rose black before me. I said it once more, but as I did so it occurred to me: "Hold on! Isn't this the face that turns men to stone?" and I woke up.

This dream was very exciting, but also a bit disturbing. It was a nice example of temptation refuted by devotion (well-aimed at my attraction to physically beautiful girls—and she was great—and my snobbery, or rather, my desire to be a bit posher).

But with my Taoist hat firmly on the other foot (as it were) I do realise the need to cool it morality-wise, lest all future nights are disturbed by this sort of "good versus evil" playacting. Just as, in the cold light of day, this paragraph is "cooling it morality-wise" playacting.

In penitence, I was up before sunrise to sweep the oratory, burn incense, and light the lamp. I took my beeswax polish, but did not use it. The damp atmosphere made the morning feel very cold.

After break I read *Abramelin*—very necessary—and the first fifty psalms. They were not much better than Genesis, which I read yesterday and which almost bored me to tears, except for the amusing little "Jewish" touches, like Abraham "doing business" with God as to how many good souls there needed to be in Sodom in order for it to be spared! So far, The Gospel of John is by far the best.

Today I committed adultery (on my old bed, so I had to bathe afterwards). Abramelin will really love me for that. But, could there almost be a possibility of classifying it under "charitable work"? I did dedicate the operation to the Earth Mother (whom I've been very lax in thanking for my good food) because fecundity was its object. It was this latter fact that finally moved me—I would not have been so happy about a fuck just for fucking's sake! So my conscience is not so much troubled by that (perhaps it should be), but it *is* troubled by my inability to remain composed. Seven days is not enough to fortify oneself against seven hours of "female" chatter ("I *do* understand what you are doing, really I do; and I *really* admire you for it ...") like the Mistral unceasingly blowing sand against my rickety foundations. I slowly collapsed. Outwardly, I did not change a lot, but inwardly, composure and calm desiccated to aridity and numbness. Women fear to see men set out on projects because they fear the projects will change the men, whereas they would rather make the changes themselves.

## Monday 18 April

Dreamed of a tornado racing across a field towards R and me. Did not feel scared as it seemed slow in the distance, but as it approached me I could see how fast it was. It gouged a channel in the field and would have struck me but for a tree that broke its force (and was itself damaged by the suction). Later I was trying to do my evening oration but without success as I had chosen a place right outside the front door and was disturbed by the family next door coming and going, and felt particularly idiotic kneeling in B's sight.

Frosty morning—not very inspiring. Hard to get up.

Further thoughts on last week: the greatest benefit of "sin" is the stimulus it gives to my sanctity. My most humble orations have followed my worst misdemeanours. I suppose this is another example of a low-grade "pact".

My "circulating the light" seems to have built up something I was unaware of until yesterday, prior to screwing. I felt a ball of fire in my inner belly quite distinct from the usual sexual feeling. I'm not sure I handled it correctly.

This morning's meditation was slightly feeble.

After break, I read St. Ignatius' *Spiritual Exercises* (up to the first week). I think I must lend them to K.

The trip to see K was excellent. I took some tools, books, and vegetables along with my lamp, on which I had done some early work beforehand. She welcomed me and we shared her delicious lunch. It was a real joy that she thought the lamp looked good. I stayed and chatted awhile before a nice cycle back.

I was haunted by Majesty today. Read about the Hellfire Club during my morning cocoa, and have been drinking odd glasses of sparkling Rheingold to test my champagne stopper. At K's I read about the amazing private car collection of some eccentric Alsatian industrialists, who have an enormous number of Bugattis. Majesty, akin to nostalgia, is a powerful and neutral spirit that I must come to terms with.

### Tuesday 19 April

Did some good reading today: Crowley's *Tao Te King* for an hour after break and after lunch while sunbathing for the first time this year—the shade of the shrubbery kept off the cool wind. Read Exodus for an hour, and found it all rather good. Also *The Magical Ritual of the Sanctum Regnum* by Eliphas Levi—the format of this clearly inspired *Book 4*, part two.

### Wednesday 20 April

I dreamt of going to the gym, then later had a dream about sleeping with "Mary" and screwing over and over again. I notice that since becoming celibate my sex dreams have improved: in the past most of them were of frustrated or incompetent screwing; now they are wildly successful. This dream ended with my being dissuaded from going to morning orison by "Mary". As I did not manage to go until six, it seems the succubus was fairly successful. A dull, damp (thank heaven) morning so I escaped the humiliation of witnessing a sun that had already risen.

When I oversleep, should I give priority to orison, and so rush through or even skip my getting up routine? I chose not, to save the situation that develops with work: once I allow myself to skip my routine, I will tend to rise later and still be too late. Instead I will do the full routine and face up fully to the consequences of my lateness.

This rain will save me watering.

In the last two meditations I was more successful at centring consciousness in my belly.

What a weather contrast! Drizzles and darkness all day. A kerfuffle about Bloaters let the drizzle and darkness into my soul, and I was faced with a testing day at last. Although I failed pretty well, I did have odd bids at "plodding on through the gloom", and it did aid my introspection—making evenmed one of the best.

I plan to go to Ben's funeral tomorrow; hence my attempt to get Bloaters a little more legal.

Thomas Vaughan's short tract on "light" gave me some light to compensate for dull sky. I always try to "transcend" symbolic interpretation of alchemy and return to a more literal meaning, as it was more difficult fixing the volatile than vice versa. When I visualised clipping a bird's wings so it fell back to the nest and had to brood, my thoughts became much quieter.

### Thursday 21 April

Moist and warm morning. Earlier on I noticed that the oil in the lamp was frozen in the morning and liquid in the evening, but over the last two days it has remained liquid.

Today is a day of distinction. 7.30 am and N is already up (his car is at the garage so he is bussing today). Must go to see the Social Whatsit people, and I think I will go to Ben's funeral and visit S on the way back. I hope that by concentrating all trips into one day I can avoid too much mental distraction.

Sure enough, Abramelin was far from my mind for most of the day—so was everything else. I spent the day cheering M and, above all, long distance motorcycling as I also went to Stroud where they fixed the speedo cable. As they did so I had an interesting chat with Vernon Gadd.

Got back to slightly late evenmed of poor quality.

### Friday 22 April

This morning's lateness was worse—and less forgivable. I was wracked by lust in the night, and lightness of sleep seemed to be induced by high winds outside despite the room's good insulation from the elements. Not sure of source of lust and there were no obvious astrological transits. Was it a by-product of the whirl of travelling? Or was it implanted by S at suppertime?

It made the morning's meditation "interesting", but not very good.

Attempted to be efficient and clear up some small items like putting up the shelf for the altar, fixing the door lintel, and washing and pressing my tunic. After a large lunch I was outrageously sleepy, but lying on my back for a short while and then sitting in an upright chair enabled me even to read the boring old Bible for two hours without dozing. Made effort not to be distracted by buffeting of wind outside.

Fixed the lintel and put a shelf inside the altar for small goods. Did all this just before evenmed.

As I was digging the ground where the greenhouse is to go I came across two large mandrakes—King and Queen. They were so large I could not dig them up whole. They did not scream, but the whole air twittered with sounds of wind. A strange flesh-like smell—veal?—came from the broken root and made me feel a bit hazy. I replanted the two pieces alongside even bigger ones beneath the elder. I am fascinated by those tuberous rooted climbers.

At evenmed a single star-like white flower[9] faced me on a branch close to the window; it was a perfect five-fold shape like an upright pentagram dead centre in the window. I wish it could stay there as it is a lovely object on which to meditate.

### Saturday 23 April

"Celibacy" justifies itself by producing a vast improvement in one's sex dreams. After the alarm woke me I dozed and was tempted by a really lovely succubus. She looked just right and said all the most flattering things, and I even "got it in" before I insisted on waking up. Never has the real thing been that promising.

Reading George Chevalier's memoir makes me feel a little small; after two weeks he had already been visited by malevolent entities. "Does 'the enemy' see so little opposition in me that he does not need to try?" I wondered. This succubus gives me hope; it suggests that the sunrise timing *is* important if two attempts have been made to confound it.

Bearing in mind Lambspring's "two fish in our sea", and remarks in *Secret of the Golden Flower*,[10] I have attempted today not so much to seat consciousness in the belly as to sift it into two parts, "male" and "female"; one resting in the head and the other in the belly. That is progress. Although theoretically understanding the four worlds division, I'd not often clearly realised it.

A day of physical labour preparing greenhouse site. My desire to prepare the site today was goaded on by the idea that not doing hard physical work would be a semi-observance of the sabbath. Read Pernety[11] and sunbathed after lunch. The sun was lovely.

---

[9]Blackthorn, I think.
[10]References to alchemical texts, *The Book of Lambspring* and *The Secret of the Golden Flower*.
[11]Dom Antoine Joseph Pernety, *A Treatise On The Great Art*.

I wrote jokey, send-up letter to the local paper, but having to give my name and address made me anxious about possible repercussions. The *I Ching* message for the day was most appropriate, referring to the need to put a "headboard on the young bull". O.K.

Evening bungle: after cleaning my room, changing and perfuming everything, I was undecided about when to do the oratory. I could not after evenmed as I needed the light, but I was keen to do it as late as possible so that Sunday would dawn on an oratory that was fresh as possible. So I did it before evenmed, which I left a bit late. Waxed floor and east wall with beeswax and sanded altar, so I was puffing, sweaty, late and in a flap with an obstinate charcoal block. In trying to be economical, I used only a small piece, but the incense kept falling off it. Also, because the censer is still on order, I placed the block on a piece of flint, but was terrified that the flint would burst with the heat. A right old shambles! So was brief and fled.

I must make a temporary censer that I can bury in the real one for continuity. Perhaps I will try a lamp-lid at the same time to keep the dust out.

## Sunday 24 April

Simply overslept—who needs succubi? A lovely clear (cold) morning turned again to shrieking, cold wind with "bright intervals"—the sun warming the earth under my greenhouse.

Went to morning service and felt rather "pagan" during it. My decision to "observe" Sunday to some extent has been uninspiring. Had intended to write letters, but too much time has fizzled. Long, bumbling and inaudible phone call from CF and a long and interesting call from SD helped to kill the time, alas. General feeling is nonsville. However I think I will continue this form of observance as an item of discipline.

## Monday 25 April

Very bleary and late. Dreams of bother and confusion with telephones (R had rung after I'd gone to bed and rang again at 7.15 today). Dull, overcast day with less wind.

Read for two hours after break in case CF arrives this afternoon. The Book of Samuel is better, spending less time in begetting and lawmaking and more action. Story of David was rather good, but I couldn't see point of Ruth.

Got some tasks completed a.m. and feel drowsy after lunch. No word from CF.

Have just read my first fortnight. Though not getting much done I am a little less shakeable and less inclined to be irritated by N's kitchen habits. Now in my meditation I am more often deliberately leaving in order to sacrifice my bliss rather than needing effort to maintain it.[12] The greenhouse is a big advance: now there is somewhere to put my seeds, which would otherwise be in danger of being blown over. The latest black cloud is the need to write letters. How about completing today's garden and "craft" jobs to leave tomorrow as letter-writing day?

8 pm. No, there was an earlier black cloud: I had difficulty facing up to pricking out seedlings. Tried to analyse why. It was associated with earlier horrors of (a) jobs done half-heartedly and in a rush (b) without adequate seed boxes (c) causing a mess around the house, and (d) often with little outcome. I realised that these problems were largely due to my having to fit gardening between a nine-to-five schedule; so this time I could, and did, do it properly.

This week's test seems to be about coping with my sociability. In fact, CF did not come this afternoon, but as I was making supper there was a surprise visit from D and A. N made the tea (for a change!), leaving me to get on with the supper without being too rude. I tell people about sunrise and sunset meditation; I think this is necessary in order to limit "visiting hours". Was a bit "malignant" about N in the kitchen.

## Tuesday 26 April

Woke early—and hungry—after dreams of roast beef, so the timing this morning was better, but still not ideal.

After an hour of Pernety, I was out weeding alongside the path. Tried a small bit in order to experiment with severe methods, e.g. sieving all the topsoil. What a job! Couch grass thunderer! Despairingly detailed work, so two hours saw about one square yard done. I made an analogy with rooting out unnecessary thoughts or, if you like, "sin". Every tiny piece of couch grass root could start a whole new plant, and even sieving let some pieces through. But that does not entirely negate the

---

[12] I think this means that I was often reaching a state of bliss in my meditations and, instead of making an effort to prolong the bliss, was opting to stick to schedule. A choice of discipline over what could be indulgence.

work for there is a big difference between a thriving colony of weed, and scattered fragments when it comes to later maintenance. Without continuing vigilance it is true that a big effort at eradicating thoughts or weeds over a limited time produces no long-term improvement. But such an effort is well worth it if a little everyday maintenance can follow it. Also; where do you stop? Do you, like N, dig around plants and leave colonies of couch grass in their roots? No, I am prepared to make sacrifices so I dug up, separated, and replanted all garden plants. But I was not prepared to really shift my ground (the paving stones). I could see some roots going under, but felt they could be ignored as dead ends; until I lifted one stone! It was a mat of roots beneath, all raring to leap out. My heart sank, but turned to joy as I resolved to accept this new challenge. For, under paving stones roots, do not go deep but skim the surface seeking outlets. So I had an orgy of couch bashing.

Couch grass root tea is said to be so strengthening. Lovely sympathetic magic. I need the virtues of couch (persistence, strength, vigour, purposefulness) so much that I'd do better to drink couch tea than lazy old lion's blood! I noted the difference between couch and bindweed under the paving: couch wasted no time and went in straight lines, bindweed squiggled and struggled in all directions forever trying to bud. (However, the predictability of couch grass in this circumstance made it more vulnerable.)

Sermons under stones.

2.30 pm, and alas it is pouring. So the awful job that became a crusade must be postponed.

Wrote one letter … a beginning! Personal discipline bad this afternoon. This tends to happen when my plans are inadequate and get messed up. (I'd not allowed for rain.)

## Wednesday 27 April

Dream: a party at the M household. A asks RM if she can take C away for a fuck. RM says yes, but later says she couldn't stand the "tomato sauce" way A asked! For some reason A expects me to come too. I am wistful for it is clear she has no intention of being fucked by me as well, so I reckon it's a bit insensitive of her.

C shows me an item from his booklist, an original documentation of the veracity of the Jekyll and Hyde story! I see my childish signature on it and recognise it as an old family possession. It is kept in a beautiful wooden scythe, but C wants to chuck that away as it is no good for a "book" list. Excited at this relic of my past I try to show M, and she recalls it (I think). My father appears and I try to get him interested. He's a bit offhand, but shows me some old photos. I'm interested to compare him and me, but am embarrassed by their bad taste ... Fancy making a tree wear a g-string, even if it is a rather humanoid shape.

Puzzling over this dream delayed me a bit. Alas, I reached oratory with thoughts buzzing. I'd gazed at Saturn as I went to sleep (I think it is important to me in this operation).

Did quite a bit today; completed the strip alongside the path, cut the lawn, washed lots at launderette, sowed brassicas, etc. But it was not a day of well-made plans. Cold, but with quite a lot of sun (*just* able to sunbathe). Very cold morning. I'd slept with window open for the first time in ages.

### *Thursday 28 April*

Cold, wet day. Bloatered to St Albans after late start and spent the morning there visiting Mrs. L. It rained from noon onwards so I stayed indoors. Very dozy reading, skipped most of Chronicles—a boring rehash. Braved the bedroom shambles and tidied up a bit after tea. Read papers after supper.

### *Friday 29 April*

Another cold day, but the sun tempted me to sunbathe after lunch. Visited K early and did lots of small seed planting and potting jobs, but did none of the big jobs, e.g. cleaning, weeding or letters, so now (8.05 pm) I feel a bit unsatisfied. Was not very "good" today. The operation slipped my mind quite a lot. I was either caught up in feelings of exultation that made me want to rush about, or dominated by thoughts that were a bit hysterical. The morning meditation was disturbed by many thoughts. Recently I've found that centering in the belly reduces verbal thoughts, but I had less success with this today. Efficiency has improved a bit with less time wasted on unnecessary journeys. Made a little temporary censer.

There was a curious difference in the style of the evening oration; it was more torrential and humble. It also felt as though someone else was doing it, but it merged into the meditation without clear distinction. Cold. For first time my room did not smell nice when I entered it.

## Saturday 30 April

Worst ever lateness. I woke up in the night, hungry and worrying about crocodile suitcases(!). My mind was in slight fizz about work that I had to do, but the little censer was fine. I have a new routine that works much better: a.m., I clean out the oratory after the oration, and p.m., I do the chamber and take a bath before the evening oration.

Efficient morning: read for two hours, did kitchen, swept the old bedroom floor and beat the carpets, and removed the double-glazing. That was really foul. I also did some digging in the sun. I was in a slight dither this p.m. as I know I am going out with N to the Flamstead craft show.

Very late evening oration, late bathing, etc., so it was almost dusk. Felt exposed, burning my lamp in the semi-dark, and imagined people smelling the incense and thinking there was a fire. I was also afraid that N would come to ask where the matches were (must get another box). Such humdrum demons are sufficient to make me waver. As I came away I realised that my meditations were very calming and clearing; Taoist, but not awesome and terrifying—i.e. magical. First days were a little terrifying (my fear of the dark). I realise that N's presence has protected me from awe, as has Redbourn itself to a much lesser extent. I only have to go back to the cottage and there are food smells, music and all is mundane and everyday. Without N, a THING would build up.

Yet Abramelin does not insist on this THING. Why else would he have allowed his wife to live with him?

Perhaps it's the Christian influence in my life that makes me feel this ought to be more difficult in a purely blood and thunder sense. There was I, nearly ten minutes late—so why did not hellfire consume me? Answer: in order to encourage me to feel that ten minutes late does not matter—nor twenty minutes, nor one hour, nor doing it every day …

## Sunday 1 May

The oil was frozen this morning. I've taken to adopting the western devotional mudra in my orations[13] (as in illustration in Pernety). It does engender a contrite heart it seems.

"Did" the psalms in one and three-quarter hours this morning! Go for it tyger! I'm warming to them, trying to follow K's system of doing

---

[13] The praying position: palms together, fingers pointing up.

them all on Sunday and thirty a day during the rest of the week (with one day of blessed relief!). No church, for SD might come at any time.

What an ordeal! Non-stop barrage of esoteric conversation. I think that those interrogators who place a tin bucket over the prisoner's head and hammer it for hours on end are struggling to achieve a similar effect.

Dreams recalled: some conversation with Hon K, who came to visit. Also, there were two mice in my helmet. I was rather revolted and tried to chuck them out. Finnegan ate one, the other turned into a book I cannot remember.

## Monday 2 May

Dream in which I was explaining why, though clever, I did not do well in Maths Tripos.

Fed up with bumbling thoughts, so I expelled them and felt ecstatic this morning. But it was all in my head and it was an exertion to maintain the belly bit. Felt randy later as I read the *Aurora*.[14] For me the subtlest pornography is to read theological rants of flesh and lust.

Vast washing dominated the day. A lot of it was old stuff cleared from old bedroom. I now have curtains in my bedroom.

Wracked by lust today; this has not happened for a long time. It can't have been due to sunbathing because that had been much earlier in the day. Hard to believe it could be Boehme, though I do associate him with sex phantasies, e.g. while reading the Bible it rested on my crotch and I longed to wrap its soft pages round my prick and jack off. (Ideally, a whole class of sexually precocious kids should do it uncontrollably as the Victorian spinsterish Sunday school mistress swoons with horror.) Writing the idea down has not totally earthed it ... don't tell me I've got to actually do it!

During evenmed, the gentle pattering of rain sounded lovely on my "felt" roof. It reminded me of Easter Sunday.

It is now 9.20 pm and I have that burnt-out pelvis feeling that I associate with resisted lust. I found the following to be the best method of control: when the vision of sexy flesh came to mind, I accelerated time (Saturn on skates) and saw the flesh age and wrinkle, then decay with maggots and then fall stinking from the bones. I'm not kinky enough to get a kick out of *that*!

---

[14] By Jacob Boehme.

## Tuesday 3 May

I don't seem able to crack the 5.30 am getting-up barrier yet. I'll have to try guerrilla tactics, e.g. a thermos of hot drink by the bedside.

It is terrible how malignant thoughts flourish in me. It is as though there was some grain of truth in the psychologist's claptrap when they say that the outwardly meek tend to be inwardly spiky.

As I meditate, a corny range of attractive thoughts assail me: (a) sheer pleasure (e.g. dreams of nice possessions); then, more subtly, (b) dutiful thoughts (e.g. plans for the day—but why make them now?); and (c) observation of the process itself—either comparing my attempts with the written word, or else the preparation of "lecture notes" for teaching other people.

It was such a dreary day that I was reduced to letter writing, tidying correspondence, papers and magazines, and other such indoor jobs. So awful are such jobs that I felt a joyous righteous ebullient feeling which is hardly justified. Chatted with N to cheer him up—that's my excuse.

Felt very penitent in evenmed, realising how I judge my days on my achievements outside the operation itself. Abramelin does allow jobs to continue in these first two moons, and nearly all, if not all, of my jobs have direct relevance; so I should not feel guilty provided I recognise each task, e.g. tidying house, as one step towards my goal. This penitence was prompted by comparing myself with the emotional involvement of Georges Chevalier. I'm not sure that it is altogether a good thing, I suppose it is guilt that makes me feel it should be harder.

## Wednesday 4 May

Dream of facing three sharks underwater. Nothing happened. Then I was at the Mill, trying to go to evenmed and all embarrassed by family. Realised oratory was not there; thought I'd slink downstream to the old magic place, but I was seen and so I just shrivelled up and put my forehead in the stream. I saw some red lettering before me.

Woke early, up at five! Out early! Pow! The rest of day, however, was spiritually unexceptional. Read lots of *Aurora*. Set bike in order (new tyre, etc.)—at length. Set up seedling warm place in greenhouse, collected dry-cleaning, and did a little tidying and sorting in bedroom. Spent most of my time in the sitting room, shirking the cold chamber. I was aware of a resurgence of some muddle-headedness: went to collect a screwdriver from the garage and on return realised I needed pliers too.

## Thursday 5 May

8.50 am. Dreary drizzle again. Woke up early, but fell asleep again so I was heartily late. It was a bit too dull for any sunrise. Dawn of a day in which I plan to go out (unless the bike collapses), so I was full of distracting thoughts. Determined to get off to a good start in the second moon, etc. All set for a lousy meditation, but on realising this I made big initial effort and banished most thoughts. Today I must remember myself frequently so I do not get too distracted.

Humph! I managed to remember myself between events, but not during. Superb craft exhibition at St. Albans Abbey was an inspiration. In Old Hatfield I was assailed by snobbish thoughts and, although I slapped them down, I have not found a way of stopping them dead; I can only push them away.

But at Hawkers I met my match. It was interesting to hear Edna say I looked happier; I was so scruffy after cycling through the drizzle in my plastic cagoule, so there was no obvious physical prompting. Found I was on the verge of smiling sublimely—that was also interesting. But when the talk turned to bitter words about Newman then I fell to anger. Cycling back I could have kicked his face in. Why? Because he had hurt my pride—apparently (for I have never met him). What everyone has said about him has created a demon—it was this demon that I wanted to maim. The awful thing is that it really *is* bad. Even in my most refined mental state I have to admit that I would like to do something about a situation where one man's reputation can put a cloud over the lives of many. Similarly tonight I considered whether I ought not to fully adopt N's manner in the kitchen, and had to admit that in most cases my ways really were the best, and that to adapt would in many cases amount to lowering my standards (not wanted in spiritual quest).

What is wrong in each case is not my basic dislike, but the fact that I allow that dislike to pass via revulsion to obsession.[15] I should either

---

[15] I seem to be struggling with a theme that later surfaced in *Thundersqueak*: to what extent is it good to stick to high principles, or should one rebel against their domination of the individual?

conquer this internally, or else externally—e.g. early on I should have been able to discuss things with Newman, in a humble and non-impudent manner, in order to defuse the potential obsession. I know I would not hurl Book Three chapter twenty two[16] at Newman when this is over, but my shame is a double one; first that I should desire to, and secondly that I am so lacking in spirit that I should weakly repress my desire. Two wrongs make only one external right.

## Friday 6 May

Another hectic day, in keeping with my plan to get it over in as few days as possible. Only read psalms for half an hour then got ready to collect K and zoom to London. Everyone in London was pleasant. (One of *those* London days. Why is everyone either charming or surly on same day in London?) Got most things done till I became wracked with hunger and became feeble. Not very attracted by mummies, which K wanted to see. The only interest for me was to consider them in relation to what I'd read in Old Testament. But there was a wonderful scarab—vast, like a pouffe.

Sunny start, thank heaven, but rain later on. On return I was sore at being out-accelerated by a V8 MG, but it was between 80–90 mph and Bloaters was two-up so I cannot complain. Indeed he saved my life by waiting till the road was clear before running out of petrol. Still, it haunted me a little. I was exhausted after trekking to S's and the whole tiring and unsatisfying evening of coming and going. I was glad to return to the sanity of my oratory and bed.

This reminded me of my weakness and low resistance. For now I am glad of two days which heavily justify my retirement, but I very much hope that the end result will include sufficient strength and resistance that I will not need to retire in order to survive.

## Saturday 7 May

Interesting thing: I had not set alarm, but just at the time it would have gone off I heard a faint, short sound of the alarm—a ghost alarm. I wasn't too late, and I cleaned the oratory quite well. There is a temptation to start

---

[16] No idea what this means.

altering my meditation technique. Easy to justify experimentation—too easy. I'd better slog on with unimaginative old technique; for me *that* is the real experiment!

I started today cleaning the kitchen and the bathroom with commendable thoroughness. Long may it last. 12.30 pm.

Jeremiah was a terrible bore and I'm glad I've got him behind me. On and on about "having no other Gods but me" is like having an owner's handbook which endlessly repeats "make sure you only use genuine XXX spare parts, or else …" Ha ha.

Trapped by "perfection" again. Cleaning the clippers for wand-cutting turned out to be much harder than expected.[17] As a result of soldiering on, the whole of remaining cleaning routine was jeopardised and late. So evenmed was at dusk when the flickering lamp made for a weird unreality. I felt something with me, one moment a tiny light crossed my gaze from centre to left at eye level, apparently one to two feet away. Concentration poor. Lateness rules O.K.

### *Sunday 8 May*

Weather is painfully miserable. Foul. No sun was rising today so the 5.20 wand cutting was a sheer formality. Cut my finger as I was snipping couch grass roots around 10.30. Did not lose any blood, but I had to suck a lot though.[18]

Rather flat feeling. "Observing Sunday" limits me to more sedentary occupations and so I really felt the cold. Was definitely shrivelled when S came. She encouraged me to have a fuck, which did warm me up and I felt glowing. I was not as aware of the "fire in the belly" as last time, but there is no doubt that it was an ace screw. I tried to hold Mars and Venus in their respective stations with some success. No weariness after. Supper was late and then a surprise phone call from Arthur Cooper has created a mini-flap.

I have put my wand in a straightjacket of wood, nails, and twine to straighten it.[19] I'm sure there is an allegorical significance here. 8.30 and S is knocking on the chamber door.

---

[17]Refers to the general banishment principle of starting every operation with "virgin" or at least clean materials.
[18]Reference to Abramelin forbidding loss of blood.
[19]I had cut a branch of almond wood as directed, but it was not very straight.

In my asana, when it was really swinging, I've noticed a tendency for lower half of me to become rigid, and consciousness to evaporate upward. So far I've tended to relax this—valuing "naturalness" above "effectiveness". (At same time my spine has tended to arch slightly forward with shoulders hunched, rather than chest out.) This evening I allowed this tendency to continue. There was a sudden welling up from belly (blue?); a semi-anaesthetic cloud which enveloped all except the very top of my skull. A feeling of great mental peace ensued. My body was dead, yet I was quite aware of the tension and my posture.

Had a dream involving a holiday towards north west of the island of my dreams. I always seem to go to that quarter. It is a hilly country. This time N had made the journey in an old hearse and was extolling the glories of the views of the hills.

## Monday 9 May

Dream of returning to study at university, a "modern" campus. I was taking over the rooms of a disillusioned student.

Full of thoughts in a.m. meditation. After break I read first two books of Abramelin; no nasty surprises so far, except that I'm recommended to *say* the psalms twice a week, not just read them! 10am.

Decided to consult *I Ching* as the second moon commences; how should I conduct myself in the second moon? Should it be different from the first? Are there any particular faults I have overlooked and any dangers I should be wary of?

| 5-4-4 5-8-8 | 5-4-8 9-8-8 | 9-4-8 9-4-8 |
|---|---|---|
| *Received* | *First* | *Second* |
| ——— | ——— | ——— |
| ——— | ——— | ——— |
| ——x—— | — — | ——— |
| — — | — — | — — |
| ——— | ——— | ——— |
| ——o—— | ——— | — — |
| | 61 | 6 |
| | Confidence | Conflict |

It seems I am correct in my conduct insofar as any other way of life would disturb me (true), and that others could be a hindrance, but I can rise above such disturbance; it would be unwise to enter into any conflict. 12.30 pm.

Wilhelm translation of the *I Ching* is more suggestive (in a way hard to summarise). There is more relevance to my meditation, the wind above and the lake below are in harmony and the "openness to truth" in between. It seems the danger is of "hidden designs" down below, and the "horse leaving the team" (aspiring) above with the result that the "lake" degenerates to dangerous "water" and the wind refines to "heaven", but instead of co-operating as before they now pull apart.

This seems somehow fitting alchemically; but is this "conflict" a necessary part of the operation?

$$\frac{\overline{\quad\quad}\ \overline{\quad\quad}}{\overline{\quad\quad\quad\quad\quad}} \rightarrow \frac{\overline{\quad\quad}\ \overline{\quad\quad}}{\overline{\quad\quad}\ \overline{\quad\quad}}$$ = blackening? Turning into evil dragon?

Or is it a danger to beware of (stick to the middle way), or is it a warning of inevitable disaster?

The answer is to brood (as in "truth" character) and to keep listening.

Very bleary reading after lunch. Really I dozed on a razor's edge from real sleep. Abramelin wouldn't like it.

During evenmed I decided that I interpreted the *I Ching* as advice relevant to my meditations: it was becoming easy to achieve an ecstatic state with the "death" of the body as I have described. Although there should be a "conflict" in western alchemical terms, it is not of the sort described by the *I Ching* symbols (it is a struggling together rather than a drifting apart), so I am deciding to be careful when entering that blissful state, careful not to let the mind float to heaven; instead I hold the two together so that the wind blows the surface of the lake.

During morning cocoa I read *The Observer*. I was very fascinated by an article on David Frost. It seemed stupid and I resisted, knowing it would be the journalist's usual claptrap about a hollow man. But then I thought I ought to be able to find a message in anything. Sure enough the article helped to illustrate the tinsel and chance nature of fame—something I believe intellectually but need help to feel emotionally.

## Tuesday 10 May

Another drab and sluttish day (weather-wise). I can quickly regain the peace of meditation. It is a help if I reject the thoughts at the very beginning, the idea of sitting and gradually lessening thoughts is often an entry to a feeble meditation.[20]

Very bad end to an ill-planned day. It became quite warm and I became aware of the big gap in vegetable sowing due to the non-stop rain of recent weeks. Press had not yet produced a cover design. Some necessary work was done: letters dominated a.m.; peas sown, ground weeded and prepared for sweet corn. But in the evening I had huge washing up and scorzonera for supper—two very time consuming things. So supper was at 8.15 and I went late to the oratory with bulging gut. Cut meditation short. Now 9.15 and actually feel hot! The weather has changed.

## Wednesday 11 May

Nice realistic dream of cuddle with girl in my room at the Mill.

A bit too thoughtful in my meditation, more spontaneous and corny in my prayer.

Another excellent and thought-provoking letter from T.

I considered the image of the wind over the lake in my meditations, and was more formal and eloquent in my orations.

Planning the advert for *SSOTBME* was a quick exercise and an invocation of the Creative Spirit. Until now this [publishing *SSOTBME*] has been, perhaps, the best thing in my life, and so has taken priority over everything (even over sleep). But now I have the huge task of making it subservient to the silence of my meditation. I can do it, but it is not easy.

Before tea, after reading Bible for two hours in my chamber (it is warmer now), I made a brief gesture to physical exercise. I am fitter than I would be, because of the gardening and a more active life; but the long wet spell keeps me inactive (comparatively) and I do not want to deteriorate too far if I can help it.

---

[20]In everyday life I often start with a jumble of thoughts, then simply observe them until they melt away. Here, after some weeks of practice, I find it better to plunge straight into minimal thoughts, strictly forbidding them to multiply.

## Thursday 12 May

Very wet morning. My oration was eloquent and moving, but the meditation was one of those where I was reduced to thinking "no, I will not move until I have attained a few moments of silence". Quite a pain.

In view of the wetness, and the need to preserve time, I definitely plan to Bloaterise this morning. I'm seriously considering re-taxing him.

2 pm. I'm very impressed by New Testament after the Old. I like this in Matthew's gospel: "But thou, when thou fastest anoint thine head, and wash thy face: that thou appear not unto men to fast, but unto thy Father which is in secret", and, "For where your treasure is, there will your heart be also."

7.35. So much of today was dominated by outside events, and tomorrow will be too; I need to develop a more disciplined timetable.

The weather does not help. Now it is clear and lovely, but all day there has been wind and rain. Progress on flower garden has halted, and it is holding up some of my vegetable plans. Even my reading has been chaotic. A very poor start to the second month.

## Friday 13 May

Dream of an acquaintance (IR) driving me up a lane. A couple drove the other way and I saw tears in I's face. I asked if it was because of the couple. Yes, he said, and he wished that he had the ability to attain that harmony with a woman. I was touched and sympathised.

In last night's oration I felt a leaning feeling—I have noticed this before and corrected it, not quite sure if it was real or imagined. This time I followed it and, sure enough, I tottered from my cushion against the side of the oratory. Perhaps that is the snag with the kneeling posture.

Too thoughtful this morning. No self-remembering in St Albans.

Day dominated by preparing the advert for the book. Did manage to pull myself together on a number of occasions—improvement. Return of foul, cold, wet weather. Miserable.

*Esdras* was good.

## Saturday 14 May

Well into my oration before I remembered what day it was. Horror, absolute shame and disgust with myself. Now I know what confession really means.

I am so badly organised, so shambolic, so inept, so vague, so incompetent, so forgetful, so pathetic, so arrogant without cause. I just felt like dirt. I asked if I should return to the house to collect stuff. Mercifully the answer came directly, "yes". So I orated twice today. After cleaning the kitchen, break and pasting up advert, it was time to visit K, and St Albans (for printing). Very little self-remembering, yet I am a better person than I was.

Really, or "ideally", I should be able to do anything provided I did it in meditation with clarity.

### Sunday 15 May

Bright morning, but I was very bleary after late night. Much too thoughtful; thinking about today's visit to Mentmore and so on. Last night was late due to dipping into Ouspensky's *The Fourth Way*; as I am not yet free of my worldly ties it seemed the best book to keep me on the straight and narrow.

After getting up "early" we went to view the sale at Mentmore;[21] the huge collection was ex-Rothschild. Fortunately our paces were different: I would have whizzed round and returned to linger over one or two items, but N went very slowly and lingered over the paintings, etc. As a result I had plenty of opportunities to pull myself together and calm my mind. But it was a losing battle. I was achieving a relative calm, a very useful aloofness, but it was far from real clarity.

Overall it was rather disturbing. I like to see such a collection and to know such collections exist. I begin to think I would like to take over such a collection, but then I ask myself what for? I would not do it justice, and I could not look after it or use it. It would be a whole time lifestyle and here I am unable to look after a small cottage and garden adequately. So why would I like to take it over? Largely in order to surprise the world, to check (in some small way) that feeling of decay and running down that exists everywhere. I suppose ideally I would like a good friend to do the job for me, a more single-minded man, and

---

[21]Mentmore Towers, built 1852–54 for Baron Mayer de Rothschild, one of several country houses built for his family in Buckinghamshire. The government refused the offer of the house and world-class collections in lieu of death duties, resulting in "one of the finest country house sales of the twentieth century". I bought a leather gentleman's picnic set. The Transcendental Meditation foundation bought the house.

so leave me free. Perhaps if I had the money I could buy it for such a friend? Strange idea.

I do not myself see this as any worse than the end of an era. Much greater collections of treasures have vanished and reformed in the past. No doubt union leaders will be building up such collections in the future.

I achieved an immense rock-like stillness in the evening meditation after a struggle with temptations.

## Monday 16 May

Dream of the great moment of decision: I had read about it, now for the experience of it. Resisting my fear, I stepped out of the elegant house into the night, and there they were, the two men. It was just as it was written, and yet I was surprised (and relieved). Just as it was written, the one on the left flapped with his little flippery hand for me to hurry. They briefed me rapidly, I was called … (I've forgotten …) and I was informed that I had to run with them and do just what they said. We ran down to the bottom of the path, when they suddenly stopped and lurked—we'd been seen. I was told to kneel and keep my face to the ground and on no account look up—if asked I must say my new name. The crowd gathered round. They sounded amiable, perhaps sinister. I could not resist a peep at one of them as I knelt—he had red hair. They questioned me, tempted me, left a piece of a Crunchy bar for me. Then they left. We rushed on up the other side—I felt I was keeping up quite well. I think this was some other test that I had passed.

Then I got distracted suddenly and realised I was meant to be high up on the frame of this building in progress. The ladder was gone but I made up for lost time with ingenuity, and again had to avoid my fear of heights. "What must be done, must be done." I caught up with the two men. They said, "Remember this, the writer's name is Roderick". At first I thought they were giving me another name when I saw the writer approaching. I greeted him. After that I remember nothing.

Crazy morning. I awoke about 5-ish and was out about 5.30 but felt terribly sleepy and fuzzy. After rather poor oration and meditation I returned and lay down to rest on my bed. I must have slept—though I was only aware of dozing—for I had a dream of watching RM lining a wall with planks—and came round at 7.30. The full enormity hit me at 8. I read *The Fourth Way* till N left, then had a light break.

As a result it felt like an ordinary day off work—it felt all wrong and shapeless. In order to limit shapelessness I washed up after break and then put the book in clamps.[22] Mrs. Smith was out so I don't have the saw. Wrote up and now it's 10.35.

The day was a little too dominated by book cover. I went to the kiosk to announce the telephone breakdown to the GPO—in case I was missing calls. The trip to St. Albans was in vain as they'd not printed yet. But Javelin had done lovely cover. Felt joyful on seeing it. Anticipating over-enthusiasm during meditation, so in my oration I modelled thanks around the joy of creativity. The meditation was very upright, and quite good. But I feel that the operation does not *dominate* my life enough. Other things are seen not as minor tasks within the operation, but as important jobs in their own right.

## Tuesday 17 May

Three dreams, recorded in other diary. [First, about Austin Spare books: one by him, one about him written by Quiller-Couch with many photos of him as a physical culturist. Second I was helping a tribe resist attack by Roman forces that were superior—except I had a machine gun! Third, about an absurd steam train load of celebrities arriving at St Albans.]

Outrageous oversleeping: woke at 6—an hour late. I had in fact not set my alarm with the intention of oversleeping. After yesterday's extremely weary start (I was fine after) and a slight impression of sickness passing me by, I thought I would "sail the wind" and allow myself a slightly later morning, but I never bargained for such lateness. At least there was no sunrise to be missed. Oration and meditation weren't very good.

This morning I have been more diligent about maintaining clarity, without, of course, lasting success. The printing for my book has laboured on till yet another day and I'm growing weary in the sun.

I "woke up" quite a number of times today.[23] Had a feeling of satisfaction because of three long-standing jobs tackled and finished; weeding by the path, binding the first batch of books and getting them trimmed, cutting and raking up weeds and grass. But I note that my satisfaction

---

[22]Refers to the process of home-made perfect binding. It was the second edition of *SSOTBME*, with an Austin Spare cover.
[23]In the Ouspensky sense of being totally in the present.

stems from such worldly achievements and everyday success instead of being from the quality of my meditation or daily consciousness.

### Wednesday 18 May

Woke at 5 and was up at 5.30. In my morning oration I considered that my idea of God is uncertain. My strongest feelings incline towards Taoist idea of the universe, or a "much out of nothing" view as in Jung's *Seven Sermons*. Yet for this operation, with its Judeo-Christian spirit, I have returned to the personified God of my childhood; so it is hard not to feel that I'm sort of "play-acting". So far I have not rebelled against this because to do so would lay me far too open to the temptation of being a spiritual nomad; forever changing my oration and never settling. Although the wording and the mood has altered, I have deliberately maintained my framework and my view of God in order to be consistent.

This morning I was aware of my intellectual difficulty. But reading the Old Testament through does not encourage trifling with different deities. I felt that it was better to persevere with an unknown rather than to flit from one to the other. So I confessed that, over the years, I had constructed my own intellectual barrier between myself and God. I saw an analogy with the long, cold winter that is still with us, whose thick cloud has kept the earth cold despite the May sun above. It seemed like the clouds were of my own devising.

I will finish with the Bible soon, so I prayed for pardon as I set out on an exploration to find my view of God in comparative religion. I said it was as though I was exploring my barrier to see whether I could find any holes in it through which God could be glimpsed. I could go on to enlarge the hole from there …

Accordingly, I prayed for pardon if in the coming weeks I seem to be playing with different deities—all along I would have just one aim before me. I will not change the *shape* of my oration, just my world-view as I do it.

As if to acknowledge my decision as worthy, the clouds cleared and the sky is unbroken. Summer has at last visited us. Noon.

Read more of Paul's epistles—they do seem crummy after the gospels and acts. He seems a weary old gasbag to me. Reading in the hot sun and the high wind was not satisfactory. The slight awkwardness prevented wandering but also hindered true clarity. N dined exceptionally early so we coincided and therefore it was a long chat.

## Thursday 19 May

Dream of Cranham[24]—the version that has interesting buildings around the chapel and Irving's area. M was involved in some WI thing in "the pavilion" which was in that area. It was a magnificent (comparatively) affair. Built of wood, with a balcony (like the Wissendens' house) and full of huge china wear. I was surprised Cranham could maintain such a collection and such a building. At first I thought it was a bungalow. I was told it was the old banqueting hall of Henry VIII. I said how funny that I'd lived in Cranham yet never known of its existence, but I knew that was untrue because I had actually known the old pavilion was there, but had never bothered to look at it, or realised its interest. I noticed that it was octagonal. B (?) told me it had eight storeys. We went to the top and I was sure we were only six storeys up. Going down again was scary; it was an outside staircase like a fire escape made of creaky wood and I was frightened on each floor as we turned. It was a bit like a pagoda. As I left, it looked huge.

This dream seemed important to me because of my lie: a place I'd known of and ignored, which I said I'd never heard of, turning out to be a treasure. The consistent eight-fold symbolism only struck me as I woke up.

I had later dream in which R was angry with me. I think it was because I was dallying, but I'm not sure. The remarkable thing is the unusualness of R being angry with me.

Bad start as I woke early and then fell asleep. I dreamt I was masturbating and trying to find a bible passage to justify me for not being celibate. I awoke at 10 to 5, and got up at 5.25. Not a very good oration. The clouds were scudding like yesterday morning.

Hectic! I was efficient in St. Albans, thank heavens—went on Bloaters. But parents arrived at 12.30. It is marvellous how I learn my weaknesses; few things rattle me it seems, like an attempt to cook a meal for guests who have just arrived and who cannot wait to talk over the meal. You really do need another person to do the chatting for you. So I was terribly screwed up and never really had the chance to unwind. I'm still doing so now. 8.10.

I still have another half hour of scripture to read. I'm so sick of Paul, I'll try the apocrypha again.

---

[24]My childhood home parish in the Cotswold Hills.

## Friday 20 May

Timing better this morning. A light morning. Many interesting thoughts during meditation, but they did not seem so "sticky" and I was able to be quite calm and attentive despite them.

Day of digging and compost shovelling. Feel weary and yet there is not a lot to show for it. Digging does set my mind racing, I can only say at least I was aware of it racing. Have just read *Seven Sermons*. Feel I would like to memorise some scriptures so I could recite them as I do jobs like digging in order to occupy my mind.

## Saturday 21 May

Late, out 5.45. Remembered clearing stuff but forgot key and had to return. Bad thoughts till I recited the Lord's Prayer.

Yesterday a huge soggy dead spider was on the floor by the altar and I cast it forth from the window (using a piece of card) whereupon the wind raged. As I concluded the oration I was surprised by the sight of a huge caterpillar on the wall, also to be cast out (by the door).

After break I read a very good *Anima Magica Abscondita*[25] again and re-learnt two chapters of *The Book of Lies*.[26] Sure enough, they filled my mind as I cleaned the kitchen, as a pop song would. 10.20.

I feel close to illness today.

Beautiful sun and high cool wind. Very distinctive day. I found *The Book of Lies* passages very helpful in my digging. Curious thing: Peckinpah (the garden blackbird) came and stood very close, his head hanging low at times. He ate the worms I gave him, but did not himself forage. He looked scruffy. Saturday: shabby blackbird—dying? Gold eyes and beak is black. Is there some sign? He returned during the evening digging.

Saturday is a day of lessons and rebukes. On both occasions I had to return for my key to the oratory!

Some torment from lustful thoughts. I explained in the oration that I was sorry for the lustful thoughts because they were a waste of time and energy. Personally I like lust, and feel the world needs more of it;

---

[25] *Anima Magica Abscondita, or, A Discourse of the Universall Spirit of Nature: with His Strange, Abstruse, Miraculous Ascent and Descent,* by Eugenius Philalethes (i.e. Thomas Vaughan).
[26] By Aleister Crowley.

however, it should be an *action* and is no justification for abstract intellectual and emotional wallowing when objects and subjects of lust are not present. I pray that this view is not a self deception.

## Sunday 22 May

Oh, glorious morning! As I had often promised myself, I took a drink to my bedside to help rouse me a.m. So I was up at 5. (Feel *virtuous* at only being quarter of an hour late—this is how bad I have become!)

I am thinking too much about the *technique* of meditation. I used to make it a rule to meditate until I'd "had enough" and then do a little more. Recently I'd dropped the second bit, but I am spending just as long in the oratory.

Sun! And at last a drop in the North Wind. 9.50am.

Overpowered by sun and fun. Read quite a bit a.m., but N's friend was a great distraction. Earlier, I've been deflected by women who talk all the time and give one no peace; but Trudy is the opposite, she's so receptive and interested that you find yourself talking all the time. Daily routine went haywire. Joined them at Hatfield and seldom woke up. I'm now seeing if I can pull myself together; my only "task" for today was to deal with the letters, and none have been written.

## Monday 23 May

Pathetic. Out about 7.45 and there was a bright sun. Not very good oration. It is now 11 with high-level clouds.

Not much of a day, except for when I read *The Gospel of St. Thomas*, which was very interesting.

K a.m. and S p.m.

## Tuesday 24 May

A little better today. Although I was up at a better time (5.05), I was very bleary. I decided to meditate longer to try an exceed the "natural" time as I had done at the beginning. I must have held asana for half an hour. My legs were asleep with pins and needles. No very obvious quality bonus, except that the meditation would probably have been very poor if I had stopped at the normal point. Too much free wandering of mind: worse than originally. Perhaps because originality has worn off. I notice during day now that, although I am "waking up" much more often, there is a tendency to make less of it: i.e. I am "half-waking" more often, or remembering to remember without actually remembering.

Sunbathing tends to evoke lustful thoughts in great numbers, but overall this is quite useful. I had been taken aback by my unusual absence of such phantasies, it was all too easy. Now I can practise resistance.

Feeling of nearby sickness today. Think I'm resisting a cold. After all it is coming up to my hay fever fortnight. My heel hurt faintly and looked as if it was cut. But on inspection it seems to be cracking. I am considering myself on Lowen[27] lines, e.g. I'd noticed in my weight-training poor development around my middle—belly and hips and small of back (backache and indigestion too) and I'd seen parallel with the weak middle zone of my letters (handwriting) and finger phalanges and therefore deduced that a consistent "middle zone" program right across the board was called for. Interestingly, this incorporates tidying up business, finance, work and everyday affairs! Just recently I'd noticed skin on my face was of worse texture than elsewhere and was seeking parallels. Now, what do I make of a cracked heel …?

I see a new blackbird is around.

## Wednesday 25 May

I think I've found where Spasmodeus lives. Spasmodeus is a particular pet demon of mine who is especially responsible for a sort of slapdash clumsiness, e.g. when I empty ashtrays into a bucket indoors—a delicate operation demanding finesse lest the ash gets spilt—I always misjudge so the lip of the ashtray hits the rim of the bucket and sends the ash flying. That is Spasmodeus's job.

Aware of vast quantities of the "fool's parsley" type stuff flowering in my garden and aware of the allergic effect from past experience, I went out with sickle and blocked nostrils at 7.20 or so this morning and cut the lot to be buried in the compost heap. I found I was stumbling and blundering. Now I feel knocked out. My mind is as though under a leaden, clammy cloth. Something heavy is in the solar plexus of diameter such that I feel a barrier to life at the crease of my groin which cuts off my legs. A similar, slightly less acute effect at arms and legs. How remarkable. Everything seems too much effort. I have taken a flower and put it in water so I can attempt to make a homeopathic remedy.

---

[27] Alexander Lowen, MD; creator of bioenergetics, author of The Betrayal of the Body.

Great peace in my last two meditations. *Thomas's Gospel, Taoist Yoga* and *Golden Flower* all point to search for a place of light in the brain. I had noticed in my meditation with eyes closed an effect which fooled me sometimes into thinking the sun had shone into the oratory. Now I sought out this effect and achieved great peace. But possible separation (going different ways) of spirit and soul? 8am.

### Thursday 26 May

Today collapsed at about noon. Up 4.45 and so out to a good start. "Saluted the sun" on the lawn as it was up and warm. Slight dew. Fairly well ordered so I was early cycling to St. Albans and saw Mrs. L before signing on. Did not complete shopping, but still I was brisk after.

But K was expected at noon, did not come till nearly 2. So I was in quandary about waiting for lunch, wanting to sunbathe, but not wanting to be caught starkers and so on. Result was flap and disruption as when M and RM came. Late and shattered routine, self-remembering almost forgotten, place an untidy shambles.

As I did not bath yesterday, perhaps there is too much dirt?

Lost the light a.m., too late and broken p.m., but still rejoicing in the peace.

### Friday 27 May

Wonderful morning, out before 5.15 and sun saluted on lawn. Washed hair and feel better for it. 8.50 am.

Did grand job: I cleaned and oiled Mrs Smith's clock and now it is going well she says. Also dug on in flower bed, but do not seem to have achieved much. I was thinking too much about whether I was getting all possible sun, and whether I could be seen from the common. Really rather bad. Lunchtime leaving drink for NF; went on Bloaters (so I could have quick lunch before going) and saw all the crowd. After supper I lay on the floor to gather energy to write. 8.45 pm.

### Saturday 28 May

Did not write up today. Hot day, visited Hertfordshire show across fields with N, George R visited for tea. Touch of fool's parsley allergy a.m., otherwise okay. Found light again.

Because of George, evening was out of time. Had to eat *after* meditation and so ached with hunger. Not looking forward to fasting.

## Sunday 29 May

Dream was appropriate: shambles of dithering involving John I and my family.

Out 5.35 on lovely dewy morning. Thoughts are too plentiful, more than ever nowadays. Writing up after the break. Will go out to read in the sun.

As I read the psalms I got an erection. Thought I would try to transmute the energy into alchemical energy. Failed and jacked off a vast quantity of semen. Somewhat amazed at my lack of control: and what to do with the output? Swallowed it (without great revulsion) rather than waste it: it was a question of "lose no blood" vs. "eat no flesh". Soon after the baking sun went in and it became a cold day! Have had to dress in wool again!

## Monday 30 May

Cold and cloudy (but not, alas, damp). I feel heavy, morose, ineffective. Today, as yesterday, I read some psalms in my oration. Meditation was much better, but must get a more comfortable mat if I am not to indulge in "mortification".

The Kabbalah is helping to reorganize the confusion of my deities: many or one? I incline to Basilides: "But woe unto you, who replace these incompatible many by a single god",[28] yet would find it hard to adapt Abramelin to polytheism and so need to structure the many into one pattern. This is not the same as reducing them to one, because I never attempt to worship the whole pattern, but only my inner "One Star in the Zenith".

After breakfast I started to re-read McGregor Mathers's *The Kabbalah Unveiled* and completed the introduction. I look forward.

Big "in the world" day (a.m.). Went to St. Albans to pay in giros to bank and have my expensive ritual haircut—relief. Some shopping, then I visited St. Michael's Church (in honour of "St. Michael and All Angels" associations). Struck by five-fold symbolism in the newer tower,

---

[28]Quotation from Jung's *Septem Sermones ad Mortuos*.

pentagon windows most unusual. Was intrigued by a 4-6-8 mandala window in the chapel, and by the *lovely* woman vacuum cleaning the church. (Can she be the vicar's wife?) Also, the first grave in the aisle which commemorates someone who "left this life" on 1 April (me?) "*Ano* [sic] *domini* 1691". Kenneth Grant would like the "Ano" bit!

On to Luton for Bloater's tax and to arrange for a new [front] fork replacement; also greeted Andy S.

After late, late lunch I wrapped up against bitter cold (indoors) and read the truly dreadful *Book of Concealed Splendour*[29]—or whatever it was. Drowsiness crashed down like a ton of dung. I had to have tea at half-time and dilute the stodge with some alchemy. Ugh. Hope rest of the books are better.

Minimal achievements in the garden. Feeling nearly ill again. Supper was foully over-salted.

## Tuesday 31 May

Untidy dreams. Woke and re-dozed and re-awoke very late. Out by 5.45. Managed to hold to light successfully while concentrating in belly, as I did last night. This seems to be a good technique. But time stands still, not whizzes. I unwind from what seems like a pleasant eternity to find that about quarter of an hour has passed!

I do not feel well. A sort of curled-inward stagnant feeling is inside me. It would be hard to "go out to work" today. I need to be at home. I remember at HSA[30] questioning our idea of illness; I was seated at a boring terminal with that sort of flu where repose is bliss and activity is hell. I felt "ill", yet was in a state most suitable for the job of the moment where a "well" me would have been too impatient. I wondered if our ideas of "illness" were not a little misplaced. Perhaps a lot of so-called "illness" is really a transient psychic state disposing oneself towards certain activities other than what is required in everyday jobs. Is pregnancy an "illness"? Is a state that disposes me to lie still and reflect for two days (something that would normally be difficult) really an illness?

Read some of *Greater Holy Assembly*[31]—much better. However, I tend to interpret it on the lines of the *New Scientist* joke: as a description of a

---

[29] In *The Kabbalah Unveiled*.
[30] Hawker Siddeley Aviation, my previous place of work.
[31] In *The Kabbalah Unveiled*.

radio/TV telephone left by a spaceman who had implanted an idea of abstract deity into primitive peoples for an experiment, or as a mission, and left a communication channel in order to control and monitor the outcome. The idea is a "wicked" temptation and I am afraid I have not resisted it a lot because it has provided a thread of interest which makes the book more memorable. But it is "wicked" because it means I have fallen back on a material image of the deity rather than an open-ended abstract one. So if the idea is historically true it would mean that it has failed: after several millennia we still prefer material idols to spiritual concepts; the idea of spacemen leaving a walkie-talkie (and viewie) is more fascinating to me than philosophical and theological speculation.

Finished *Greater* after supper. The above-mentioned enthusiasm had fizzled out. I was only intrigued by my efforts to translate the "dirty" bits in Latin. Reasonably solid achievement in garden in view of my slightly poor condition.

Malignancy against N was prominent—until he appeared to be sad. It seems that I have so much sympathy for the underdog that I do my best to keep people down so that I can be sorry for them.

### *Wednesday 1 June*

Day of (a) sun, (b) washing (big laundry job), and (c) weeding the flower bed. Blew my gut with asparagus and malta mosseline sauce p.m. Re-read *The Cloud of Unknowing*. Good. Relevant to final two moons.

Now running late. 9.20.

### *Thursday 2 June*

Did not get to bed till nearly 11 after bath last night, so "allowed" myself to sleep till 5.30.

Took extra blanket to soften my mat. Used mantra, yesterday tried OMNIL,[32] today AUMGN.[33] In time to out- and in-breath. This was inspired by *The Cloud of Unknowing*. There were still many thoughts, but perhaps they were in some way more distant? Held the light. Uncomfortable rigidity came. I managed to relax it without losing light.

---

[32]Suggested by William Gray for his instant banishing ritual in *Magical Ritual Methods*. It neatly encapsulates *omnis* ("all") and *nihil* ("nothing").
[33]Crowley's extension of AUM, from *Magick in Theory and Practice*.

Wish fulfilment dream last night—showing FV around a house I'd bought. It turned to shambles despite mental effort to make it a smart Elizabethan manor.

9.20 pm. Oh hell. I'm furious with myself. Everything ran late and pathetic. Read about Sufism today. Just getting back to efficient timing as I put supper on before 6 when Mike F turned up and evening wasted till 7.40. Bloody chaos. I'm in a mental muddle: (a) hopeless planning shattered by surprise visit, (b) getting in usual flap over a visitor, (c) not waking up then, or after. Bloody pathetic. Reduced to swearing at myself.

I certainly will not go to Mill on Saturday. If it were not for S I'd cancel tomorrow. And I have not checked Bloaters or washed up.

## Friday 3 June

Out 4.50. Read psalms in morning gloom. After a period of holding to the light and circulating with AUMGN a series of rushes of energy moved up my back. Not what I would expect, i.e. a serpent up the middle of my spine, but more a wave which was felt across and especially at sides of my back. Washed up to heart level. Found I had been out nearly an hour.

Plenty of stupid thoughts at breakfast about all the magic spells I am going to do. Now 7 and must get ready for Cambridge trip.

Alarmed by bloody egg at breakfast. Think I removed all the blood. (Without touching it!)

Day in Cambridge. Little of worth.

## Saturday 4 June

Up 5-ish. Still feel physically tired after punting yesterday. Kitchen cleaning was hard. Now 10.35 and hazing.

Oh gosh, how tired I am. Tried early lunch so as to recover for dynamic afternoon. But now 5.10 and I've dozed through Iamblichus[34] and lingered over tea. Fragmented, pottering activities. Must do some cleaning ere NGT comes.

Did so, and it helped make evening less inefficient. N did not come till about 10.

---

[34] *Iamblichus on the Mysteries of the Egyptians, Chaldeans, and Assyrians* in the horrid translation by Thomas Taylor.

## Sunday 5 June

Rain, glorious rain. I feel it moistening my soul; I also suspect I have a cold, dammit. Now we have a West Wind at last after weeks of North Wind.

Held light and AUMGN and felt rushes of energy again for a short while. They shoot up from my pelvis to the middle of my back then seem to reappear, or induce a pulse, in my scalp. The effect occurred again slightly after break as I read the psalms. I can produce it now.

Complete nonsville for operation. Read for one hour after break and another after supper. Otherwise it was solid collating[35] with records playing so I was not even very good at waking to alertness. Realise this is an obvious blow; tomorrow will be similar. But my main priority is not to get rattled. Events hinted that that was the test. This week the pressure for visits is huge. But a complete book binding (or as near as can be done) would be such a boon.

Now I must read Abramelin for guidance on the next two moons.

10.25. Supreme bliss in my meditation. I had an inkling of it in my prayer and then it came. It never left. It grew dark and I could have stayed all night. Difficult, for Abramelin says I should now start to extend my prayers "to my utmost". As it was I felt I had to drag myself away. Why? (a) because I want some sleep, (b) because after a crummy day op-wise what merits such bliss?

It is not deserved, and is more than even kindness can give. So is it temptation? A false path? I said the Lord's Prayer and a chill and goose-flesh washed over me, but no pain. Now I'm still zonked. I am very grateful for this oasis in a desert of incompetence.

I will strip my wand.

## Monday 6 June

Absolutely shagged. Late night after surfeit of bliss and stripping wand. Alas, bliss has not vitalised me, I am in a state of semi-coma having nodded my way through Thomas Vaughan. Cold and wet morning—never best for vitality. Oration and meditation quite good, wished I had not been so weary.

---

[35] Refers to collating *SSOTBME* pages for binding.

My tongue is peeling again, after months of relief.

Today was another fiasco. Read for one and three quarter hours and that was all. Awareness went to the winds when Chris M brought friends around.

## Tuesday 7 June

Today was no more than a singularly unproductive day off work. I don't know why I go on—I suppose there's nothing else to do. I've got no money, no job. I could go home, but it's a bit cold for the journey. I could garden but it's too cold and too much effort. I could go to S or W for a bang, but might not get it up. I'll go to bed.

*PHASE TWO*

# The second two moons

The second two moons mostly require an intensification of what has already begun:

> The two second Moons follow, during the which ye shall make your prayer, morning and evening at the hour accustomed; but before entering into the Oratory ye shall wash your hands and face thoroughly with pure water. And you shall prolong your prayer with the greatest possible affection, devotion and submission; humbly entreating the Lord God that He would deign to command His Holy Angels to lead you in the True Way, and Wisdom, and Knowledge, by studying the which assiduously in the Sacred Writings there will arise more and more (Wisdom) in your heart ... You shall also wash your whole body every Sabbath Eve ...
>
> I have already given unto you sufficient instruction. Only it is absolutely necessary to retire from the world and seek retreat; and ye shall lengthen your prayers to the utmost of your ability.
>
> As for eating, drinking and clothing, ye shall govern yourselves in exactly the same manner as in the two first Moons; except that ye shall fast (the Qabalistical fast) every Sabbath Eve.

The routine was still being disrupted because of weather changes, visitors, and arranging a second edition of *SSOTBME*. But here is a typical day:

> 4.35 am get up.
> 4.50—5.55 Oration.
> 6.15—6.45 breakfast.
> 6.45—8.45 read psalms and *Thrice Greatest Hermes*.
> 8.45—9.55 planting vegetables in garden.
> Made coffee and breakfast for visitor, then walked to high street for cheese.
> 11.20—12.30 sowing vegetable seeds and weeding.
> 12.30—1.20 lunch and light fire.
> 3.30—5.15 reading *New Scientist* and *Thrice Greatest Hermes*.
> 5.15—6.40 planting out brassicas in the rain.
> 6.40 cooked and ate supper.
> 9.05—10.05 Oration.

## *Wednesday 8 June*

Kicked off with a big one; I dozed on till 6.05 so was over one and a half hours late! Lovely sun has since been joined by a few clouds.

Taoist dream (amongst several other dreams); a judge who, whenever forced to convict a criminal always convicted himself in some way. But it was pointed out that he need not have worried, for he was such a good judge that the accused never noticed him at all, just assumed that his punishment was the work of natural justice!

In today's morning oration I yearned for guidance, so far had I wandered off the rails. Square centre of the window, standing apart from its neighbours was a leaf which was fresh and green yet severely deformed, with two large notches on the left side, and one small one at the top of the right side: somehow it recalled my early dreams of the left-hand side being beyond my ken and yet the right-hand side also being tainted (the crooks on the right-hand side of the house did live upstairs).

*I Ching* divination: in the light of the last two moons, how can I improve myself in the next two moons? How can I make better progress in the second two moons?

| 9-4-4  5-8-8  9-4-4 | 5-4-8  9-4-8  9-8-4 | |
|---|---|---|
| *Received* | *First* | *Second* |
| ───── | ───── | |
| ───── | ───── | |
| ── ── | ── ── | |
| ── ── | ── ── | |
| ───── | ───── | |
| ── ── | ── ── | |
| | 59 | |
| | Dispersion | |

Again, Willhelm was most useful: "Wind blowing over water disperses it into foam and mist. This suggests that when a man's vital energy is dammed up within him [...] gentleness serves to break up and dissolve the blockage [...] Through hardness and selfishness the heart grows rigid and this rigidity leads to separation from all others. Egotism and cupidity isolate men. Therefore the hearts of men must be seized with devout emotion. They must be shaken by religious awe in the face of eternity—stirred with an intuition of the One Creator of all living beings and united through the strong feeling of fellowship experienced in the ritual of divine worship."

I especially note that I did *not* get six in the fourth place which would have suggested that I should not give in to sociable contact with my friends.

An especial worry of late has been the chaos in my life that outside contact causes. So should I be more isolated?

The suggestion seems to be "no". What is wrong is not my friends but my own egotistic rigidity which cannot be flexible enough to adapt to contacts. My friends are not invaders, they are parts of me. Therefore there is no reason why my routine should be shattered. What I need is a little more devotion in my wooden "ship" (the oratory!) and a little less worrying about people as intruders. For "little", read "a lot".

Rest of the day reasonably ordered and constructive. Some tidying, laundry, correspondence and gardening. Held off stupid thoughts better than of late. It is now 9.30 and I have not yet bathed. Poor oration.

### Thursday 9 June

Alarm did not go off and I did not wake till 5.30—out at 6. Very cold morning. I am *angry* that in mid-summer it is still too cold to germinate my beans.

Yesterday I had further revelations/ideas about the other half. I recalled past dreams of fighting a strange man in my house, and not being able to chuck him out. I have always become irritable with partners, and I get angry with N. So other people in my house align with my other half. In N's case, my irritation is linked with his weary behaviour—so like my behaviour with my family. This links with Mars in Pisces (N's sign) which is the only planet on the left-hand side of my chart, and the third house.[1] I am very critical of N's unhygienic and untidy behaviour (Mars opposition, Jupiter in Virgo). Certainly, energy (Mars) is my most out of control part; I can usually conjure up sociability, tact, intellect and so on, but energy is sometimes there, and sometimes not.

3.45 pm. How angry I have been. In St. Albans I could not get the printing done, which was frustrating and time-consuming. Awareness of time wasting. Was held up for lunch waiting for SB. Phone call postponed till "mid-afternoon". Lunch was not fun. I felt a bit abstracted from tales of "good old Lionel". I suppose I was glad S was not there. Felt a bit tipsy on very little. On return I wanted to doze but was angry with myself, so I cut the lawn, then hoed in preparation for planting brassicas. Returned to change and lie down. Dozed slightly then meditated. Now there is a little sprinkle of "rain". Is my anger related to above recognition of Mars?

Help! SB staying till Saturday. But this is good as it means I can get on with my jobs and not spend rest of the day entertaining. I feel more relaxed.

### Friday 10 June

Woke very early—4.10—and dozed till 4.35. SB was up for a pee. Lovely morning, damp and warm. Just what garden needs. Gosh, sparrows look untidy compared with most little birds.

Last night I was uncomfortably aware after eating too much: my heart thumped irregularly and not only distracted me but occasioned anxiety. A pulse went right through to my temples.

---

[1] I later discovered my true time of birth, so this last comment is actually dependent on the system of houses used.

This morning I separated fine from gross and waited till it pattered like rain. To some extent it helps to let my mind wander (without losing observation) because it saves it from too actively considering the actual processes.

Last night I noticed how my prominent leaf had sunk out of prominence, this physical disappearance reflects psychic relief. Also happy that S has left me in peace.

Pretty distracted day. Lots of welcome rain and planting of brassicas. Late supper so I expect poor evenmed. T's letter came; it looks as if fast (now begun) is the big one.[2] But for tomorrow I will allow myself couch tea and ginseng I think.

## Saturday 11 June

Thoughts were bad yesterday evening and this morning. Curious effect this morning; starting at the neck and spreading, my flesh felt as heavy as lead. Heavier and heavier. With *I Ching* comment in mind I relaxed and eventually effect eased. Then the electric flashes up my back, which I encouraged.

Cold bright morning has become cold and dull. Shame. Though not hungry, I am always thinking about food.

Feel okay but wan, as when one is in bed after flu. No pain localised in the stomach, but rather a numbing of the brain (could get a headache). I put on coffee for SB and N.

I don't like fasting very much. It must be a help if you believe you are doing good—which I do not. I had a regulation cup of couch grass tea at noon for a fling. Day collapses as I stand around in a haze. Read quite a lot and did some planting out in the greenhouse. Intended gardening was frustrated by heavy rain. 3.40.

Thank heavens it's over. Day ended with "boring" sherry party. I had tried to back out, but it was clearly making N a little anxious so I had to wash my hair and dress up. It was a smoothies do; ICI directors, barristers and so on. I was trundled around from group to group like a tray of stale food. Fortunately, my faster's haze enabled me to not care greatly. I can sip the embarrassment like an unhurried gentian bitters. But my fast was broken by orange juice (semi-excusable and

---

[2] He explained that the fast should be in the Jewish tradition, i.e. starting at sunset, etc. But I chose not to forbid myself water for health reasons, and actually allowed couch grass tea for its symbolic significance (see 26 April).

anticipated), but also by a few "cocktail sundries" when my excuse of vegetarianism was challenged by vegetable delicacies. That was unnecessary, and weak, and wrong. I was moved by Jesus Christ's saying about not looking as though one is fasting, accordingly my one consolation was that I did not mention the fast as a conversation piece, and that was my justification for taking orange juice. Of course the evening was disrupted, late and chaotic. Despite relative detachment I was left with the usual rubbishy thoughts; imaginary conversations when I let slip to impressed interlocutors that I am posh, taught at Eton, etc., etc. Keeping up with the smoothies. All in all I regret that more than the broken fast.

## Sunday 12 June

Slept late, late, late. But I had allowed for this with one drawn curtain and no alarm clock. After the fast and furious I was a wreck and wanted a "together" day and not a prick-kicker.

I did not like fasting. The temptation to eat, in a mechanical or animal sense, was not strong. Old bod simply faded away wanly and I had a mild headache like slight hangover (which persisted next morning till after break). I do not feel I achieved a glorious victory over the flesh (I lost anyway). The battle was with my more intellectual fear that I was damaging myself, for I have always tended to thinness (I've lost a stone already without fasting) and so I have always laboured to feed myself up. Therefore I did not have the consolation of more beefy or fat brethren who can kid their flesh that it is being done good. What is more, such accounts as Philo's "spiritual athletes" letting their bodies waste away to pale skeletons in order to come closer to God, do not inspire me so much as revolt me. I feel that so much of what is vaguely called "lust of the flesh" is no such thing. Is it a "lust of the flesh" to stay up all night drinking, smoking, gambling, socialising and fornicating? Not at all. The flesh is happier for a good night's sleep, a good meal with wine and a good screw. All multiplications of these to excess are not on behalf of the flesh, but on behalf of some demonic temptations to be "with it", to "prove oneself", to be "liberated", a "go-getter" and so on. So, for me, it is no glorious battle against the flesh to fast, it is a rather mean attack on a poor animal.

But does this mean that I should not fast? No, because there *is* a worthwhile battle; my intellectual fears are a limitation. Whilst apparently protecting the flesh they, in fact, constrain it. Of course, I cannot harm myself by one day without food! I must fight against fears which make me muddle-headed. The physical weakness highlights bad planning, by withdrawing reserves of energy.

I notice that the pain of quitting my asana is melting away.

This morning I felt randier than of late, without any obvious justification.

My lopsided leaf rose again to view for this morning's oration. I wondered why. Sure enough, I had committed a wicked sin against myself this morning; I spoke a saved-up bombshell psychologically aimed to hurt. My only hope is that I am so blinded by my own inner division that the hurtfulness is in fact my own projection; and that the remark passed unnoticed. For me, "three's company, but two is war".

Thank God for the lessons of yesterday (and this last). Would that I could LEARN, LEARN, LEARN.

What a feeble day. Unless I get more done on Saturday, I ought to give up my Sunday observance.

Evenmed poor. Masses of thought about yesterday's "party", also recurring tunes from last weekend's record playing, and even a vision of Mentmore. Each break haunts for long after.

Great black veil descended over me. I'd risen to finish and resumed in self disgust. Raining again.

## Monday 13 June

Monday, Monday .... Slept late and arose like lead. Everything is a chore. Dull and wet.

Held the light and was better at discouraging thoughts.

Decided I would go to the gym. It poured with rain and I am like cold wet earth.

I did go to the gym, and got other jobs done! Yesterday I made a written plan for this morning as an experiment. Timing was haywire, I thought I'd be back around 10.30 and not 11.30. Too shattered to do much, I needed my planned half-hour break. Now I have a lunch invitation so I can kiss other open plans goodbye. So I'm glad I have gymed. It was awful, hard work, but I hope it is correct to include it in my operation. It *should* be a meditation.

Shattered day. Worst part was complete forgetfulness of my operation. In fact I got a few necessary things done, but it was all as nought before such sin. Only read for one and three quarter hours so as to wash up before evenmed.

Poor start, surprised by lightning, or something. Scratchy twigs on door which had burst open. So thoughtful that I had alternately opened and closed my eyes each time I needed to make a break. Rather heavier and damper blackness descended, more a damp cloth then a veil. Wonderful feeling that something had happened. Blackness was entire and a pile of greyness in it washed me from head to foot. Did I come away too soon? Distracted by exciting motorbike.

## Tuesday 14 June

Woke in time but was scared of the thunderstorm. (I was also scared of getting insufficient sleep after the gym.) Held to the light. Thoughts were bad but I just took my time and eventually won. Was not scared by slight return of storm.

Another waffly day. So wet and dull it did nothing to compensate my aching body after yesterday's gym. I notice a feeling not unlike a beginning of a cold. This rings a bell of other "day after" fatigues. The cold is said to be a physical symptom of the body's need to flush out "poisons". Is this pseudo cold a symptom of fatigue toxins being eliminated? As it is a hindrance (excuses, excuses), should I therefore drop idea of going to the gym? At this stage I think not, for I have decayed to the point where any effort would evoke fatigue. Had I not better make an effort to get fit again before it is too late? Hope that is correct. Tomorrow I'll go again and expect—from past experience—to be cured.

It is difficult to recapture the alertness and awareness of the operation (I scarcely had it anyway). This is certainly at least a twilight of the soul, but love has given me much worse treatment than this in the past, so I will not call it "night".

A ridiculous sparrow chirps monotonously on the shed roof before me; all fluffed up and spherical like a fat retort. Chirp, chirp, chirp ... he quivers his wings and puffs up all fat and ragged and helpless—looking upward in his repetitive prayer. He must be a fledgling, thrown out to fend for himself (he still has untidy fluffiness in his feathers) but still, with beak raised to heaven, expecting to be fed. No-one comes. When he flies to other sparrows they desert him.

Is this a message? Is it really time for me to stop praying for the goodies to come my way, and to go out instead to find them myself? I find it hard to believe. Surely my lack of problem is my lack of faith, and my inability to wait patiently? Could it apply in a limited sense e.g. in my reading? No, surely I am the infant until my Holy Guardian Angel makes me a man?

I worry, with justification, about my incompetence at getting jobs done. I forget my priorities: those jobs are just distractions (the only reason to do them is the limited one that *not* to do them is even more distracting and upsetting); the worse fault is my mental decay which goes with the inactivity.

## Wednesday 15 June

One hour late again. Little incentive on such wet mornings. Absurd sparrow appeared at the oratory window again, still cheeping. But this time Mumsy appeared and fed him. Moral? It's the early bird that gets the worm! Nice one, God!

When I got out of bed I found another of those soggy black dead spiders *in my bed* (see 21 May). It seemed a good anima image. Last night I had looked at some of *The Secret of the Golden Flower* and got even more from it. Today's meditation went smoothly with fewer thoughts, but I really think I stopped too soon.

Not so thrown by the gym today; I was weary and needed recuperation but still managed awkward and fiddly job in the pea enclosure. I was tempted to think in terms of "time wasted", but this is probably an illusion (or will be when I'm fit again) on the lines of those athletes at school who bemoaned the time they had to spend in training and yet got just as much done as me in the rest of their time.

Nice letter from Tanya H was a thrill and occupied my mind excessively today. Just after I had read the comment on Pythagoras' dictum on harbouring swallows!

Rather poor oration full of thoughts.

## Thursday 16 June

Woke on time but abysmal re-doze. Oration besieged by thoughts, but discipline was strong. Especial struggle with a Linda Ronstadt song that kept recurring.[3] No great effect, just good containment.

It was yesterday when I began to apply *Seven Sermon*'s dictum about "distinguishing" to my soul. So instead of tormenting myself with

---

[3] "Desperado", I seem to recall!

*enveloping* guilt for my laziness, etc., in oration, I instead prayed for my soul to be purified. This seems to help separate the gross from the fine, and to improve discipline.[4]

Blasted song persisted for a long time. Rather unsatisfactory after-lunch reading in the chilly sun.

## Friday 17 June

Gosh, my timing is bad. This week I've averaged over an hour late in the morning I guess. But there has been no sunrise in ages.

Last night's oration was bad. Although supper had not been very large or very late, I suffered from thumping heart, and so the meditation was really irksome. Each time I breathed I waited for the jolt from my heart. Twice I broke off, shifted position and resumed. The only obvious thing about supper was that it was high in what S called "acid-forming" foods, and there was quite a lot of tobasco. Bread does not always go down well.

This morning was not very good; being late one feels downhearted and tempted to rush it all. Lots of movement from anima though not a vast amount of actual thoughts. But I stuck it out until she separated and she became quiet. It does seem that gentleness and understanding can be helpful for a change—as suggested in Taoist texts.

These last few days I've had a cleaner feeling of the anima soul, so I felt the nature of her femininity. I see a "Garden of Eden" analogy to her corrupting the animus spirit. I also see that I have been unaware, and so negligent and unkind; and it is that ignorance which has given her the power to take over. *The Secret of the Golden Flower* is helpful and illuminating.

But *Seven Sermons* is of increasingly limited use; apart from advice about "distinguishing" there is not enough potential instruction. It is best as advice about what not to do: e.g., I approve of the idea of not trying to confuse the "incorruptible many" with the "one God". People always suggest the pagan idea is "primitive" and has evolved to more sophisticated monotheism. But in Iamblichus and such we find the idea of an Ultimate among the many gods. This Ultimate is no everyday scrubber of a god, in fact it would be an insult to worship him in such a

---

[4]Don't recall what this means, except that "distinguishing" felt a little like Buddhist "non-attachment".

way. It would be an insult to represent him, sing to him, or burn incense, or even think about him. The only acceptable worship is silence and a quiet mind. So they have a god purer than ours. Our god is a jack of all trades and gets all the songs, images, and incense. We do our best by dividing his facets into Father, Son and Holy Ghost—but even the latter is a dove.

But *Seven Sermons* does not say what to do about these gods. We are only to pray to the inner sun, what do we do about the rest? How do we best pray to the inner star? How "inner" is it?

Thumping heart mucked up my oration again; I'd eaten early, but had last glass of milk before fast. Slight pain in pelvis persists. I might have to spend £5 at the osteopath if it does not clear up. It is only in my asana.

### Saturday 18 June

Ghastlily and sickeningly late. At least it shortened my conscious fast by nearly two hours! It's back to alarm and morning drink I fear.

Fast was better today. What with re-starting gym and having lost so much weight, I have made an effort to stuff myself up during the week and I might almost have something to burn up as a result.

I notice one wonderful thing about fasting is that it gives T-I-M-E! A vast expanse of endless day with no meal breaks. As a result I seem to be tackling jobs in such detail as to take me right back to my pre-office job days. Since I've been nine-to-fiveing I have never felt able to take on big jobs as my routine has been like an obstacle course before me.

This morning I used a koan to tame my soul. I used Spare's one about "if not-white is black, and not-black is white, and both black plus white is grey, what is not-black-nor-white"?! Soul seemed to relish struggling with this, tied herself into a knot with it, and became still. The koan served as a "vessel" to contain her. It produced quite a good thoughtlessness. Usually Saturday is difficult, with all the cleaning to do, and incense burning and so on.

Tried to meditate for an hour after cup of couch tea, but it was more like a doze. 5.45.

Evenmed not very good—some heart throbs despite having no food! Started and finished so early I'm having to fill in time till it's dark enough to eat! A spider walked over me as I meditated.

Last night I dreamed of returning to Eton—quite peaceful and pleasant.

## Sunday 19 June

Less late, but I slept light so it was a battle. Nasty cold morning too.

Vast bliss in oration; started reasonably free of thoughts but had Austin Osman Spare's neither-neither koan up my sleeve in case of an upsurge. As has been practice of last few weeks I held to clear light in upper storey, but held thoughts down in my solar plexus. Then the two evaporated to an unadorned pale twilight of great vastness. I extended from the atom to the stars. Did not entirely lose the body but it shrank from being the oyster's shell, as it were, to the grain of sand that needed to be a pearl: a tiny intuition. Held this for a long time and even now it is close. Returned slowly to small world.

Not a very good day—a lot of time-wasting. Fell into phantasy ("living thundervision"[5]) by suppertime. Had two battles against desire to show up N. He tends to leave things boiling too hard, wasting the gas. Two nights running I have turned out the light from under a blackened potato pan. Today I wanted to leave it until he made the discovery.

Evenmed blew my mind again. Not so clear, waves of thoughts—but non-sticky ones. They did not hinder trance. It was good in that it dissolved a left-right distinction of imbalance felt in my body (this feeling has tended to make me imagine I was curling over to one side in my asana), but in general it was rather a bogus sort of trance with flapping visions, e.g. slimy black tentacles which I dissolved with .... wait for it .... LOVE. (I must try that on the scale in the w.c. pan next Saturday.)

OK smartyboots, at least trances make a bit of variety.

## Monday 20 June

Overwhelmed by cold.
Discipline bad.
Backache from gym.
Impressed by re-reading *Aha*.[6]

---

[5] An idea I had for a 3-D cinema experience that began with an old man cranking a black-and-white projector then, as the screen grows coloured and larger, it turned out that he had simply been a holographic projection. Next the cinema interior turned out to be a similar projection and it too melted away to leave the audience totally immersed in the enfolding scene.

[6] Liber CCXLII by Aleister Crowley.

### Tuesday 21 June

Uprising has defeated me. I set alarm and it went off and I awoke and stretched, but just dropped off for another hour. Maddening. What is more, I awoke a wreck, so I cannot even say extra sleep has done me good. I feel a cold lurking inside me.

Very bad morning meditation. My spine seemed to warp; I was aware of uneven pressure on my heels despite most careful seating. I wanted to be balanced because I had strained my back with gym and gardening. Over and over I had to adjust and restart. It became utterly wearisome. I was at it more than one hour and only left when I had attained a modicum of composure.

S is here this morning with a view to sex magic. At least that will keep me from gardening and give my back a chance to recover. At worst it will conspire with my cold and desolation and lack of discipline to make me forget the operation. It is fearfully cold today; I have both night store heaters and a roaring fire going and I am sitting in my overcoat with a warm vest, woollen shirt, jersey, woollen trousers, and socks. I wonder if I got up at "sunrise" time whether it would make the sun rise?

Too much sex tends to make me ill.

I must have some couch tea for my back, and yarrow to save me from cold; if it is not too late. But first I will close the door and meditate.

Held out for about eighty minutes but then it escaped, but I felt better after than before. The day was largely wasted, but with my back plus quasi-cold it would not have been all that great anyway.

One of the best evenmeds yet, but I was only out for about forty minutes. After a bath my thoughts were quiet. But when it came to the meditation I kept my eyes ajar and steady (in order to avoid the twisting body illusion) and entered a great peace. Alas, I was sweating a lot (perhaps due to the cup of yarrow tea prior to the meditation?). Good Heavens! The sky is clear and I see a crescent moon; I'd forgotten what it looked like.

My wand is still crooked.

### Wednesday 22 June

Dull and cold again. Rather good morning meditation on same lines as last night except that I spoilt it a bit at the end.

In yesterday's copulation I managed to hold to clear idea with a lot of success, and did not fall into *narrow* sensualism. I did achieve a measure of oneness and drew some energy back up to solar plexus.

Floperoo of a day in Luton. It turned warm and sunny and when I got back I only had time to do the lawn edges. It is a lovely clear evening, but my joy is tarnished by my sense of waste.

## Thursday 23 June

Dull but mild. Very bleary after a night of sweats and broken sleep with tons of thoughts, as if to prove I'd made no progress. I also had that lopsided feeling; it was so convincing that I turned my mat around to see if this reverses it.

It did—so it must be uneven. Bad evenmed. I was aware of my thumping heart, although it was long after supper. Is it TVP (textured vegetable protein) that does it? Or turmeric? I struggled to no avail.

## Friday 24 June

Intriguing dream; I wish I could remember it more clearly. K (?) had stolen a box of necklaces from somewhere and we bluffed our way out of it with the police. Somehow this brought her into contact with a very rich man who was interested in magic, and she convinced him that she was a great initiator who could somehow guide his magic. Having performed one great operation he was completely hooked and more or less married her. The girl was becoming younger and younger. But as the preparations for the final Great Initiation were underway, it became clear all was not well. The girl had transformed into a tiny tot and had become quite sinister—we heard it cursing and screaming upstairs (in a room where it should not have been). When we went up it had turned into a baby, drunk and blasphemous. This was a blow to the old man who loved the girl. The baby fell into a deep sleep and somehow things were defused.

It does not seem very significant except for the deterioration when it went upstairs into the "forbidden room". This could bear upon my meditation.

Not particularly brilliant this morning. I can slow down and (for a while) check my thoughts (or rather reduce them to an occasional trickle), but the feeling can be sterile. In a sense I have made no progress at all. All techniques which have been breakthroughs—e.g. mantra, koan, finding the light, concentrating in the belly—have never produced a lasting change in my meditation. It has all reduced down to random progress.

I'm beginning to miss the bliss. 7.30.

Reasonable amounts of digging and letter writing today. The sun faded however.

### Saturday 25 June

I awoke on time and deliberately re-dozed. Sigh. The oil had run out in my lamp so I cleaned and refilled it. A symbol of improving aspiration?

Wand is still bent! (And cracked.)

Not a bad day for work. Started later, after one and a half hours reading, and plodded on. There was no one big achievement like last week, but minor achievements all add up to an equal, or bigger, total. I did not have my couch tea until nearly six.

I had noticed that I'd got into the habit of realising I was "asleep" and promptly forgetting again. In order to elaborate the realisation into greater permanence, I invented, and slavishly repeated, the following litany:

> "What are you doing Lionel?"
> "I'm doing the Abramelin Operation."
> "But you appear to be cleaning walls, weeding, washing the sink, etc.!"
> "Oh …. oh that! Well it's just part of the Abramelin exercise!"

8.30 and the shades lengthen.

### Sunday 26 June

Real eye-opener: I had not expected to *finish* embroidery today, but nor had I expected the culmination of nearly three hours to be just one hexagram on the crown. Gosh. Some useful planting out. Berkhamstead trip, a bit of early sun, otherwise not much of a day. Nearer bliss in morning meditation. Still have fasting hangover, alas.

## Monday 27 June

Good meditation this morning. Up early enough to see the sun to at least have a "just risen" look. Last night and this morning I used sexual phantasies to burn up thoughts. Past experience suggests I should be careful of suggesting that any new technique works better, suffice to say that these last two meditations have been more inspiring.

Especially notable today was a feeling of "completeness". Yesterday I came round to sex, today I kicked off straightaway. Body evaporated a lot, and so did the world. Felt purified by a gentle fire. When I did the tarot trump "Strength" bit, I entered a region of bliss. But on some previous occasions the return from such a state has been rather artificial; a feeling that my time was up, or that I was overdoing it, or uncomfortable. This time I just floated back without effort and was swallowed again by the body as in the last few pages of *The Book of Lambspring*.

Last night the final words of my oration became a mantra of great vigour. They were something like:

> "Let us become one, in your honour."
> (The "us" represents my warring parts.)

It is now 7.45 and I still feel sexy. A rather haphazard day, but useful work was done. Felt a little ill and squittery earlier, but a slow, thorough workout at the gym cleared that. Two bad points: my reading of the psalms after lunch (as I had *not* done them on Sunday) was slow and interrupted by fantasy; then the evening was worse—after worthy weeding I made tea at six and collapsed into an excellent *Atalanta Fugiens*[7] so that supper was very late, 8.45–9. As a result of this I went to evenmed with a bulging gut. I suffered all the worst physical symptoms: thumping heart, agonisingly claustrophobic sweltering so that I wanted to rip off my warm clothes and plunge into cold water. Shifted and groaned and prayed. Relief came after a break when I resumed with total lower belly breathing. (As on previous occasions when at my wits end I had asked "Should I go on?" and heard the immediate answer "Yes". The voice was inner, very definite, and did not wait for question to be completed.) This eased the physical symptoms (I was moving my lower belly in and out like bellows) and I grew quiet.

---

[7] Alchemical work by Michael Maier.

Then blackness descended and I *shrank*, very small. Then I came back to "reality".

## Tuesday 28 June

Late and bleary again.

Puzzled by seventeenth emblem of Atalanta Fugiens. I had compared the first two emblems with the idea of breathing through the heels to the lower belly. But what are the four spheres? Top is Apollo and so I felt should be solar plexus. Vulcan? Could that be earth again? (as is breathing through heels). I could imagine Yesod as a moon sphere and the lower belly child as Mercury, except that the order is wrong. Anyway, I tried it as the morning meditation. It went well—good and unspectacular.

Wracked by lust at breakfast and reading. It is now 9.30 and I'm exhausted.

I have felt a bit ill all day—squittery sort of gut feeling. Plodded on with sewing symbols on the crown and the whole day's achievement consists of three pentagrams. But I was quicker with practice.

My concentration has been deteriorating, my mind wandering far from operation.

This is also true during orations, though there is usually a point about half hour later after which I am silent (comparatively).

Visiting time is starting: Skinners and Susters on Sunday, and PF on Thursday.

## Wednesday 29 June

Overslept very badly, till 5.55. But in the past I have had the idea that if ever I missed alarm (or it did not go off) I would take it as permission to rest longer. I am still ill; though it is mild, it is debilitating and I was a wreck yesterday. I will forsake gym but hope to press on with cleaning the sitting room.

So far it is a clear and promising morning. Let's hope I can rest in the sun.

In my orations recently I have begun to use the "Royal We". I am more aware of a political problem in me (us). We are a divided kingdom. True, an upstart "I", full of righteous pomp, has jumped into the throne and said that the kingdom was going to do Abramelin this year (Six-Month Plan) and become a Super Kingdom! But how well did he consult the other citizens? He did study Astrology, *I Ching* and his life history so I think that the basic idea is right; but still he did not obtain prior co-operation with his rivals. Lack of unity is weakness. That's us folks. Dare I say it? That I think his overall plan is correct? But on the other hand I note the feeling that when the HGA comes and unites this kingdom and makes it whole, old you-know-who expects to be on the throne. In other words, I will not have changed.

What to do? Thinking in terms of "us" during oration might humble him, and an attempt to realise a greater openness in future possibilities. But how is the trust and cooperation of the rest of us to be gained?

Operationswise, today was from zerosville, but achievementwise it was alpha. Feeling too unwell for gym or garden I set to at 8.30 and spring-cleaned the sitting room—the big one; I even laundered the chair covers, polished the pictures, and beat the carpets and cushions. Now I could eat off it. It took all day, 8.30–6, with only a short cocoa break and soup for lunch.

This was very relevant to the operation; I had realised before I started that cleaning the rest of the house (as well as the garden) was a necessary banishing. I somehow thought it would be done in the first month, not the third. Now the dining room (less vital), the garage, and tool shed remain. The "clean" feeling should help break with the past.

However, my day was so solid that I was not able to read. What is worse was that I spent all day ranting about the fact that N never spring-cleans. Time and time again I told myself off and yet later found that I was thinking "N would not have done this", or, "would not have done this so well." Of course, nothing came of it—when he returned, all was joy. But this thought was so recurrent I even wondered which part I should repress. Perhaps my true nature should be more brash and critical. Perhaps I should not repress my critical nature but express it as B would. That would take more courage and skill than it would to banish these thoughts (I *believe*) and so is less likely to be "me". 8.55.

### Thursday 30 June

Equally late, for same reason. Humph.

Distraction day. PF came to visit. Collected him from the station after "signing on". Tried to sunbathe, but it was not much of a day. I did not get into the usual "visit" flap, and I did one and a quarter hours reading after lunch.

Evening meditation a real pain. Tons of thoughts, stifled feelings, falling over feelings, desperation. I challenged the enemy to show itself, but it was not so generous. Comparatively early night.

### Friday 1 July

Forgot to set alarm this time. Woke up at 5.10 and leapt out, so I was comparatively early (i.e. only half an hour late).

Bleary during oration—rather poor. Meditation very simple, no clever stuff to banish thoughts as I had started pretty clear. So it was good. Thoughts started towards end, rather than dying out towards the end. Had that leaning feeling, though. I wish I knew what I was doing.

Tried tantric screw again, a big flop as I only lasted twenty minutes. But I did attain a wonderful feeling of completely evenly spread near-orgasm; a state of calm thrill where a waggled toe would have ejaculated, or a brushed hair, or a fluttered eyelash.

More humiliating and futile was a second go; when the pressure was low, I was reduced to fantasy, and it was all less cosmic—despite lasting longer.

That wasted the rest of the day, as I felt washed out. (I'd had a fairly thorough session at the gym just before.)

### Saturday 2 July

Nice sunny start. Fairly thoughtless meditation, quite good. Feeling connection between child being created, future ruler of the kingdom, and HGA. Anima needed a baby. 8 o'clock.

Easiest fast yet. It was a hot, sunny day and that kept me above food. Less physical work, large reading afternoon in sun. Allowed water drinks after about noon. Did not flake out after reading, cleaned Bloaters and weeded. Late evenmed and not very good.

### Sunday 3 July

Summer is here. After meditation I only put on trunks. Day of preparing food. Morning med nice and internally peaceful (despite too many thoughts). Watched changes instead of trying to make them.

Terrible day for op. No reading. I prepared food *all* morning. Poor planning meant I had vastly overestimated lunch and created a mountain of chaos. It tasted nice. Hot sun meant a swimming trunks day and evenmed just in judo suit. Summer is here.

I was a bit of a gasbag, and very much a flapper, but there were times when I was relaxed and was sensible. The fault of the meal was poor early planning, in fact I produced it quite efficiently in view of its complexity.

I was more alert than I would have been in the past, when a day of entertaining has passed like a dream.

The greatest joy was that I did not magnify my work in their eyes, or particularly devalue it. I spoke little about it.

Evenmed not brilliant. Short and thoughtful.

## Monday 4 July

Oh bliss! I was out before sunrise (wearing only judo suit). Morning meditation not brilliant despite this my greatest triumph. Though not hearing church clock I was out more than an hour. But as I took asana I realised one foot hurt slightly so as to unbalance me, and despite usual numbing I did lean very much. So a measure of bliss was arrived at, but it fused with a measure of physical pain. Too many thoughts.

Grim thing; a lot of yesterday was marred by painful peeling of my tongue—worst ever. What causes this? Was it a nervous effect from having so many to cook for? Was it an allergy? (I noticed it first when licking a mayonnaise spoon.) I had eaten aubergine and tinned loganberries, everything else is everyday fare.

Not a bad day opswise, little achieved otherwise. Tried sunbathing. Crowley yoga asana; a hopeless jumble of useless thoughts. So bad it makes me realise how good my oratory meditations are! At half time I decided that instead of feebly going for "no thought" and being swamped by rubbish, I would encourage useful thoughts. That was better, it reduced the flow!

*Chuang Tzu* was excellent.

Distant distractions in evenmed; heard Phil talking to N. But such obvious distractions can almost help by diverting the attention so that room can be cleared.[8]

---

[8] Not sure what this meant, except that when internally tangled an outside distraction can pull one out of the situation and create a break for a fresh return.

## Tuesday 5 July

Another "on time" day. Although in theory the sun was already ten minutes risen there was no sight of it on the horizon here. Good calm morning meditation, though bleary to orate. Held asana a bit more naturally.

Very hot day. It began a little hazy, but even that cleared by mid-afternoon. Wind saved it from being too uncomfortable. Sunbathing ruled today, so did all work and reading in full sun. Finding Geber very interesting so far.

Sex meditation in sun after break. I did not time it, but it was under an hour. As I read psalms, an absolute riot of lust hit me and I ejaculated. This took me by surprise; I'd have thought it too hot for such a sudden happening. Absolutely wonderful feeling. It is as though my bestial and "higher" sex natures were both coming together and cooperating. Great improvement.

Evenmed too thoughtful, wallowing and crummy. I welcomed the pain of posture as a distraction from other thoughts!

## Wednesday 6 July

Horror! No sun! But was up before "no sun" rose. Good morning meditation. Steered through the reef of bliss to a calm re-entry.

Days have been dominated by sun and so rather unplanned. But it has made for extra meditation. Attempted Crowley-type asana (hanged man or corpse) while sunbathing, but without success. They collapsed into reverie, or else were very dry.

Took advantage of no-sun to go to gym for good session. Terrible blow as I left; far from regaining weight I was down to 11st 9lb (74 kg). The full horror of this sunk in during the day. This was the biggest sacrifice so far. I was close to weeping. "Thy will be done". I knew sacrifice would be necessary. The Lord giveth and the Lord taketh away. The years of exercise have been a great joy; through times of the dreariest jobs it has been the guiding light and hope, and the one creative and original thing in my life. Everyone else says I look well on it.

The Lord giveth and the Lord taketh away. S came and was sleeping in my old room. I ignored her, knowing I must sleep. But I thought I could hear her masturbating (through the dividing wall) and was so moved by the idea that she could not control her lust in the way I was doing that a rage of delicious lust burst over me. It was exquisite;

I'd always been ashamed of my control and longed to be a raging beast, like lovers portrayed in films. I'd even admired the spirit of the rapist. So here I was, out of my mind. Erect and throbbing I rushed next door and ripped off her clothes and mounted her. In my fever I even lubricated her with my tongue, something I've never before dared to do for fear that revulsion would douse my timid desire. If she had said "no" or that she had her period, I doubt if I would have stopped.

Again and again I thanked God. It was as though my dithering and warring parts had at last, for the first time, united in pursuit of my Will. Oh heaven, oh bliss, oh stainless wonder.

## Thursday 7 July

Groaning wreck, not having got to sleep before midnight. Lumbered over to the oratory at 5.15; late, but no sunrise. Good oration, but I fear I cut it short.

Again, sex was king. I'm a bit puzzled as to what to do. The tarot trump "Strength" shows the jaws of the lion being closed gently. It seems clear that I must "control" to some extent, just as I did not wallow in meditation bliss. But I do not want to banish it because this lust is the most delicious thing I have known: "Abramelin Improves Your Sex Life". Of course it is illusion and must be transcended (e.g. when I am dead) but it would seem ridiculous to transcend it now for it is the breath of life. I would be as foolish as the "Adam" figure in the Sumerian creation story if I were to throw away the greatest thing I've experienced just on account of the wisdom of old books. I can happily forget St. Paul's rantings, I can see the Hermetic anti-flesh propaganda as a misunderstanding, but I come to grief on the Taoist works. To be without desire, or to be in ecstasy of desire (as in *The Book of the Law*)? When I am free of lust I am not free of lust because I admire those who are not free of lust, i.e. when without lust, I lust for lust. I have always realised that there were some things (sin?) that I could only rise above by experiencing them. For example, I have never known torment like that of a virgin teenage male knowing that his peers are "having it". Now I am above that through having lots myself.

So do I simply wallow? No. First, I realise that lustful distractions when, say, reading, are no good unless the means of exercising that lust are present and keen. Secondly, if I revere lust I should revere it in its purest and hugest form. That means stripped of phantasy. (If, for example,

I imagine breaking into a girl's college at night with a cock like a telegraph pole and screwing a hundred virgins, then I have set limits and reduced and constricted lust—why only one hundred? Why not a giant redwood?) Thirdly, I must distinguish lust from evil (à la *Seven Sermons*). I cannot see that the greatest thing I *know* can be equated with "bad", but I can see badness being swept along in its wake, hiding in its shadows, etc., etc.

### Friday 8 July

Morning oration was good, as was meditation once I had cleared waves of thought.

Crummy day. After morning drink I decided to try sex meditation in the sun. Snag 1: no sun. Ended up as just a glorified shag. I only realised my mistake afterwards; on other occasions my desire was spontaneous, this time it was contrived. I had to *work* on it. Immediately afterwards I might have admitted some success. But the rest of the day collapsed into sub-mediocrity. Again, I do not know why I'm going on. My tongue peeled again before evenmed. Seeing the Big Sweat coming I thrice broke meditation to strip. To little avail. I'm sick of it all now. And cold.

### Saturday 9 July

Rather cold with the North Wind. Dejected, but worthwhile meditation. Thoughts held less sway. Not very alert this morning. Still want to doze.

Getting up is no longer a problem, but wandering abstracted attention is. It's moved to first place I think.

### Sunday 10 July

Oh my! A time of lessons! Set about cooking for guests more calmly and purposefully than last week; but then at 10 the visit was cancelled. So there I was with this heap of food. Did not cut my losses and go on to have a constructive day. Instead I went for a long ride in search of alternative guests (cf. parable of rich man's banquet). Eventually K came to a late lunch. She stayed till evening and the Rs came really rather inconsiderately late. (I fear they were curious to see me orate.)

So, what with taking K home, I was orating from 9.45 without having had supper. Late night.

## Monday 11 July

Disgrace. Woke too early, wanting to pee. Then I dozed till an amazing 7.15. It was a surprise, but I knew I was late because of that "oh well, I know I'm late so there's no point in hurrying now" feeling. By the time I returned N was having breakfast, so I wrote up, and was horrified to see I'd not written up Saturday morning.

My dreams confirm yesterday's warnings about guests. One was about surprise arrival of crowd at the Mill and me being all in a social flap trying to put M at ease. The other was about an embarrassing guest being here and me trying to keep out of his way.

Fast was easy—I even shopped for food at lunchtime. But after about 7 I actually felt *hungry*, as opposed to the pain of fasting; so I was ravenous after my meditation.

## Tuesday 12 July

Much better! Only one and a quarter hours late! Puzzled by this, but it became clear I had a slight case of flu. Did laundry instead of tidying garage, dozed before lunch, and had long leisurely read after lunch. Now, 8.55, I feel a lot better.

Since Saturday evening I've used a new technique to banish thoughts. Instead of relaxed "Taoist" idea of observing thoughts until they no longer stick, and then drift away, I have been applying rather rigorously P.G. Bowen's maxim of "observe the observer, etc."[9] This is rather more aggressive; if a thought starts, I "blame" the person in charge, and keep my eye on him. From the start it was very successful. At first there was a tendency for the place of concentration to rise gradually out of my head as I went higher step by step. But yesterday I sought to work *inwards* in an onion-peeling manner.

The result is long periods of silence. No bliss; indeed meditations have been shorter as I have not got used to the slow passage of time in such intense concentration, uninterrupted by thought. And when I stop meditating and open my eyes, the world is vivid; there is none of the

---

[9] The Occult Way, by P.G. Bowen.

gentle return to reality. Whereas in my previous meditations I started with masses of thoughts and, if I was lucky, ended with none; now I start with almost no thoughts and they only begin to appear towards the end.

Sunday evenmed was very late and therefore dark. I noticed a curious visual effect: I thought my eyes were open but deduced they were not because all was black. Then gradually I began to see, without the feeling of opening my eyes.

For now I will persist because it is good to be so thoughtless, and the dragging of time is good discipline.

## Wednesday 13 July

Still slightly ill. RM was here till noon. Mostly dozing and reading on the camp bed (*Plotinus* and *Turba Philosophorum*).

6.35 and I will consult the *I Ching*: what should I do to make progress this moon? No.

Should I behave differently—No.

Should I make any changes in order to progress during this fourth moon? Yes.

5-4-4   5-8-4   5-8-8   9-4-4   9-8-8   5-8-8.

| Received | First | Second |
|---|---|---|
| ——— | ——— | ——— |
| —x— | — — | ——— |
| — — | — — | — — |
| ——— | ——— | ——— |
| — — | — — | — — |
| —o— | ——— | — — |
|  | 22 | 53 |
|  | Grace | Gradual Progress |

"Grace": light within the mountain: still without, glowing within. Elegance is merely outer. (Suggestion of triviality?) 1: Must work at it, if offered a quick way out but better to walk if that is dubious. (Tantra?) 5: Withdrawing from luxury lovers into spiritual heights, this will require humility, but it will be accepted.

"Gradual Progress": now mountain within and wind without, a suggestion of the volatile having been fixed and the fixed made volatile?

A little fuddled by hunger and flu. I think message is to eschew elegance and outward show, though my first impression was that it should be encouraged, but recognised for its limitations. This has one definite local relevance; I have to visit London "on business" and had wondered if whether I should waste time at the sales. 7.35.

Evenmed was bad, a little late and I did not watch the watcher, but had erotic visions. (Much more fun. Ha, ha.)

## Thursday 14 July

Overslept again. I have been bad all week but I'm not confident about fighting it as long as the flu persists.

Poor meditation (oration okay). I tried to watch the watcher but my heart was not in it. Tunes, and thoughts about the operation, and possible trip to London, all got in the way. I had delayed the technique in case it was just another flash-in-the-pan improvement. Perhaps it is.

London trip was almost a complete forgeteroo, and I spent a (comparative) fortune. But even that was a huge sacrifice by my usual standards. (I looked at only one sale and bought *nothing*!)

Mike F came and I knocked up supper. Pub trip made for a late evening. 9.30 meditation. Very determined; no London thoughts. It worked! "Watch the watcher" took on new meaning as I stampeded after Mercury! Very interesting and I look forward to the next episode.

## Friday 15 July

Miserably cold morning and on with the central heating. Out in good time, but meditation was short. On with the hunt. I was confused between the two and the one; between seeking Mercury and seeking the two fish. I fear my revelations are just distinctions and diversions, but without them what is there? Though my path is mystical I'm more interested in magic in the long run.

Today was to have to have been the ultimate tantric sex. But yesterday it was cancelled by Hecate.[10] It is going to be difficult to make myself use the God-given free day profitably. I feel a yearning for diversion.

And got it. Long delay at the gym from chatty people. Read magazines for rest of morning. Thorough read after lunch. Only other achievement

---

[10] Do not recall the would-be partner, but assume she cancelled with a period.

was to prepare pattern for embroidering robe. Not bad, but quite a lot of sex phantasy late afternoon.

### Saturday 16 July

Unfortunate start: I was hungry, for I had not had a very big meal last night. Feeling wan. I read before getting down to jobs. N up early to go away home for the weekend. Sunny morning (but debilitatingly cold) later turned to cloud, and stayed cold. I had read the Abramelin book and realised what a lot I still had to do.

Important day; I started reading Crowley thoroughly, *Magick in Theory and Practice*: it was too familiar to be exciting, but I look forward.

I was rather idle in my weakness. Because of cold I rested in the sun whenever it appeared. "Finished work" about 3.30 and broke off reading to curl up in bed to try to get warm. In the evening I bathed with exquisite Blenheim Bouquet bath oil and it raised my consciousness but alas raised it into snobbery as it was such a majestic smell. Very solar?

Great joy! A *very* appreciative letter about *SSOTBME* from someone who had really *used* it and was ordering six copies for friends! What happiness to be useful as a teacher! That is what I would like all my books to do. Thanks be to God.

### Sunday 17 July

Lazy start after lateness of yestereve. Trouble with posture in meditation; I am screwing sideways again. Cannot so far trace it to internal imbalance as I *think* I am conducting an impartial inward search—but as I write this I have a doubt, after all "watching the watcher" is a more aggressive technique and so perhaps is imbalanced. My head goes to the left and my body to the right.

Long meditation, but not good as I was searching asana.

Horrible thought this weekend; have I misjudged timing? Is a moon twenty-nine and a half rather than twenty-eight days? I was judging my moons by her return to zero degrees Aquarius, but should I have judged them by her passing the last quarter? It would make a ghastly extra ten days or so. Unfortunate to spin out the hell, sure, but my main worry is the *change*; the old timing seemed special, as its final week covered the feast of the HGA, and coincided with Jupiter transiting Saturn in my chart, plus other aspects.

I have not studied the timing based on twenty-nine and a half days so much but it does not look good.

Feel very sexed up again today. Warmer, with drizzle. A curiously unproductive day, time simply passed. No psalms, but lots of reading of *Magick in Theory and Practice*.

Evenmed well balanced, physically and metaphysically.

## Monday 18 July

Operationswise nonsville. Late up, very late. I was semi awake, but not enough to make a decision, so it was a shock. But I felt a little ill so that might have been it.

Fortunately I screwed myself up to go to gym and seemed thereby to banish sickness. Rest of day was lost in a daze of excitement entertaining Tanya H and family. Surprise visit from B too, very good as it provided a car for transport. It is now 8.50 and I'm still dazed. She lives a glamorous life which dazzles me and could be too much for me; it is certainly not right for this retirement. But I hope that *after* the summer I will be strong enough for it. If not I would feel that I had a long way to go, and that I was not yet calm in the centre of circumstances.

But Abramelin was right; the children were more disturbing than Tanya. One expects an adult to understand my retirement to some extent, but the children are less forgiving and I was scared to disappoint them. 9 pm.

10 pm. Oration good, but meditation disgracefully thoughtful. I wondered what was wrong with today? I never remembered myself, in fact I was in a dazzled dream, i.e. was not "myself". Who was I? I was the person who has always taken over in times of stress, interviews, P's wedding speech, when important guests arrive, etc. The person who does all the work on those occasions and gets all the blame after. I do not recognize this person in my reflection in the mirror, but perhaps it is that rather embarrassing person who I see in photographs of those occasions (un-photogenic me). This person gets the blame because *l'espirit de l'escalier* is in fact the ordinary "me". I come away thinking, "Now why didn't I say *that*?" or, "Why on earth did I do that?" It is the social feminine "me" perhaps? The one who I cruelly crushed at puberty when at school and I wondered if I was homosexual, felt my nipples and was terrified I was going to change sex. Having studied autosuggestion,

I hypnotised myself to sleep with "I am a *man*". Is this then my contact with my soul? Is the dazed feeling because of lack of communication? (Understanding?)

Meditation was bad, but I did feel an unusual new realism in my conception of the anima in my belly. I encouraged it at the expense of clarity and calm and it ruled the roost for a change.

I look back to 8 June, the still relevant hexagram for these two moons, and I realise that I am learning from my painful brushes with the outside world. I re-read the commentary on 59 and almost sobbed with relief. Tonight in my meditation I thanked my other self for its work. The exhaustion comes from the tension of the absent monarch.

As I left the oratory an eye-level nettle stung my hand. And a night scented stock has miraculously appeared after all the others have stopped. 10.25.

## Tuesday 19 July

Late again.

Again too thoughtful. Lambspring and others talk of two fish in the sea, I have tended to be one fish trying to find the other; this time I was the observer to the two fish. Is this outside observer the one to eliminate, or vanquish?

Twice yesterday and today my "voice" accused me of not liking sex. This seems absurd, but as the accusation was repeated in different contexts I had better keep an eye open for an understanding of this. (On both occasions the message came "on holy ground".) It is true that I have sometimes felt obliged to pretend that I liked it more than I did. Odd.

In *Magick in Theory and Practice* I find an interesting comment upon what I earlier called my diabolical pacts, e.g. when I make use of the invasion of foolish anger to overcome a different vice such as sloth. Crowley commends this (whereas I had slight doubts) because he claims that the useful exercise of the "demon" serves to dissipate it. I do believe he is right, provided the *decision* is conscious and controlled.

Unsuccessful sex magic. Held off for ninety-five minutes and whole act was two hours, but somehow the flame went out. There was none of that searing elixir. What was wrong? For a start she was not red hot, that had not occurred to me, for usually it is the other way round and I thought my gusto would enflame her. So is this an example of seduction rule: do not act too keen if you want to attract women?

Then I noticed a split in me, I was not "myself". But who was I? It did not seem like a socialite persona, it was more of a frozen thing.

The message here I do not understand.

## Wednesday 20 July

Quite an intriguing dream with K: the black cloud which passed over turned out to be made of many thin layers of little clouds. And I was having a new pair of haunches made for me.

Feel a bit dead today. I tried to find the mean between the hardness of "watching the watcher" and the softness of reverie. I was quite calm and lifted out towards the end.

Very poor. Slow and miserable stitching—actually swore at it. So dopey after lunch I "dozed". Lovely Ruth came with Rs for high tea and I was late and full of thoughts of Ruth for evenmed, but managed some sort of control.

Terribly dead beat day. Squittery gut.

## Thursday 21 July

Late and pathetic. Meditation became good and quiet. It is not difficult, it is just that I am drained and listless so even such a simple job as this is too much. I could not face gym (bad), but at least I got washing before St. Albans (good). Lingered in shops (bad) and eventually resigned to going to coffee house and seeing if I could relax over it (better).

Now morning has gone with no reading and no stitching. Oh how I hate stitching.

Another nonsville day except for slight stitching breakthrough in evening. In evenmed I asked why I had suddenly deflated and gone from vigour to collapse. Vision of visit to Silcox came and I could not understand. Seemed to be some allusion to red and green (he had very red hair) so one idea I had was that my energy and my lust (Mars and Venus) had played the part of two devouring beasts and had annihilated each other and turned to putrescent slime. Another was that I was anaemic, and needed iron—but my hands do not look anaemic.

Early night at least.

## Friday 22 July

Two dreams. Second one was of exploration of a recently discovered ancient Jewish holy place. The scientists and archaeologists had done their bit and now I was in as an occultist to study the books and remains. After the first day, more or less finding our way around, I was shutting the place up at night when I heard organ music. Intrigued, I followed it—in case it was something magical. But in the crypt was an organ and some Christians were singing hymns around it. I said to them "Time Gentlemen, please", and they took it very badly. They were scientists in lab coats. They stalked out with angry and malevolent faces. As I went back some shadowy trendies released their big dark Afghan hound. It leapt snarling towards me. It had four eyes. I knew it was the hell hound and I had to grab its muzzle and hold it shut. This became an ordeal; I knew I must not relax my grip (like "watching the watcher"), despite various distractions. I succeeded and the dream fizzled out. [It would have been braver to let the dog go and see what happened.]

Morning meditation rather thoughtful, with calm interludes. Today more than ever I feel gently putrid. My crap stinks and my tongue is sweaty and I sweat in the night. Horrid, like the weather.

10 pm. Weather bizarre. It remained utterly overcast; but at about four I noticed some people stripping on the common and reflected on youth's (fool) hardiness. Then towards six I stepped out of the house and had a shock! It was like a sauna. Evenmed in just vest and tracksuit bottom under judo jacket, and sweat was dripping down my face. Not very good, most thoughts gone but I kept being amazed by heat. Defied my voice and left early as I felt grubby in my sweat.

Sex seemed better today—not sure why. Divided it into two. Spirits low, but I was quite keen and so we made love from 11 am–12 pm, without orgasm. Resumed at 2 pm. I was not at all stirred and had to make an effort, but a good state of ecstasy ensued. It somehow seemed good. Came after only about twenty minutes, but dozed in situ for a further forty or so. Feel better for it.

It is funny how often my sex life changes along with the weather.

## Saturday 23 July

Very, very sluggish. An hour late and none the better for it. Bleary oration. Meditation quite good as I "watched the watcher" quite thoroughly, in honour of it being Saturday. Strange warm weather persists, orated only in judo suit.

Later, wind arose, so evening was less torrid. A poor day for achievement—too many loose ends to tie up—and operation. Instead of alert I was in a faster's daze. Tried to work towards a resigned acceptance of my awfulness.

Evenmed was quite good; I could hear the church clock so I "did time" and was quite calm and clear. Orated with feeling. Oh, but food was bliss. Orange juice, avocado, lovely bean stew with some brown rice and exquisite minted mange touts from the garden, strawberries, milk and a brewer's yeast tablet. Yum!

## Sunday 24 July

Dreamt that my mother had had a baby in the night! The baby was quite robust, just able to rise to his feet and so on.

With alarm clock I managed to be less late.

It is not easy to decide between an "all out effort" approach and a "relax and let it happen" one. The parallel in meditation is between "watching the watcher" and just observing. As a result I tend to waver and fall between states. I make little effort, yet I worry (that's me to a tee). "So then because thou art quite hot, and neither lukewarm or hot, I will spew thee out of my mouth."

Everyone else thinks I am marvellous, "brave" and so on. But I myself think, "In view of what is offered by Abramelin can I not even pass one single day in faultless concentration upon the work, or even perfect oration?" How little I have progressed. I read with admiration the appendices of *Magick in Theory and Practice* and see how great are the achievements of the lowest grades of the A∴A∴.

If only I had set myself, say, daily tarot practice as well!

During evenmed I struggled with very slippery and fluid Mercury but eventually pinned him down (watching the watcher). When I do that I achieve a blissful stillness. I *think* this is an improvement upon the bliss of early days, because I think it is more solid and down-to-earth. The volatile is fixed in the vessel rather than carrying me away to heaven. I use these alchemical terms because they fit my observations and because I want to know their meaning by experience, not because I already do know.

I must have sat in an unsymmetrical way because a needle of pain entered my back. It vanished when I shifted a bit, but I did not completely renew my posture so I came out with an aching ankle.

## Monday 25 July

Something I am always giving thanks for in my orations is the way in which my errors are regularly made into lessons. This morning was a really crummy lie-in, despite alarm, of the type that says "as I'm late anyway why hurry?" Ended up about one and a quarter hours late, and feeling worse for it. But I managed to detect the pressure in me of an illness generator (or evoker) creaking into action. It is the bit that learnt at the prep school (and which was thoroughly reminded at HSA) that the only sure way to get some peace is to be sick. Unfortunately nowadays there are conflicting interests, and so inner tension and I do not get all I might from my bouts of flu.

A similar screwing up took place as I contemplated going to gym. Recognizing it and relaxing it reduced its effect.

Morning meditation was good. Happy making. Noon.

## Tuesday 26 July

Groan; it has happened. I've caught my cold and it is a miserable morning. Good meditation. Last night's was good but with some slumping and it did not last very long. But this morning I found slight help in posture from holding my chin in, like a yogi. One of the best meditations because I held the silence for most of the time, and it was a long one.

On return it was so cold that I remained in my warm underwear and I will continue so until the day warms up a bit.

Crummy day as I could not back out of Berkhamstead trip though feeling bad. Too late to bath in the evening.

## Wednesday 27 July

Day in bed with cold. Reading and writing notes on the psalms. Terrible to be so ill, but it did rub my nose in my retirement. I actually had to spend the day in the chamber as I'm supposed to.

## Thursday 28 July

Still have my foul cold. Last night I had a bath and yet in two of my dreams I was having a bath (in a more or less public place).

I am perplexed by the "two fish in the sea" (*Lambspring*) and the "one thing that is two" (almost every alchemical writer). At first, using Taoist yoga as my guide, I felt two consciousnesses; one in my belly (anima) and one in my head, betwixt my eyes (animus). That seemed to fit the bill, but it got me nowhere. I began to wonder about the consciousness that flitted between and recognised these two localities. Was this the mercury and were the other two salt and sulphur? Now I concentrated on this "finer" thing the original two seemed rather bogus, they were really "thoughts" that I had stuck in two places.

But Mercury has a male and female element; so should I expect to find two parts in this consciousness? In trying to fix Mercury, I always seemed to end up in the upper locality. I was aware that this could be wrong, could be a male overbalance. This was the "watching the watcher" bit and I have been ill since it started. But on the other hand it did seem to be the beginning of the end for my thoughts, so I persevered.

In more recent "watching the watcher" I have considered this tiny volatile consciousness closely. One analogy to me was splitting the atom; should I continue to hammer away at it till it split. Would huge energy be released? Could a chain reaction set in (not if I succeeded in removing all other atoms surely?). And have I made myself strong (and directed) enough to control this energy? Another thought was an awareness that the female could lurk behind the male; there was the consciousness which had thoughts, and that consciousness which was aware of the fact that there were thoughts. The latter lurked within the former when I was awake. Perhaps they reversed positions in dreams? (So that the occasional "conscious" feeling in dreams was the reflection of the occasional "fully awake" feeling in the day.) Certainly there is a male and female feeling about the two consciousnesses.

In yesterday's evenmed I went for splitting the atom. Huge pressure formed in the upper chamber and consciousness descended into blackness. There was a shape suggesting that I was in a fish's belly. If it was the thirty-second path I never persisted till Yesod. Time passed in an interesting sort of way, so I feel Saturn was in on it.

This morning I plugged away at the male and female consciousness. Time crept. Every now and again the odd thought diluted the mix, but I returned pretty conscientiously. I was in a semi chinlock position (like a yogi) because I hoped it would stabilise asana. So there was a slight feeling of looking down from above in my consciousness. Then it reversed, and I was looking up. My consciousness had drained down to my solar plexus. Now it was in two phases, and in a rather more convincing form than in my early attempts; for there was nothing else. Time went more quickly then.

Wretched in my sickness, I orated very late and with great feeling today.

## Friday 29 July

Oh how I wish I could have this week again, in health. This seems like divine judgement for last Sunday when I went out to lunch, for my hostess had a severe cold.

Weak oration; like last night I linked my misery with an early childhood memory: I had fallen on the stairs and broken something belonging to my parents. So I cried, pretending I was very hurt in order to deflect anger from the damage I had done. Now my performance in this operation has been so bad as to amount to a broken vow. But I have been anxious at God's kindness for there have been so few difficulties from outside. So now, in my guilt, I am crying with pain in order to make it difficult. Being of the age of slave gods I imagine sacrifice to be necessary.

In meditation I concentrated on the point. The feminine bit spread out huge and misty and enveloped the world in a Nuit and Hadit sort of effect. Then it condensed into my belly. Good separation but still something scuttled to and fro, stirring the sediment.

After yesterday's pathetic and sick-making day I have returned to bed to stew in my own juice. To hell with achievement, why pretend I am capable. I had intended to complete my preparations for the operation this week so I could enter the final phase with a clean sheet. But sickness spells "NO". I must not get tangled up in outer details. The rot is here.

Have just read up my last dreadful month. Amazing. Despite sickness, sex aches, confusion, visitors, and pathos, all the progress I can think of seems to have happened in this busy four weeks thanks be to God.

## Saturday 30 July (written up on Sunday)

Pretty rock bottom: very late start and combined horror of fasting and non-improving cold together with "outside" jobs to be done like laundry (needed for tonight's clean sheets, but at least I could do both weeks' in one wash!) and trying to find a censer.

I had ordered a nice silver censer with copper fire basket to be made for £100, but it was not made in time. It seemed too bad not to be complete for last two moons (but I have already fallen from that ideal with the help of last week's sickness) and there is clearly a lot of work still to do. So I gave up that censer as a bad job. (The wasted money seems the least misfortune.) So what to do? Lash out for more silver? Surely not, for I had failed before. So could I use a little silver bowl lying around my bedroom? Originally I had dismissed this as it was not virgin: it had been sold to me as scrap, and used for incense, pins, etc., by me. But what choice was there? What if I saw the perfect censer in an antique shop, even if it was suitable, how could I be sure of its past? This little bowl had at least been in my possession for a year or two without showing signs of being a cornucopia of malevolent demons.

So I sought a copper (or even brass) liner. In vain. But in St. Albans I found a stainless steel ladle which snugly fitted my bowl. On the other hand I could not even get a plain copper sheet or gauze to do my own liner. (Thank heavens I was in no state for craft.) Iron and carbon (Mars and Saturn?) seemed a poor substitute for copper, but it was at least *stainless* and that seemed symbolically delicious to my foul sickness-wrought mind. What makes stainlessness? Is it chrome? I liked the idea, it was sort of "new-aeon" and let's hope HGA rides in on a Van Veen![11]

I thought I would have to cut off the handle, and bought a cheap hacksaw, but in fact curling the handle over made a rather elegant handle for carrying the liner and looks good in situ.

This shoddy bodging, and the way that sickness seems to have tripped up my plans to be complete for the last two moons, has since recalled the month's *I Ching* line: "the roll of silk is small and of poor quality—disgrace followed by ultimate good fortune". The commentary says that a man leaves the luxury-loving lowland people in search of a great person in the mountains whom he would befriend. His gifts are few and poor so he feels ashamed. But, as it is not material gifts but sincerity of feeling that count, all will be well.

This is, of course, *very* relevant. I only hope I live up to the "sincerity of feeling" bit.

---

[11] A luxury Dutch rotary-engined motorcycle that I lusted after.

Yet the £100 censer seems correct. It was my way of honouring the event and I do not regret the failure. I will have a silver elephant on my hands. Oh my!

As that line proves so relevant, what of the other line?

"Elegantly shod, he leaves the carriage and walks [...] The beginner must take upon himself the labour of advancing: there might be an opportunity of surreptitiously easing the way (symbolised by 'carriage') but the self-contained man scorns help gained in dubious fashion. It is more graceful to go on foot than in carriage under false pretences."

What was the carriage? Only this moon has my reading advanced to Thelema and I welcomed the idea that the universe is Joy, not sorrow, and that it was typical Christian negativity to feel that sacrifice and pain is essential to advancement. This idea was helpful, and it linked with Taoism to relax me and to reveal that a sort of negative action of conscience has made me make worse of my dilemmas, to create trouble in order to feel I was suffering duly. (This effect can be very noticeable in other people's behaviour, particularly very "devout" people who are forever shouldering burdens and telling everyone else about them.) But it was not quite what I expected of the carriage because, taken in its fullness, Thelema is very hard work. It is, in quite a profound sense, not "me"—as I am much too timid. So, though it was an inspiration, it did not really strike me as a short cut or an easy way out. For example, this sickness: by Thelemic standards I would say, "Brace up Lionel, be honest; it is not really hurting you as much as you make it out is it?" Whereas by "old-aeon" standards I would say, "This illness is not to be avoided, it is a test, it is a necessary pain or purging because of my sinfulness and imperfection". But in both cases I am ill, and each is simply a way of helping one through the illness.

Then how about "watching the watcher", etc. Though hardly a free lift, this did speed things and banish thoughts and bring alchemy to life. But somehow I began to associate the fierce concentration in my head with this long-lived congestion of my catarrh. So I am now (Sunday) trying to return to a more relaxed and passive contemplation. I've had a nice trip in this carriage—at least it has shewn me there is actually something up the road—but now, perhaps, I will try again to walk. Let us hope we will then attain "gradual progress".

PHASE THREE

# Final two moons

Things shift gear for the final two moons:

> Morning and Noon ye shall wash your hands and your face on entering the Oratory and firstly ye shall make Confession of all your sins; after this, with a very ardent prayer, ye shall entreat the Lord to accord unto you this particular grace [...]
> Ye shall do this same at midday before dining, and also in the evening; so that during these two last Moons ye shall perform the prayer three times a day, and during this time ye shall ever keep the Perfume upon the Altar. Also towards the end of your Oration, ye shall pray unto the Holy Angels, supplicating them to bear your sacrifice before the Face of God, in order to intercede for you, and that they shall assist you in all your operations during these two Moons.
> The man who is his own master shall leave all business alone, except works of charity towards his neighbour. You shall shun all society except that of your Wife and of your Servants. Ye shall

employ the greatest part of your time in speaking of the Law of God, and in reading such works as treat wisely thereof [...]

Every Sabbath Eve shall ye fast, and wash your whole body, and change your garment.

Furthermore, ye shall have a Vest and Tunic of linen, which ye shall put on every time that ye enter into the Oratory, before ye commence to put the Perfume in the Censer [...]

Also ye shall have a basket or other convenient vessel of copper filled with Charcoal to put inside the Censer when necessary, and which ye can take outside the Oratory, because the Censer itself should never be taken away from the place. Note well that after having performed your prayer, you ought to take it out of the Oratory, especially during the Two last Moons, and ye should inter it in a place which cannot well be made unclean, such as a garden.

British Summer Time means that noon oration takes place at 1 pm. Rather than orate on a full stomach, I decided to have lunch after oration and do my meditation before the oration as preparation. So now a typical day might be:

5.30 am up. Oration 5.45–7 am or later. Breakfast then reading till 9.30 am. Gardening or chores until 11.30 am or so. Meditation till 1 pm then at least an hour of oration before lunch. After lunch reading for a couple of hours then tea. Chores till supper. Reading then in oratory around 8.30 pm to 9.30 pm according to sunset time.

## Sunday 31 July

Cold is slightly better. But still I shatter my routine and leave bed open in case I want to doze after break.

Up in much better time; really almost worthy were it not for longer time needed to prepare the new censer and get ready for the new oration.

The linen robe fits! I was afraid I might have found that the summer would be so warm that I would be orating starkers, instead of in woollies and scarves. I was alarmed to find I'd left my college scarf in the oratory overnight—there must be a load of malevolent vibes in that four feet of wool.

I also nearly performed the bloody sacrifice, but prepared myself against it as best I could. Yesterday came with bad nosebleeds[1] and enough lost blood to feed an army of "denizens of darkness". Today it promptly restarted, but fortunately held off during oration. Blood on the linen ("not to be removed from oratory") would have posed practical problems!

The incense burner looks good. Anxious moment; the overhanging handle parts the rising plume of smoke. Apothis and Typhon? Duality invoked? Mercifully, no. Aerodynamics ensure that the divided flow swims around the handle and reunites to symbolise the alchemical process of the ONE thing which is made TWO, to be reunited in a higher ONE. Phew!

On Friday evening and Saturday morning I pressed on with "watching the watcher". There was the upper point like Hadit. The "other" bit spread out like a cloud till it filled all space, like Nuit. Then the cloud condensed, falling inward to a dark star in my solar plexus. The two were in the chambers. I drove (enticed, i.e., from above/below) the upper down to the dark region. The first time it descended in heavy wet stygian dark and came up in flaming rocks like a volcano. Later times it knew the way better; going down then floating up, then down again and up again, etc.

After all that, today's return to relaxed positivity seems sissy and too thoughtful. But I'll give it a fair try. Anyway it is better, from what I have achieved and remembered. There is more to look for. A very soft circulation along spine and down front did take place. 9.30. What a long write-up.

## Monday 1 August

Terrible oversleep till 6.30! I had bad nosebleed in the night. Out about 7–8 am and had only porridge break as a result.

Lovely warm sunny day so I had large laundry of blankets, my meditation "suit"—tracksuit, etc.

---

[1] Reading this in 2017 I am reminded that South African San rock paintings often show nosebleeding as a sign of intense spiritual activity. It is a nice idea but, at the time, I was only aware that a severe head cold had caused the nosebleeds.

Unlike Chevalier, the noon oration does not disorientate me. The whole timetable of orating is so different that at first I did not think the meditation fitted in any more. I do not do it at noon. Because of Summer Time noon is 1 pm and I have to lunch after oration so I do not want to be left hungry at 2. So I do Crowley-type asana in my room or garden from 12 and then orate.

I must slick up the incense act. Being mingy with charcoal means I am having to interrupt my progress to balance grains of sticky incense on a tiny piece of hot charcoal. And with my lingering cold I am coughing and spluttering in the fumes.

Midday oration in briefs and evening one in shorts; the weather has cheered up. To me it feels correct to be praying with less clothing. Pagan!

Oration said with feeling; I'm trying to spin them out to same length as old type.

Meditations feeble. I'd much rather do something fierce, but re-reading Jung's commentary on *The Secret of the Golden Flower* reminded me to be patient. In that respect I made a big effort this evening. Also with noon meditation, agony of thunderbugs[2] crawling over my nostrils and tickling me to death (not quite, alas).

### Tuesday 2 August

Late again, and I am still ill. I felt furious to be still suffering after a week; tickling throat with coughing that really hinders meditation. Yet I did it for a long time this morning and got foolishly cold. (I wore a tracksuit instead of my thunder undies because, having washed the latter, I wanted to wait till I'd had a bath before donning them.) Also, very irritating incense. I'll see if I can arrange for it to smoulder on a tray over the charcoal. I think my home-made stuff does not smell as good as that which I bought, but having suffered a cold which ruins my senses ever since starting how can I be sure? How can they be different if we both obeyed the recipe? And Starchild[3] provided the materials as well as the mixed incense (with the exception of the lignum aloes, perhaps that is the culprit and it has gone off over the years I've had it).

---

[2] Tiny flying insects that sometimes appear in sultry weather.
[3] Occult book and supplies shop founded by Bernie Ratcliffe in Luton. It later moved to Whitby, Yorkshire.

Last night and (I think) the night before I dreamed I was packing up and leaving my flat. A rather boring older man was moving in. He had a shoddy gramophone he wanted to plug in.

10.30 am and I will ask *I Ching*, "How should I best conduct myself during these last two moons?" This is a general question, but I have two particular uncertainties. One is in my meditation; how hard should I "try"? and if so, what? Second is equivalent; what should I do physically? My sickness seems to have coincided with my attempts to keep fit and stop the loss of weight. I wonder if there is a message here that I cannot face? So, as to keeping healthy and strong, how hard should I "try"? I hope the answer will bear on the question, otherwise I will ask separately.

9-8-8  5-8-8  5-4-4  5-4-4  5-8-8  5-8-8. Moving lines 1, 3, 4.
44 to 61. "Coming to Meet" to "Inner Truth".

| Received | First | Second |
|---|---|---|
| ——— | ——— | ——— |
| ——— | ——— | ——— |
| ——o—— | ——— | —  — |
| ——o—— | ——— | —  — |
| ——— | ——— | ——— |
| ——x—— | —  — | ——— |
| 44 | 61 |
| Coming to meet | Inner Truth |

Oh dear! The first hexagram suggests that the innocent-seeming feminine element has crept in and must be checked before it grows, i.e. a temptation must be spurned. "Even a lean pig can rage around" suggests that I (long pig) should not worry about becoming thin because (commentary) later I will eat and be fine. "No skin on thighs and walking is hard, but if mindful of danger no great mistake is made" seems relevant too. "No fish in tank" means I've been "out of touch with the people"? Neglecting true needs because of what I think is good for me?

But what is all this about a dangerous temptation that I will be unable to accept but which will hurt me? I thought I was past that. I thought the fierce and glamorous meditation practices were the temptation that I had successfully avoided. Is in fact my dropping of them and returning to simplicity an evil temptation? How very original! Quite unlike the punch-line in a corny occult novel!

Similarly I had come to terms with the idea of giving up gym and obeying instruction to "retire". Is this the cunning temptation? How puzzling.

I will have to think a lot about these.

61, "Inner Truth" or "Inner Confidence" takes me back to the first *I Ching* answer. Does this mean that, if I try very hard and am very lucky, I might just make square one? Oh thanks!

11.40 am. Actually, "Inner Truth" depicts an outcome that would be most desirable.

Asana at noon for forty-five minutes. Very calm, plagued by shabby spider or thunderbug causing tickle agony. Longed for the end so I could bash it (or even revere it for creating such psychic pressure). Come the end, I could not see it.

After reading the superb *The Supersensual Life* and am again amazed at how bad *Aurora* was. It was my long acquaintance with former that made me want to read the latter.

In my noon oration I recalled a previous time of great change; on leaving school. Through occult studies I had developed inner silence—my "neo-hip". I was aloof from the world, yet did not despise it. For I became dissatisfied with my lofty height, all the more so when MW came to stay. She, to me, embodied all that I lacked; vivacity, naturalness, moodiness, femininity, youth, and colour. To my silence, she had noise. I recall a conscious desire (at the Fiddler's Elbow[4]) that I must fill the silence of my mind with pop songs and chatter in order to become like her. I was aware of loneliness because of the created gulf, so instead of attracting (or advancing to) a loved one, I had to invoke the desired qualities in me or become the loved one myself. It was a sort of pride that made me fear to be the awkward adolescent lover. So I changed. From being the "mature" and silent schoolboy, I became the naive and amusing student and now my contemporaries speak to me as the image of their past, their student days. It is I who have not aged.

But now I seek to undo MW's spell.

That was the time that I should, according to earlier intentions, have been doing the Abramelin operation! Earlier this year, when persuading myself it was the right thing for this summer, I was aware of that fact: because my not doing the operation marked the point of downturn

---

[4] A notorious bend on the A46 between Cranham and Brockworth in Gloucestershire.

in my fortunes (in the sense that, having risen from village schoolkid to Cambridge Maths scholar, I fell from reluctant schoolmaster to being a civil servant and office stooge). 8.45 pm.

### Wednesday 3 August

Terrible lie-in till nearly 7. Disgusting with phlegm, catarrh, and head like a septic tank. Clumsy blundering on the way out, spilt sand from censer.

So revolted that I prayed to God to kill me. When he failed to deliver the goods I tried twice to suffocate myself by not breathing. (Meanwhile I had asked Michael to chop my head off, then to throttle me, but neither did much good.) After that a sort of lurex feeling came over me, distanced me from my sickness. I orated with fervour and meditated a long time without any physical pain or desire to fidget. Thoughts wafted around but they were, as it were, cirro stratus rather than cumulo nimbus. After reading *The Psychedelic Experience* (by Leary et al) I decided to re-enter as a calm and purposeful personality.

Yesterday and today I put my incense in an open cover of foil. This made it burn more slowly and with less heavy fumes. This morning the incense actually outlasted the charcoal. 8.45 am.

No better, I discovered. So I forwent breakfast and made do with tea and raisins. What with that and death posturing I've been high all morning, and quite useful.

Asana was late (shopping delay) and rather bad with thoughts. More death posturing and scream in my oration. I felt blackness gush out of me, most of it was taken away too.

Letter from C.F. Russell, refusing (politely) more information on his Holy Cube. This is a pity because it has for many years struck me as the basis for my perfect system; I did not understand his attributions, but thought the framework superb. For about five years I've been trying to get his Primer of the Holy Cube and meaning to write to him. At last I've done it, without success.

Could this possibly fit yesterday's *I Ching* remark: "there is a temptation to fall in with an evil element offering itself—a very dangerous situation. Fortunately circumstances prevent this; one would like to do it but cannot." Certainly I would have been embarrassed had he enthusiastically offered instant enlightenment at £100! But does this really merit that warning? And if not, what does? Is it my death posture? But that is not hindered by circumstances but positively encouraged. (I no longer notice cold.)

Heaps crummy p.m. Three hour phone call with K—time flew. No time to read anything. I'm warming to the idea of giving up my weight; after two months of difficulty in maintaining eleven and a half stone, I'm now quite keen to see if I can I lose another one and a half stone. If I cut out eggs and dairy stuff which is what S has long suggested anyway—and cut out gym and wrap up warmly and move around very little I think I could drop to ten stone. It would be a sacrifice. I'm beginning to feel quite masochistic about it; "all those who criticise my diet, and mock my enthusiasm for weight training, just you wait; I'll show you what becomes of me when I give it up. I'll die—that'll show you!"

Accordingly, I am going to bed with elderberry cordial instead of milk drink.

Evening oration poor and meditation positively bad. Ended up "doing time"; just sitting, looking at my watch every half minute.

## Thursday 4 August

Up nearly in time, though still felt a bit low. Oration a bit tame. In meditation I circulated the light with breathing (as I have been doing more thoroughly this week) and began to attain that concentrated consciousness. Noting thoughts I sought their source and obtained a different consciousness, rather "everyday" yet pure and clear. It was as though I was behind myself, around the middle of the spine. I moved to and fro between states and collected other consciousness into my belly. Again a more realistic feeling of the separation into two, of the child in my belly.

Dark cool morning has lightened to clear (hazy) sky.

Hung on to operation fairly well in St. Albans. Very poor asana as the tickle in my throat gave me hell. But managed to unload ego in my oration. There is still a fairly vigorous tendency for ego to make best of any decision—e.g. making masochistic thing out of my resignation to ill health and scrawniness—and I am still thinking in terms of "my God, I'm gonna be a real spiritual smoothy when this little number is up; look out world!" whenever I have any victory over my ego. But it is better.

I think this could be the next big struggle; against dreams of the future, something I have always enjoyed and yet has never been correct.

## *Friday 5 August*

Another dead beat and hopeless start. Woke too early and fell asleep and felt leaden on waking.

Circulated the light until calm and gathered and then made the division into two and went to and fro between states.

Just as I am warming to the idea of staring the pig into submission, and trying to destroy all my dreams of the future, I am interested to change my handwriting,[5] because I recall that that was based upon some sort of contrived image. So if I let it lose its character then it can re-grow into whatever it wants. I noticed a recent tendency for words to be written strangely, often with two letters interchanged.

Asana for fifty minutes, too thoughtful but quite pure and clear all the same. I circulated light for long time then worked at separation; not much spatial difference felt.

I've been hungry most of the morning, I'm following S's suggestion and cutting out milk and eggs. I'm still having milk in tea and will have eggs in made-up dishes for a bit longer. Gosh, this new writing is quite nice.

## *Saturday 6 August*

Quite unjustifiable late rising; having had early night (not long after 10) I slept through till 6—giving myself eight hours at last! But instead of feeling refreshed I was so shagged that I dozed till 6.30, and even then I was below par. Perhaps it was a reaction to too large a supper last night? Certainly I felt much less enflamed and spiritual yesterday evenmed and oration, as though there was some truth in that bloke's quotation about feeling one can know God when one has a naked body and an empty belly.

Fast not too difficult this morning, so I'm not taking water yet, in order to tighten it. 11.30 am.

Did bathroom cleaning when I would normally do asana, so I incorporated latter into oration in the normal way. Too many thoughts. Lovely rain continues to fill the water butt.

---

[5] This sudden and unexpected change in my handwriting was quite dramatic. The old style returned later, and for a time I slipped between the two. Ramsey Dukes' signature adopted the new style; Lionel Snell stayed old style.

My desire to crush thoughts of the new smooth post-operational me has made me wonder anew "what *will* I be like?" Ghastly is the thought that I might become a simpering Christian wet like Boehme or Bunyan—as depicted in their respective works. How could I face my family and friends if I become "religious"? M would be quite happy for me to be religious if it meant doing some discrete good works and ending up marrying the bishop's daughter. But if I joined a monastery (especially a Catholic one) it would blow her mind!

I would claim it to be a good thing if, after this, I became rich, handsome, extravert, clever, and sexy. I am very suspicious of becoming "above" things of the "world" and "flesh" if it means being no good at them. When S speaks of withholding herself from orgasms during the period of my sexual abstinence, it does not turn me on. I'd much rather she cut the spiritual bit and glutted herself in order to make me jealous. I would be, but I like to think I could survive it for this operation. I was much more excited by her parting remarks (as I yearned for food in my fast) that she was always much more interested in the "other appetite". Thinking "dirty" has an exquisite quality which has yet to be matched by spiritual experience. I do this operation because it is my nature, and because I believe in giving things a whole-hearted try (though I so seldom practice my belief). I have no illusions that this proves me better than others. Sure, I'm better than LBS who has not done this operation, but I'm no better than a successful Casanova, say.

I see a little more clearly the nature of the deception; there is a sensual picture of Linda Ronstadt on N's LP cover which peers at me through the chair legs. I can spurn it because I realise it is a fraud, not because the lustful feeling is evil. I realise that the suggestion that she is a hungry bundle of pussy is in fact a lie dug up by the viewer's mind; in real life that idea would be swamped by complications, e.g. S, who turned me on (unknowingly) by expressing an attitude to the "other appetite", but who can turn me off by diluting it with a load of old "spiritual beauty" stuff. Cf., "the sexuality of man hath an earthward course, the sexuality of woman a spiritual. Man and woman become devils one to the other if they distinguish not their sexuality" (Jung's *Seven Sermons*). When S gave her sexuality an earthward course she became a devil to me. This is because she gave her sexuality a masculine form. This is the secret of the succubus. Apparently both incubi and succubi are in fact male spirits—they can impregnate a woman but only drain a man. The picture of Linda Ronstadt portrays a male "earthly" sexual quality which is a lie because if you knew her no doubt she would give you all the usual feminine twaddle about "is that all you ever think about", "don't just look on me as a sex object" and all that. It is only when women are devilish that they excite like succubi—that too is why real randiness tends to come at a later age; the mature woman who is less "feminine" in nature and who begins to live up to the male ideal of cock-hungry "I'm-a-woman".

What's all this got to do with Abramelin? Well, like you can see, I really dig what a succubus can do to me (and to other people), and so far "Spirit" has not matched it. I do not mind becoming dead to the succubi charms to show that I see through the fraud, but if I was simply *left* dead to their charms I would feel that it was a swindle, I had been diminished. As a mystic, I would feel that Abramelin's operation should end with the knowledge and conversation of the Holy Guardian Angel, and that the follow-up, about commanding spirits, was a rather grubby appendage. But as a magician I think that is important. Having died to the world I want rebirth at a higher (more able) level.

So instead of being satisfied if I came round all pious—"above" the lusts of the flesh, and no longer moved by them and keen to dissuade others—I would in fact want to press on to being in control of those lusts, in their purest forms. So that I might be open to the odd jibe of being "sexless" because I was not interested in going to amusement arcades to gaze at uninteresting and uninterested females; but on the other hand, when I was with a woman whom I felt was cramped and in need of experience I would be glad to be able to conjure up the full succubi experience—make her a real devil and give her the wildest time of her life. I would also like her to realise what had happened (it need not be worded in terms of magic), lest she associated me too closely with what I had done, and become enslaved to me.

Oh dear! What a way to fill a diary! Have I got incubus and succubus the right way round? I've always assumed an incubus stuck it in, and a succubus sucked it out, but perhaps the medieval church had the Chinese deviousness to reverse this. 3.15 am.

Survived my fast. Really quite relaxed, and when it was over I only had a small supper so I felt hungry. Wish I had left as in fact I stayed telling N a full account of "Slow Joanz".[6] How foolish, all that prattle and in my creative fervour I did not get to bed till midnight, and then had to fight myself to sleep. Set alarm however!

---

[6]The title of a novel that I started but never had time to write down fully.

## Sunday 7 August

Overslept tragically, never heard alarm. Very groggy, I wilted over to oratory. Despite large porridge, I remained hungry all morning. 12.50 pm.

Stopped just short of my fifty minutes time—I thought the timer must have stopped! As ever, too many early thoughts.

Over the last few days I've noticed a tendency for the old dream to recur in a flash during the day, in a *déjà vu* fashion. I suddenly get a glimpse of some "unreal" dream event or situation or atmosphere, without any clear link with what I'm doing. Often it is of an old dream, far fom my mind, and forgotten.

It has rained again, lovely wet soil, good for the garden.

Afternoon passed to nothing as I read N's Sunday paper, went to discuss design of my now redundant silver censer, and returned via K, where I stayed till 8 pm and so had no time for supper.

## Monday 8 August

Another bad, late morning. This time the alarm was faultless, I awoke on time, but in my bleary running over of dreams, etc., I couldn't believe that a whole hour slipped away![7] As ever, of late, the extra lie-in did me no good at all.

Still resigned to thought in my meditations; they do not hinder a lot, but who knows where I would get to without them.

Reading of Rosenkreutz anthology started after breakfast. As I start re-reading *The Chymical Wedding*, I wonder if the seven days fit in with the six moons (they both begin at Easter). Then I wondered how they compared with, say, seven years. That set me to examining my last seven years.

1. 1970. This was a stinking year. I was a teacher at the world's most famous school, but was not sure that my life was right. I wanted to experience a more humdrum life, partly to see if I could stand it, but also because I felt there was a need to make basic changes to myself.

    It was a year of wonderful holidays, to the North with FV and to Scotland on my own. I had Blavatsky (the lovely Lea Francis

---

[7] An example of trying to integrate too many systems. The work of recalling and noting my dreams for divinatory purposes increased the likelihood that I fell back into sleep. A more single-minded aspirant would just leap out of bed on waking.

saloon), which made travel a pleasure that has only revived with Bloaters.

It was a year of crisis; my miserable and unhappy termination of "affair" (too one-sided really to justify this label) with BB. The only thing to keep me alive was Austin Spare's philosophy of the "death posture", and the joy of travel.

Blavatsky broke down, never to recover; there was a crisis of a wonderful holiday in France which began with last-minute rush, twisted ankle, and severe cold, and no money at all. On my return I had my one and only court case and news that my job was terminated. I expected the latter (and was relieved) because it was the day of Uranus on my MC (it had crossed Neptune square Saturn at time of BB-achs) and several other relevant aspects.

2. 1971 was a good year (starting autumn 1970). Knowing that my future was not fixed I felt free and relaxed and I taught well and had lots of pupils. People said nice things about my teaching and I was offered a job at Clifton which I shyly turned down because of the above-mentioned need for experience. Again, wonderful shared holidays. Began regular attendance at the gym and knew new health and vigour. Contact with S and happy sexual relationships. Lovely sunbathing and rowing. In autumn I had brief "retirement" and wrote my first book. Finishing it lingered on.

3. 1972 was sour. Staying on at home and trying to finish writing and re-writing, encouraged by Gerald Yorke. The book was shown to publishers and had lukewarm reception. Job hunting grew important and dull.

4. 1973. The cursed year of entering the Civil Service (burial in the grave). Amusing times with PR, lovely hot summer and first astrological conference. Very striking "rebirth" type aspects; the solar return was very like my birth chart and was just at the time of moving to Redbourn (near my place of birth). Saturn crisis imminent. Autumn disaster; another painful non-affair with another K collapsed me into misery. Again suicide ruled, only tempered by Austin Osman Spare. Started writing (unfinished) "Slow Joanz". Began to hate my job.

5. 1974. Escape from Civil Service. Also sold taxi, after years of burden Very unusual year in that *I* made the decisions (rather than fate, or other people). Unlike previous jobs and situations, Hawker Siddley came from my own decision; true fate showed it to me and I had no illusions that it was aught but release from Civil Service. I actually published a book (correction: *SSOTBME* came out in 1975) and for the only time in my life it was I who first asked a girl to sleep with me

("Legs"). Of course all these great decisions ended up as flops, but they were at least made.
6. 1975. Selling my book. Riding Ivan (my Ural motor-cycle sidecar combination). Learning my limitations. No holiday except anxious week in Northern Ireland being PR's "best man". The big come-down.
7. 1976. Death. A.O.S. sigil magic brought me money, "enough to be free". The freedom was in the form of Bloaters (my Moto Guzzi I-Convert). Travel was now a joy and yet I had no time to do it. Work was complete purgatory, I felt it as an ordeal of darkness and swallowed it accordingly.
8. 1977. Abramelin. First time I deliberately shun exercise.

This week I am not reading the psalms! I'm on strike. Having opened the mighty Rosenkreutz anthology I think I'll give that my full attention for one week at least.

ML is keen to visit before October. Oh dear. I said I would not be very prominent.

In evenmed my lamp burnt low literally and I was slightly scared it might go out. Shortish, sweaty evenmed. I am not sweating at night anymore (due to eating so little?) but I am sweating and stinking in my meditation.

## Tuesday 9 August

Still late, but a bit better. Very clear and detailed dreams of friends, of a crazy American whose all-absorbing hobby was firing heavy guns at an old Trident wing, and of a sophisticated girlfriend of Dick's who slept with me and gave me all sorts of advice on my lovemaking technique.

Good meditation, perhaps the best yet. Very gentle and calm concentration despite music from Francoise Hardy and Lindisfarne in my mind. Clear feeling of something large, diffuse, and heavy sloughing off from the upper point of concentration and drifting down to its own place. Perhaps an important point was that I did not follow it, but hung on to the upper light. Practice for this came last night; poor meditation with very lumpy heartbeats and sweats and worries. In desperation I watched the watcher and became aware of hanging on to something that forever changed its shape, as in the myth of Proteus.

Also this time there was a definite ending, an awakening to clarity. After that, Rosenkreutz seems a load of rubbish.

Asana fairly poor. Tried to continue morning's good work but a cold in the throat and hunger and general crud did not help.

After lunch I read Rosenkreutz till I felt like screaming. There was only one good bit, a page in *Secret Symbols of the Rosicrucians* showing the tree of good and evil and hands grasping for its fruit, leaves, and branches—very AOS.

Good evenmed, though too thoughtful. Managed to minimize heart-throbs by same gentleness; felt that in theory they could be banished by that method. Definite feeling of "as above, so below" circles with water surface separating them. I think I stopped too soon.

## Wednesday 10 August

Ghastly lateness, all-time low.

Dream of being on a small island in the South Pacific near South America. With someone else I left by the sea and landed at the end of the world, the very tip of Cape Horn. As I beached I picked up some stones, lovely clear pieces of crystal, irregular smooth shapes. I wondered if they were of glass but because they were full of bubbles I, for some reason, decided they were stone. I was very much aware that this was Tierra del Fuego. We walked north past some natives who, to my relief, did not accost us. The countries were very small, a short journey and we had crossed two. These countries were keen to trade with Europe. In a car we collected a young man keen to be a sales representative. He was the brother of Dominique or some French-speaking paying guest of the Mill. And so on …

Could not leave my bed; lay there thinking that it was so late any-way. Lay there hoping for a miracle, a sudden fire to make me leap forth full of go. But it never happened. So, rising at 7 was as much agony as it would have been at 5.15. I was out from 7.15 till 9, determined to go for a long time, at least till N left.

A good oration. More to confess! Also full of feeling. In my meditation, I applied the gentle insistence of recent times, and felt the separation. Yesterday, I likened this gentle holding tight to holding a frog spawn in a pair of tweezers; it was holding something slippery, yet delicate, which needed maximum concentration and minimum force.

This time I considered Suchten's[8] thing about making one into two, and making a third from one of them. Previously, I'd thought in terms of dividing the upper, having "cleared the dross from it to below". This time I considered the lower. Conscious attention was in the upper and the lower squadge sort of became two lots of mud. The image suggested itself of the two balls hanging below the erect penis. This seemed to fit the image of the upward pointing triangle too.

Came together and separated again.

So late was I that as I finished the sun shone in on me through the window.

Crummy midday meditation, lying in the sun and eventually defeated by thunderbugs crawling on my face. But it was amazing how much I managed to put up with earlier.

Crummy evening meditation too. Got excited beforehand by the idea that *New Scientist* might accept my book for review. Managed to fight that off, but succumbed to palpitating heart. Oh hell, I fear I'm allergic to chocolate. I must repeat today's supper without it and see. Why can't I be allergic to something foul like pork pies or Wall's ice cream? Chocolate of all things! Having decided that was it, my meditation went for a burton; I sweated and my mind wandered everywhere. "I'll do it right next time," I promised. In fact I could do quite well banishing throbs for short periods, but never for long. It's the old thing of making sickness an excuse.

Abramelin says I cannot eat flesh, S says no eggs or dairy products, and now aubergines and chocolate are out. I'll end up on water.

## Thursday 11 August

What a struggle, with long alarm and about three runs of my little timer, I croaked out of bed at 5.35.

Poor oration—not fully there. Good meditation. First separation of lower element was like earth and water separating (earth to the right). Then there was a fairly confused interval and return. The second separation (a new sort) of the lower was into light and dark, also warm and cold in a Sun and Moon sort of way. The Sun was on the right.

I wasted time till 9.

---

[8]Think this refers to Alexander von Suchten, but I forget which book.

Late and crummy start, and loads of snags en route, but Bloaters went like thunder and I went from signing on at St. Albans at 10.10 (there was a queue) to Gnosis, to the Zodiac Emporium, to the Susters, to Petersham and back to Redbourn by 12.55, in time for noon oration. It was a sunny afternoon so I read and sunbathed.

The day was too exciting so my meditations have been very poor, but the actual oration this evening was good.

## Friday 12 August

Slightly later today. Meditation no good, too many thoughts. My wretched book and its prospects keep intruding. I don't know whether writing *Thundersqueak* would be good (letting the pressure down) or bad. Too much excitement in my life. Had a second try. Held on for a while and the vertical separation took place, but instead of the base dividing in two, a very bright light glowed over "the waters", which was around the solar plexus and chest area, but it nearly joined the upper and lower.

Oh dammit. 12.45 and I've just given up my asana as it was so spastic. Just thoughts, thoughts, thoughts. The only time I made any progress was when I was ill. Perhaps a few more days in bed is what I need. Oration was different; several times over I willed myself to death by not breathing. When I began to feel dead and empty, having prayed to God to kill me and clean me of all personality and encumbrance, I then continued but prayed impersonally, never for myself. For example, instead of praying for knowledge and conversation of the Holy Guardian Angel, I prayed that at the end of these six moons there should be a clean and empty body for him to inhabit, to take over as an instrument of God's will. I have continued to see the Holy Guardian Angel less and less as a sort of decorative additive and more as the real thing, i.e. me as I should be. So I want there to be nothing left of me but the Holy Guardian Angel.

Oration for fifty minutes. Still feel blown. Good. I'm very cold. (Corpses can't have everything.)

After lunch I huddled in woollies, thick trousers, dressing gown and eventually I had to lie down under my duvet to read. N agreed it was a bit cold, so I must have generated a psychic chill! Plodded on with dreary Rosenkreutz. But I will finish it this week! Great!

Life had returned partly by the time I went to evenmed. But still oration and meditation went well. The latter nice and simple; by avoiding too conscious a circulation of the light I bypassed heartthrobs. It is that concentration on the breathing which seems to cause or make me aware of the trouble.

Vertical separation (above and below) took place after longish spell of my trying to keep the tiny star (or seed) in view. But the lower separation was not very clear. I tried to extend it into a four-fold separation into elements. The ending was a bit confused.

## Saturday 13 August

Dreamt I was riding a large horse in an indoor riding school sort of place. Didn't like riding and, realising horses can sense a timid rider, I was anxious and awkward. To my relief, the brute was more human than usual and spoke quite well. I was relieved when it said it would rather stay indoors (where I felt safer) and when it expressed an interest in an archery demonstration at the end of the hall. I was able to pull off my old boast about having been Vice President of the Eton College Toxophilite Society. Even horses are impressed by that.

Leaden awakening. Dead feeling. But whereas yesterday it was the bad bits that were dead, today it was the good bits. So I could not get any verve or interest. My meditation was pathetic and full of half-hearted thoughts. It was not for lack of trying as I was out there for about one and three-quarter hours.

Returned to bed to try to get warm. Read relevant dates of Chevalier's book.[9]

He seems to have had a much more exciting time and made more progress than me. No-one would publish my diary! In my defence, I might suggest that he is perhaps more prone to self-deception than me; but, wow, that is a big claim.

To save me from getting up I'll describe my orations. They used to change a lot. Although at a higher stage I'd consider such inventiveness to be good, I reckoned that for me now I should curb creativity and vanity and try to be monotonous. So they settled down in the first four months to:

1) Thanksgiving. I started by giving thanks for birth and upbringing, then worked towards the present. But in the good summer days I often entered oratory bursting to give some immediate thanks for

---

[9]*The Sacred Magician* by George Chevalier.

something (like sun or a good cabbage) so I changed to immediate thanks for THIS and everything that made THIS possible—the cottage and garden, my sympathetic family and friends, for N's tolerance, T's wisdom, K's enthusiasm and help, RM's understanding about my need for the freedom to leave my old life, and for the laws of the land which made it possible, then for all the signs which had helped me to make up my mind, including the pattern of my life which has led to this, then for God's grace in my life at making my errors into lessons, for my formal education, for the inspiration of the beautiful places in which I have lived, for my parents and the qualities I've inherited from them, for God's creation (the heavens, the elements, life, lust and laughter), and for my privilege to have been born in a rich and pleasant part at a time of peace and plenty, for magic and the freedom to pursue it, for all the meaning and purpose it has given my life, and above all for its leading me to THIS.

2) Confession. I would grovel a bit about how I've wasted all God's gifts and lessons, and corrupted talents (e.g. turning appreciation of beauty into covetousness and so on). I'd moan about my poor time-keeping and concentration.

3) Aspiration. I'd rise from prostrate to kneeling position and ask for strength, wisdom, and green shield stamps; so that I could aspire to the knowledge and conversation of my Holy Guardian Angel at the end of these six moons. That through him I could know my true will and become good and useful, clear and strong, a joy to God and a joy and inspiration to the world so I could repay the trust of my family and friends.

Then I'd meditate. Quite often I'd lob in a psalm or two, or TB's collects between scenes.

But the final two moons need a different format, no mention of thanksgiving and more emphasis on outcome. Still, if I was bursting to say thanks I'd tend to kick off with it, but only very briefly. I'd begin to prostrate myself and spend some time trying to find some sin in my spotless life worth confessing. This is very much spun out in order to make the time up to the half hour that K and Chevalier manage—I think they sin more than me. If really miserable I might death posture a bit. Then I make a general confession for sins and omissions against God's divine will, whether committed consciously or in ignorance.

They say that my sins cannot harm God, but I regret them because they form a barrier between me and God, and so I am blinded. Here I have an analogy which I can amplify at length: at birth, God planted a seed in me, which was my true will, but instead of tending it I have lost it under a rubbish heap of lies, illusions, fears, misunderstandings, malice, and feeble distractions. It is that shifting rubbish heap that is now me, because I've lost my will. So please send down the gentle dissolving rain (universal solvent) so as to dissolve this heap, kill "me" and let me rot down to black compost. Let the moisture and warmth of God's love thus find its way to the lost seed and quicken it. Let it come to life and spread its roots through the blackness that was me. Let this matter be transformed by my will (the plant) into new growing life and let the plant (the new "me") rise up towards God's light, growing straight and strong. So saying, I rise to the kneeling position and pray for the grace to complete the operation worthily, to have and endure visions of angels and the knowledge and conversation of the Holy Guardian Angel. That with him I may achieve Abramelin's magic and have the power to command spirits, the confidence to command them well and, with him, the wisdom to command them according to God's will so it may be done upon earth. Sometimes I make a few impertinent suggestions as to what God's will might include, just in case he's short of ideas.

Then I usually need to stoke up with incense again before praying to angels:

Oh Holy Angels of the Lord, hear my prayer and come to this oratory.

Oh Holy Angels of the Lord, come to me, stand around me. Stand around and be my fortress, a wall to guard against outside hindrance in my work.

Oh Holy Angels of the Lord, come into my heart and mind. Make them clean within me and save me from internal strife that would weaken me in my work.

Oh Holy Angels of the Lord, stand before me. Make straight my path before me and lighten my way so I may see where I must go and step forward boldly in the way.

Oh Holy Angels of the Lord, come and go between me and God. Come and go and be messengers of God's will and judgement so I may know what must be done, and whether I am doing it.

Oh Holy Angels of the Lord, be with me in my reaching. Give me judgement to find what is good, learn it, remember it and apply it in my life, so I may grow in worth and strength.

Oh Holy Angels of the Lord, be with me as I end this operation. Let me merit the vision of you and be strong enough to endure it. Let me grow from it and have the knowledge and conversation of the Holy Guardian Angel.

Oh mine angel, mine Holy Guardian Angel, be with me, come to me and be known by be. Be one with me. Come into me and make me clean. Bring my warring parts into harmony and the strength of oneness. Lift them up and make them noble. Let us together have power to command the spirits, the confidence to command them well and the wisdom to command them according to God's will, etc., etc.

Oh Holy Angels of the Lord, be with me now, be with me at the end of this work, and be with me evermore. Amen.

That is basically it, but made rhythmic with repetition. In these more desperate days "me" hardly comes into it. The message is more on the lines of "kick me out" and tidy things up so that the Holy Guardian Angel can have a clean and empty vehicle to take over and transform for his use!

How modest can you get, I'd like to know! Oh God, I really would!

There is a hedgehog very close to the oratory. He stirs and scratches at the time of evenmed and sometimes a.m. too, like today. Perhaps it is a distracting elemental—but I know there is a hog around.

What a deadsville day! Stayed in bed all morning, shivering with cold. Stumbled out of bed to dress and "meditate" for just over an hour. In fact, very crummy with thoughts as I felt a sort of hangover from yesterday's furious oration and wondered if by starvation and not breathing I was destroying brain cells, and would therefore achieve simplicity by "physical" means. Was this why spiritual people seem simple and childlike? Except ye become as little children ... Is cleverness the great handicap? And the Tree of Knowledge the original sin? This seems to fit evolution for it is the clever people who are always being bumped off once you quit the wild state; and a country bumpkin, or a cretin in an institution deep in the country, will have a much better chance of surviving the next war than will a city slicker.

Die on, it's a crazy feeling.
Die on, it's got me reeling.
Die on, by revealing
My love for you, God, God.[10]

## Sunday 14 August

Happy day, besieged by phantasies and old temptations to anger and distraction. Bought a suitcase in an antique shop.

Dreamed of the sewage system under houses; they all had a sort of reservoir of sand to absorb moisture "lest the system should dry out in a drought".

Started reading *Faust, Part One*, having finished the awful Rosenkreutz anthology.

At lunchtime my alarm was not heard so my asana went on for an excruciating hour and twenty minutes before I gave up in disbelief.

Orations have been relaxed and meditations not too bad considering the attacking thoughts.

## Monday 15 August

Forgot to set alarm and was late, despite waking on time at first. Embarrassing dreams about a party.

Last night I seemed to avoid heartthrobs by starting meditation with less emphasis on circulating and more on cutting my mind off from my body, so that my head felt it was on a plate. Did something similar this morning.

I have not written a lot since noon on Sunday. My mood changed dramatically then. It had been a "hard" week and I was struggling into a calm state by being almost suicidal in my zeal.

After an hour of fruitless meditation at noon I went to the oratory in desperation and asked God for a miracle because I had no idea if I was on the right lines at all. Then God split in two.

Yes. He did just that.

The sentences in *Seven Sermons* came to mind; they're about the closeness of God and the Devil (e.g. God is the sun and the Devil is the empty space filled by the sun) and the idea that our striving after God gives power to the Devil. I had noted that the big "progress" of the last two

---

[10]Sung to tune of "Rave On" by Buddy Holly.

weeks was questionable. When, for example, I took the advice to forget the desire and stay fit and healthy to concentrate on the work, it became a sort of masochistic desire to starve to death; also the achievement of a state of fervour and absorption in the work to the exclusion of distinction to a large extent was only achieved by reaching a sort of raging negativity. As is suggested in *Seven Sermons*, the pursuit of the good will only lead one to fall into the bad unless one distinguishes oneself from both.

So anyway, in my agony God split in two and it was rather striking. Of course the idea of a God of many faces was not new and I had made a point of thanking "Mother" for food and all that is in *The Gospel of Peace*, because that part of my life was best distinguished from my orations in the early stages. But I had left the *Seven Sermons* because it did not fit in, the Abramelin operation did not lend itself to multiple deities. So it was good of God to split for me, it felt very peaceful and relieving, as though big God had decided to do some of my work for me.

It prompted the reflection on the mysterious secret of the alchemists. Why was the first matter, Mercury or whatever, always described in terms like the Tao (it is everywhere and it is despised as the lowest thing yet revered as the most precious thing, it is water and not-water, etc., etc.) Could the matter be God? That was the only justification sufficient for such secrecy, for who would dare write a book saying that it was necessary to split God in two?

Anyway, an idea, which had been with me for years nevertheless, was rather striking when it stopped being an idea and actually happened.

How to address the split God? The English language does not lend itself to that, hence our ideas of an all-male deity—for apparently, in the Jewish Genesis the word for God is male *and* female. So, in fact, I kept silent mostly as I went through the stages of oration. What to call the two halves is a natural but perhaps useless question. *Seven Sermons* would say God and Devil, but there is a snag in that we use the idea of the Devil in two ways that interfere. Devil can mean a polar quality of God, as in the *Seven Sermons* (God = effective fullness, and Devil = effective emptiness) in which case God and Devil are like the two aspects of God in Boehme, the Devil being the dark and wrathful aspect of God. But Devil also means a rather crummy by-product of this division. When the Devil is described as an imbecile nature spirit as in parts of Eliphas Levi (he says the Devil is utterly unintelligent and below reason, yet can still defeat intelligent men by his persistence), or as God's henchman sent to ginger up the creation as in *Faust*, in these cases we are obviously not discussing a polar balance to God. Indeed, in the Abramelin system

"Satan" is one of the demon princes who will be subject to the magician's command. At present I am most aware of Devil being the dead weight of old prejudices and time-wasting phantasies and debilitating illusions which hinder me from doing anything positive; this Devil is obviously not to be revered, being lower than Saturn. It is more like the one referred to by Levi.

But anyway this was very helpful. For example it helped one dilemma; what had God to do with lust and sensual pleasure? I had, for purposes of this operation, given up both and indeed in my negative state I was really not too keen on either. Yet memory and intellect reminded me that they were awfully good things and God either should have a share in them or else have a very good excuse why not—better excuse than any I'd found in scriptures. Now I was relieved to be given an answer: I had been climbing up God's right leg, that was my choice (via Abramelin's advice) and it would get me to the same place as the other route.

Since God split in two I've felt very different—a bit like my old self dammit! (But I hope I've come back higher up the spiral.) There has been a riotous uprush in distracting thoughts and phantasies to waste my time. But, taking a tip from a divided God, in my confession I do not apologise for those phantasies so much as for the (lesser) extent to which I get distracted by them. I no longer see them as part of me, but invading and tempting demons. (I think that although when faced by a really scary or disturbing demon, it is good to remind yourself that it is "only" part of you; on the other hand it is psychologically healthy to disown the trashy little demons.)

Seeking an idea as to how to come to terms with this event in the practice of my oration and meditation, I realised that God had simply done what I had done. When I had split into △ God had split inversely into ▽ so together we were ✡ *comme ça*. If I could achieve a ✡ "ping"! It would be a mystical experience. If I could press on to "crunch"! It would be to achieve this work, the Holy Guardian Angel being the centre of the star. (Then I would continue my life with my sights on a "higher" or purer vision of God.)

To leave a long story long: I had rehearsed this in my meditation today. When I had divided up, after a while the upper ▽ descended and it was, as Austin Osman Spare would say, "amiable".

Somehow, this writing up, plus a letter, have passed a whole morning again. But I might just have time for the lawn.

### Tuesday 16 August

I don't know what to do about capitals in my new writing. Yesterday evening I again rehearsed ▽ bit. I was aware of doing the work this time. According to a lot of theory, I should really just wait for God to do it, and to enact events is to bring mumbo into my meditation. However, I decided to do this again to try it. It is a sort of ritual playacting, necessary to try it in case it rings bells or sets something in motion.

This morning on the other hand I started with a campaign against heartthrobs. The "head on a plate" effect was found to arise from an overflow of the devotional oration feeling into the meditations; in the oration I am aspiring up and am "out of body", whereas in the meditation I am holding down to the centre. But if I let the former feeling continue into the meditation I don't really start in the centre, but a bit above my head. This avoids the heartthrobs. I then gradually work into meditation gear. I also hope to avoid the persistent pressure feeling; it is the feeling one has called "a lump in the throat", except that it is elsewhere. Right now I have it in the bridge of my nose. It is like catarrh congestion. I did not succeed in avoiding it altogether. I note that Chevalier had pressure in his head and it grew bigger. My head is already big enough thank you.

Sinking down happened, so this time I acted out the decapitating of the dragon, fermenting it in its blood, distilling off the liquid (up) and heating the earth to whiteness, remixing the fluid to give a red tincture. Nice one.

Now I must do some gardening for a change.

Great stuff, some good work done except alas for longish break partly to blame on Mrs Smith feeling suicidal as I cheered her with coffee. I made that a priority over the garden.

Real floperoo meditation at noon. Found I'd slumped and was so fed up with the pressure in my head I threw in after half an hour. Stood on my head for a short while hoping somehow to effect my head.

Oh doctor, my brain hurts.

Evenmed illumination concerned the armour I'd made within myself. I'd ascribe this to memory of being bullied by my older brother. I quickly learned that I had no hope in combat being five years his junior, so I bottled it up in silent rages. This same block keeps me from revealing myself in love. But it is a vertical block—it does not stop steam escaping sideways. So when the pressure is really high, I am no longer seen as cool, indeed the only person who does not know my feelings is myself, e.g. there have been occasions when my embarrassingly obvious passion has been joined with impotence—my consciousness being in a dazed vacuum.

## Wednesday 17 August

Did not write up today, cannot remember it much. Very wet, so I stayed in and wrote letters a.m. Read early so that, after lunch, I could go to see CF in hospital. We were able to go out to a tea house. He was in because he'd been miserable in love and so had been deported from Holland on psychiatric grounds. I was able to give him much comfort and advice, but I noticed him shrivel again as we returned to the shrink house.

That reminds me of lunch oration; I was so fed up with being haunted by dreams of what I wanted to be and do when and if I succeed in this work, that in helplessness I described those dreams in detail in my confession. This afternoon's event promptly recalled one aspect of my dream that I'd dealt with insufficiently, and that was the desire to heal; especially people like CF who tend to come to me.

I would like to follow my visit with a long letter, something for him to keep in case his memory of our talk fades.

## Thursday 18 August

Appalling lateness, after an interesting and frightening dream. The dream was in a place shaped like Cranham. In a place vaguely situated, I'd say, between council houses, church, and Mann's Court, but which was "on the moon" in the dream. I was in a curious space ship or "living module" amidst a lot of clutter, and there was an appearance of a herd of horrible, small swimming horses with fangs bared. I cannot recall what it was all about, but a surviving "moon family" appeared with a rather lovely daughter who said that everyone dies who came there. (I think that was what I was investigating.) I felt anxious for her safety.

I returned "home" down to the place where Mill would be. As I went along the drive there was a wooden box by the stream, nicely polished and in a net. It moved towards me and sprayed aerosol jets over me and in the air. Somehow I knew this was a plot, and sure enough I grew numb and bleary and made my way to the large modern plate glass building where the Mill should be. I managed to reach my friend, but we were seen by the police car which stopped us. "Milko!" cried the policewoman. My suspicions were aroused by a police car selling milk. Sure enough it tasted odd, so I warned my friend in time. As I grew even blearier I realised it was drugged milk. By only pretending to drink it we managed to keep awake. We were being watched by sinister men outside. We pretended to fall asleep and an imbecile crowd came in. Three of the crowd were huge and clumsy (I think the rest were small). They bellowed to be worshipped. I felt that the idea was to photograph us as though we were taking part in this. The small idiots lined up to kiss and serve the giants. One, a negro, insisted that the worshippers bugger him as they worshipped. He gurgled absurdly.

I awoke a bit scared and haunted. It was very dark with clouds. Despite setting the timer, I fell asleep for another one and a half hours or so and awoke so disgusted that I could not stir myself till another three quarters of an hour had gone. (Second dream was of visiting N's mother in hospital.) This seemed to illustrate the dream; I was late there, very bleary, and had a dead feeling.

Not much morning left, all spent in St. Albans. Only forty minutes asana on my return, but it was good. I've been going for a very simple state, and almost achieving it.

## Friday 19 August

Only half hour late a.m.! Wow! Slept through second alarm even though it was in my hand.

More constructive day; I tried to steam my wand straight and vacuum cleaned the sitting room meanwhile. Afterwards I pulled weeds despite light rain. Virtuoso.

In meditation there was a great pressure in my head, p.m. I wept over my inferiority phantasy as I made my confession; it was very clear how it had sabotaged my last two jobs (perhaps teaching too).

## Saturday 20 August

Further revolting lateness. Worst of all I think I woke in time today and was simply awake and zombie until 7.20 or so.

In my meditation I held simple state on high. It descended thrice to my belly. The second time was spectacular, a very clear descent after which I had a funny feeling that I was only wanting to breathe *in* and a corresponding rushing up my spine. I anticipated a return match, when I would be only breathing out, but it never really happened. Last descent perhaps too soon and forced.

On return I wrote up two days.

Crummy sort of day. After cleaning the kitchen and the bedroom I did the laundry, and I had to wait for drying machines too as it did not look like a day for drying outside. Read *Cloud of Unknowing* again—salutary. That took me up to noon meditation, etc. Reading went on all the rest of the day, from 2.20 till 6.45 because, when I was about to get up and do the garden, it suddenly rained. This happened twice. Final reading was of this diary up till the start of the last two moons. What a dismal bore, oh what a bore. What a bore. What has God had to listen to this year? He'll abdicate if I threaten to do this again.

But I wish I could have disposed of a few garden jobs. Today's fast is severe; no couch tea, no water, no nothing.

In evenmed I was calmly concentrated on the upper part and it went down. Some consciousness obviously stayed up because there was a feeling of something leaning on me and plunging out of sight into a dark mass. It surfaced and soon went down again and then resurfaced. This happened with increasing rapidity. There seemed to be a stirring of the blackness which came higher, and the light grew more grey. Eventually I halted it as it was getting late.

## Sunday 21 August

Hooray! I was out in time! Too many thoughts, I more or less overcame them, but it took time so nothing else happened. Some sun at last, between the thunder clouds.

Trying today to make sure I do not start to prompt the events in my meditation again.

In the evening as I held to the upper vessel there was a strong feeling of its being occupied by something greater. It too went up and down. I recalled the parable quoted by Ouspenky of the shambolic household which elected a deputy steward of some sort to get the affairs in some sort of order until the proper steward could be found for the job.

## Monday 22 August

Out by 6.15 today, very hard work.

Usually in my confusion I try to probe around for past sins to flaunt, spending quite a while reflecting. This time I simply plodded away at the usual ones in a humdrum manner. In meditation this time the "deputy steward" or organiser sunk down. This meant that there was not that constricted feeling in my head. However, that feeling has returned during the day.

Hooray! I actually pressed on with my robe embroidering today! And I recorded the *Seven Sermons* to be my accompaniment.

Lunchtime meditation was not very good, lots of thoughts and it was short (forty minutes) as I was late. At the end I became like an enormous prick, and a black goddess—Nuit—descended onto me. Rather impressive. In the following oration I waxed very penitent and tore my soul to shreds with furies and lightening. So I felt very cosmic and blown at the end and fell into the meditation. Again I was a prick and a huge goddess was over me. Went on longer and there was even a sort of orgasm. I was full of joy after, running through the rain. Evenmed was humdrum after that.

## Tuesday 23 August

Late again. A cold morning which cleared to sun, but still clouds around. Yesterday's evenmed was plagued by heartthrobs. This morning was clear of that, in fact it was very clear. I was plagued this time by all the most ensnaring thoughts and really did quite well driving them off. Came to a very ecstatic, blissful, rising feeling, but as I came out of it, I noted that my leg muscles had been tense during it.

All morning at K's, and C and H fixing replacement forks for Bloaters, so I only had time for forty-five minutes asana. Efficient afternoon;

I read, mowed lawn, pulled some weeds, and finished my hexagram on the robe. Even managed an early supper and read after.

But at 8 my will broke. I consciously read a magazine instead of getting ready and so was twenty minutes late. Crummy oration and meditation just "doing time" to make sure I got no laziness reward for being late.

## Wednesday 24 August

With a bit of effort I was out before 6 on a cold, dull morning. Good meditation held off thoughts pretty well and nothing funny happened. Quite an invasion though as I read the psalms.

A morning of drawing the squares,[11] until it occurred to me that I had better get them Xeroxed! I was tempted sorely by thoughts of the sexy things I could do with them, and my hour of asana passed all too quickly as I was wracked with lustful visions.

Evenmed unusually crummy. I tried quite hard, deliberately being undeliberate, hoping to ease my headache. But I burst into fearful sweats and all the claustrophobic feelings that entails. I gave up at quite a cosmic moment—the point was that I really had no sign that I was doing right. Without that, should I struggle?

## Thursday 25 August

Still a struggle to get up, even though I now have the possibility of seven and a half hours sleep.

This morning I photocopied the magic squares of Abramelin to save a bit of tedious copying of squares which I have little intention of using. This goes very much against the Goetic spirit—where I should really not just draw my own, but also make the necessary paper, ink, and pen from scratch. But it seems to fit the spirit of Abramelin who says that all that sort of thing is for the diabolists. Anyway, I already have my own hand-written copies of the basic squares I really want and I'll ask the Holy Guardian Angel for advice when the time comes.

After the headaches of recent days I'm trying to be very gentle in the upper storey; trouble is this tends to produce a consciousness in

---

[11]That is, the magic squares of letters in the last part of *The Book of Abramelin*.

the throat with extensions to head and belly, rather than the whole lot in one.

## Friday 26 August

Poor day. Late start without much excuse. Dream involved a party of friends making our way back for a walk. Came to a flooded river blocking our return. Help! But I explored and found narrowest bit for possible jumping. But it was Ruth who actually dared jump first. Then I followed. After her courageous start I did well and landed without dropping the coffee cup. Then we came to a high wall and I climbed a tree, hung over and let drop. This time I was the first. But I'd forgotten my cup and glass. Oh well! N could pick it up. He and his friend hadn't even jumped the stream yet.

Decided to find out about Malta ferries. Slight guilt at such un-divine pre-meditation made me want to get it over before last moon was in full swing, but on the other hand I did not feel I could just leave it in case I had frantic query from Major.

That planning, plus the news that Chris Murphy sells Van Veen motorcycles, kept my mind buzzing all through the brief meditation in all the time that was left.

I'm continuing the very gentle meditation. My earlier worry was that when I stopped my strong concentration within my head, the consciousness tended to rise up out of my head. This seemed wrong until I recalled the illustration to the text accompanying *The Secret of the Golden Flower*. Not that I believe I could be so far along the path without being more vividly aware of the ground covered (at least I hope not), but I do believe stages are lightly rehearsed at all points along the way. This is why I was not over-worried by sensational events in my meditations such as the splitting of God and the descending $\triangledown$ and the ascending $\triangle$—I never felt that "It Had Really Happened At Last", but rather that I had been invited to rehearse at a humble level.

As I was about to throw in Ouspensky in disgust, I actually found some good bits! Skipping all his crappy terminology and concentrating on chapters on "self remembering" and "not identifying" at last I find it beginning to fit other systems. "Not identifying" I now recognize as a familiar aim from schooldays onward; it is equivalent to the Taoist "non-attachment" and to *Seven Sermons* advice on "distinguishing oneself from qualities". Also, the explicit statement that one should become more emotional was a relief, in view of the "cold fish" impression often given by the Gurdjieff schools.

However, I still have doubts about curbing imagination as much as he says. I note, for example, how very bad he (and most writers from that school) seem to be at illustrating what they mean. They usually resort to lame repetition as though they had lost the ability to paint a verbal picture for the benefit of others. Crowley would never be short of ideas to illustrate a term used, and he would give it more penetration by his use of humour.

## Saturday 27 August

Dreadful. Woke feeling hungry and suffered all day. Did not write up till next day.

Not a lot of rain. After noon I transplanted the chicory plants. Nearly fainted each time I stood up. That activity was a much better training for banishing negative emotions; it is a pity that manual work is rather frowned upon by Abramelin in this last two moons. Of course I failed utterly, but felt I would like to try again when not fasting. There seemed to be an avenue for improvement. I had wanted to complete robes, etc., today, but when I thought of stitching without food I decided I had better leave it till tomorrow.

Evenmed noticeably hurried, not quite one hour! Tut!

## Sunday 28 August

Woke about 4-ish and did not go back to sleep so was up at 4.30 and had breakfast and shave before orating on time! Extremely cold. It must have been around freezing point; clear, still morning.

As the garden was so desperate for warmth, and as I have noticed how the worst of the weather has (unusually) concentrated in this area of the country, I vowed in my oration that I would not go out to enjoy the sun if it stayed sunny today. I'm afraid the garden has been suffering weather aimed at keeping my nose to the grindstone.

I will ask the *I Ching* if it has any advice for this last month to further my success in the Abramelin operation, but first I will re-read the reading for the two moons.

Background thoughts for these two moons: should I start to write my book? Should I starve more? Should I narrow my studies and reading? Has the weak "feminine" element been thwarted (re: last hexagram)?

| Received | First | | Second |
|---|---|---|---|
| 5-4-4  5-4-4 | 5-8-8  5-4-4 | | 5-8-4  5-8-4 |
| — —  — — | — —  — — | | — —  — — |
| — —  — — | — —  — — | | — —  — — |
| —o— | ———— | | — —  — — |
| ———— | ———— | | ———— |
| —o— | ———— | | — —  — — |
| —o— | ———— | | — —  — — |
|  | 34 | | 15 |
|  | Power of the Great | | Modesty |

This looks good, but it is not easy to interpret as specific advice.

I feel confident that the weak thing in the two-month hexagram is now under control, for the "great" have power.

It seems that a time of breakthrough is forecast (hooray) both in the general meaning of 34 (in the "judgement") and also by line 4. Warnings are:

a) That I should be careful of being intoxicated by my own power and so forgetting to ask for what is right ("judgement") and also of not waiting for the right time ("judgement"—I hope that does not mean I'm wrong to take a "moon" as 27.5 days as in the ephemeris).
b) That there is too much power low down which would want to be forceful but should not.
c) That I shouldn't be exuberant (line 2).
d) That the power is best applied inwardly and not outwardly.

This last warning is the nearest thing to a judgement as to whether I should write; that would perhaps amount to an outward expression of power which should be contained in order to transform me.

In the commentary of volume two there is an extra idea that "strength makes it possible to master the egotism of the sensual drives". That's good.

"Modesty" speaks of "if you have it, don't flaunt it" (in contradiction to the BMW adverts, so I'd better not buy one it seems). This would be relevant because I'd just love to tell the world I'd "done" Abramelin and was a "spellster"! The first shall be last and vice versa.

I do hope this is not a ban on stately homes, Van Veens, and Bugattis. I'd be glad to be limited to a small mansion, and had never really entertained the idea of a Royale, just one of the little saloons; but a Van Veen is a Van Veen for all that. But at least it is not a car. Though I hanker for silk suits, I'd rather they were of a demure design.

Sigh.

Felt rather proud and immodest during the rest of the day, because of that encouraging forecast. Very poor midday meditation, but I "did time" and so it improved. I've tended to feel a sharp pain in the right-hand middle of my spine in the midday meditation (on that occasion only—when it is done before the oration—I'm sitting in God-form position rather than kneeling. This is comical; I chose what I considered to be the more comfortable position for the longest meditation, and now it is turning out to be not only less comfortable but also often no longer!) But as I "did time" and did not give up, the pain eased.

Dreadful psalm reading p.m.—did not even complete the wretched things. I'd love to drop them from the routine, but the *I Ching* did seem to suggest a real old stickling to form this last moon.

Late evenmed. Late because I sat resisting, giving in, and again resisting the temptation of Bendick's Bittermints. Since my "lean pig" diet (i.e. not bothering to eat well) has been in force I have felt cravings more than in the past. This is good and bad; good because it has revived manifold joy in simple things, like hot buttered toast, boiled eggs, and mint chocs, but bad because I now have a fierce and concentrated craving to overcome.

But also late because I wrapped up my "completed" scarlet robe (with two gold edges, gold pentagram on the front, and gold hexagram with crux ansata and three yods on the back) and crown (with gold snake band, gold hexagram on the back, three gold pentagrams on the front of which the middle one will accommodate my diamond tie pin if the angel approves—for although it is a large diamond it is rough—and the other three symbols containing the gold tau crosses) and I oiled my wand till it gleamed like silk. Then I took these and tried to fit them into my tiny altar. (I forgot the girdle.) The only way I could fit the wand in was by moving the shelves and replacing them so that they are balanced and resting on the wand. A rickety arrangement and one needing delicate handling or it will collapse. It symbolizes the fact that much now rests upon my will and, because that is lacking, great delicacy is now required of me. Thanks!

Cruel trick—I am flea-bitten and cannot find it. (From the hedgehog?) What a distraction—I'm always imagining I can feel it during meditation.

## Monday 29 August

Very late. Did not hear alarm so it was a late awaking which disheartened me. Then I was slothful and finally I decided to wait until I *wanted* to get up, to see what happened. My mind was awake first, but my body was a definite hindrance; then wakefulness in my body moved downwards, arms being awake before the feet. Key moments were: (1) opening my eyes, (2) moving my arms from under the duvet to behind my head, (3) bending my knees.

So if I could arrange tea in bed, it would work because it would exercise the upper part of me without needing my legs to move. This used to work well when I was at Eton; but there, I had a plug for the kettle, whereas here the wiring is crummy and I only have a two-pin horror.

Very, very cold outside and in the oratory; wore tons of woollies. Meditation distracted but "persistence brought reward".

Another crisp, clear morning; how long must I stay shivering inside in order to preserve the sun for the garden (as in my vow of yesterday morning)? Can I read outside now? Sigh.

Launderette was full so I was not back till late. Went a little early to oratory and meditated after. Long oration, short meditation; but it was so timeless that I was surprised it was so short. Now I *will* read in the sun. 3.30 pm.

Hooray! The sun did not flee as I lay in it. Such a welcome warmth, but one cannot help but note how low the sun lies as August ends (like beginning of April).

Help! As I put on my supper in quite good time, there was a surprise visit from FV and DH. I whipped out a bottle of wine and foolishly offered a bite of supper. Nice chats but, (a) it disrupted my planning—a small point, (b) it made me marginally late for evenmed—also rather small, (c) I got excited and my consciousness was altered with only a brief awakening—this was bad, and (d) I was sorely tempted to boast about my retirement and tell all—this was outrageous.

Confessed as much in oration, and wondered why? It is not really a pride in being one-up on someone. I'm not innocent of that because I feel that relative to N: i.e. if I thought he was going to get an expensive new job and a luscious girlfriend this summer while I was stuck meditating on the dole, then I'd jolly well hope for three million gold florins and a super bunch of familiars. No, it is not so much spite of putting others down; but it is a desire to justify myself in other's eyes—partly to show them that they need not worry about me, and partly because I'd really like to prove that a spiritual path is not incompatible with a happy sensual life. (Indeed, I'd really like to show that the latter depends upon the former.) When I show off my friends to people, it is true that I like to elevate myself thereby, and quite often at those people's expense (one-upmanship). But when I show off my books, I do not want to create envy, but rather I really want to share my pleasure in them (this is why I lend so freely). This is because I feel a bit guilty about having so many nice books lying on my shelves. Between these two extremes, if I show off Bloaters I do hope to gain some reflected glory, but certainly not to create envy, which would embarrass me (again I feel a bit guilty about having a better vehicle than I deserve); most of all I like people to enjoy Bloaters, to share my pleasure at experiencing such wonderful things. In some ways, I never really feel that I own Bloaters—he's more of a friend.

My oration was very stark and simple. In meditation I was a shade "bolshie" and coy as suggested in *Cloud of Unknowing*. I melted and spread to the stars. When I came round and opened my eyes it was unreal—not at all as vivid as after "watching the watcher". So I closed them again and began to concentrate as if to "watch the watcher". It was a slow implosion—like a gravitational collapse of a gas cloud. In four minutes my universe fell and kept falling. Interestingly, I began to sweat a little, for this recalled the later pages of *Lambspring* where (a) the spirit takes the soul to a high mountain and shews him the kingdom that could be his, (b) the soul thinks of his father the king (who is described as "the body") and returns to him, (c) the body swallows up the soul, (d) the body spends a night sweating and ill, and (e) the happy family is re-created.

Anyway, I came round feeling nice. A large glass of Marstern Kapellenberg 1971 on an empty stomach might have helped.

## *Tuesday 30 August*

Not a very good start—lazed a bit in bed. Dull morning, but warmer.

In thinking of pride I realised with unease that there were times when pride seemed appropriate. Yesterday I realised, without too much self-deception, that there weren't many occasions when I indulged pride in the sense of putting others down relative to me (as opposed to a positive rejoicing in something). However, this morning it occurred to me that copulation fosters a joy in putting others down relative to oneself. When screwing, it is not nice to feel humble, it's nice to feel decidedly one-up on those not having it. One wants to feel magnificent and to brag to one's woman and mock others. This does not come very easily to me because my everyday modesty is somewhat bloated into a degree of inferiority feeling which is merely negative. (This was illustrated when I did N's book of personality tests; I knew I was not exactly proud but I had not realised that the average was so high relative to me. I almost went off the scale of inferiority!) So a natural and—let's presume—"healthy" desire to say things like "I'm a man" and "I'm the greatest" when I fuck is stifled by my exaggerated everyday feeling that it is not altogether true. This undoubtedly hinders ecstatic communion. In this situation, modesty is a vice. This is not an unbalanced idea; for, after all, how unattractive is the modest girl beside the randy flirt?

Why should modesty be a vice in these circumstances? If you are fucking your wife and do not, at the time, think you are a demi-god, then what the hell are you up to? You are selfishly enjoying yourself at the risk of propagating the second-rate. If you are humble it would be wicked to nobble the chances of your family by continuing your own seed, and you should be unselfish and let the much more handsome and witty milkman bless the future.

I'm sure that the only humility allowed in copulation is humility before the God and Goddess—in order that they may visit the act.

Another situation where modesty appears undesirable is in children—though I'm on less certain ground here. Surely a parent does not like to hear children at play being modest. This is not just true of his own children, in which case you could say it was projected pride, for schoolmasters tend to get excited over "one-up" children. Adults would rather hear a bit of a squabble over who is going to bat first than hear the children say "Oh no, John, I'll go after you. For your superior skill will surely be an example to me." It is the mistake of "mother's boys" to be modest. There is a letter in *The Sun* which is so funny because it is so "classic": it is of a mother lamenting her lonely son's failure with girls. He has a car, so the girls get him to take them to pubs and discos and then promptly drop him for the "fun crowd". The mother laments this, saying that her son shows "good old-fashioned kindness" to girls and it doesn't seem to attract them, not like a friend of his who "treats girls like dirt and they love it". I know his problem so well! He is a "mother's boy" for sure. It is a mistake to act upon what women say rather than what women do. The most basic misunderstanding between the sexes comes when men assume that womankind use the tongue as an organ of communication in the way that men usually use it; in fact, they often use it as a weapon. So when the sensitive male hears a girl say, "I just can't stand so-and-so, he's so full of himself. He's just a great big insensitive bully out for what he can get", then he makes the mistake of believing them and encouraging his own sensitivity and courtesy.

It is not actually a lie when girls say they like gentle and sensitive men. They do like them around, like Kleenex tissues, for mopping up the odd tears. But not for "real life"! The rugger captain will get his girl—even if she admits it could mean an old age of discomfort and disagreement, somehow the sacrifice seems worthwhile to the knowledge that you have "lived". So I guess old "lonely" was taken in by his mother's words of "always be nice and gentle and show appreciation, my son, then you'll get a nice girl" and he modelled himself on his mother's words instead of rebelling. Now he doesn't know how to get the not-nice girls![12]

My mistake was to believe my mother when she said that I was a peace lover, not the sort to pick fights. And I grew up a "wet". Team games were out—not feeling aggressive about the goals meant that the pain in reaching then seemed utterly unjustified. I was wrongfully dismissed from Eton, but did not stand up for myself because I felt kindly towards the brand new headmaster and his embarrassed giving of notice—after all, I quite looked forward to changing job anyway. But I never bothered to point out the good standard my pupils had attained, the praise of parents and other masters, and that most of the criticisms stuck to me were in fact unacknowledged errors of my alcoholic head of department that I felt it would have been bad etiquette to point out. And now, having modelled myself on what my mother said, I find with horror that she would like to kill terrorists and beat up communists! (In the name of "peace" of course.)

All this is a long-winded proving that there are departments in life where pride seems desirable. Which is worrying, as the *I Ching* has said I must be modest. So how do I resolve this bummer? For a start, I'm not allowed to fuck for another month anyway, and I'm not competing in the world, so the whole debate is just a distraction in order to stop me

---

[12]This is the classic "mama's boy" lament. In the postscript I discover and explain where it came from.

from surrendering totally to God's will and trusting him to resolve the paradox. Checkmate. (Yes, that's what I'm talking about—pun.)

Hell's bells! It's "pride day". All day I've been reading, in horrified fascination, N's book on Hitler. It confirms all that I thought about politicians and how I despise them. And it provides a balancing sermon against the other sort of pride. I'm not innocent of spiritual pride myself and often found myself thinking "go for it Adolf"! It would indeed be refreshing for the soul if I were to start a movement which ended with all the members of all governing bodies of the world hanging on gibbets—as long as it did end there, when its job was done. Sigh.

My hour of meditation was painful, but I persisted—like a fanatic—until the pain faded into bliss. Because of the need to be on time for the oration, I was not able to earth myself as before so went, still sent, to the oratory and was out for fifty minutes—and the Black Goddess had herself off on me again. Even then I did not come down to earth so must try again tonight. I think that Ahriman is displaying his wares to me and offering the idea of revolutionary fanaticism to brighten my life and fan my pride. But I feel cheated; in the past (and even in Chevalier's book) these devils appeared in person and scared the life out of one. Whereas I have to be my own devil. The do-it-yourself age.

A fiery Mexican bean dish awaits me—that should bring me back to reality.

Nasty coughing fits and the crawling of fake fleas made my oration and meditation a trial.

Now I'm sad because I've lost two and a half stone and am terribly skinny and weak. Why the hell do so many people want to lose weight? It's a foul feeling. Soon I'll weigh less than N.

### *Wednesday 31 August*

Hard getting up and now a drab wet day. Uncomfortable meditation as I felt unsymmetrical and squiffy.

Spent most of the morning sorting out those wretched magic squares. I hope I can have a new lot; these do not cover my needs (wants).

Felt lustful again today and prayed to be liberated from phantasies in order to enjoy more of the real thing.

In evenmed I ensured that I never lost my concentration on God. Must have been at it for over thirty-five minutes and I do not think there was a break when I lost it. There was not total one-pointedness, often the concentration was shared by invasion, but these invasions never broke the continuity. However I had a lot of pressure and slight, yet anxiety-making, pain in my head; but I received the message "trust me" so I stuck it out. Consciousness of both time and the rest of my body was minimal.

## Thursday 1 September

Bad late start after involved dreams. This morning I did not hold that strong upward concentration but was receptive in my forehead and noted that there must have been around ten breaks, all very brief.

The morning was wasted in St. Albans. But it was nice to meet DH and go for a coffee. On my return from the shops there was a traffic warden to tick me off on behalf of Saturn. Returned too late for prior meditation so I did it with the oration. I did not concentrate hard; I think, after being out, I really should have done so, but the distractions didn't really relate to the morning all that much.

In prayer, I bemoaned the fact that, although I am subject to the tyranny of time, I lack any time sense. I said I was afraid lest I should attain nothing in these six moons—not so much because I had doubts about the operation, but because I had doubts as to my own ability to merit Big G's attention after just 6 moons' footling.

This evening I commented on something I'd read in Hitler's biography. Hitler was furious at a rebuff and ranted about die-hard old reactionary do-nothings and so on. It was said that it hurt his pride to be told off by a "bigger" man in a way that made him look like a silly boorish upstart. I rather agreed with Adolf. If I sent my crummy, ill-printed little book to *The New York Times* for review and they ignored it with a scornful snigger, instead of admitting that I had aimed too high, I would make a note that at some point in my life I must get my own back on *The New York Times*, and put *them* down. My friends think me modest; if someone is neutral to me I am modest, if they praise me I'm positively embarrassed, but if they squash me I'm furious—but often do not reveal it. It must be very tightly bottled-up because I remember slights for years after. This can be very debilitating because others can make me angry just by telling me stories of mean people. One of the most irritating phantasies of mine is that of being able to use my magic powers to out-nasty nasty people. I used to get very upset as a toddler when I heard adults talking of the wrongs of the world. They never realised how much it touched me as I was so young, but it hurt me to hear my big formidable father telling tales of woe and mistreatment at other's hands. I believed his (probably) one-sided accounts and burned for him. I knew that being bullied by a brother five years older meant that I bottled up my anger because I was intelligent enough to see that I was powerless. Perhaps, also—as in a recent speculation—my mother's assurance that I was "peaceful" meant I further bottled up my wrath. There are a lot of signs of aggression in my horoscope with all its Aries and fire signs and so on; and yet I appear very mild, to the point of being an ineffectual cipher. I am amazed by my lack of energy, yet I do feel this bottled-up useless wrath. In alchemy, dragons are meant to be sealed hermetically, and they eventually turn to medicine. The trouble is that their heads have to be cut off first. Should I leave that to Michael? I asked for guidance. My image of the rotting compost cannot include unexploded pop bottles.

In meditation my consciousness went walkabout in my head, to see if there was a better magic mountain to be found. Down to bottom where bottom joined skull, then up the back and over the top.

At the bottom point it was very black and cosy and I saw an image of the planet Saturn. (I see lots of second rate images so normally never refer to them—I only noted this one because Saturn I feel to be important in this work.) But "voice" didn't seem keen that I should dwell there nor on the summit of my head, but only back in the old jade palace. So I just returned there and held it. After a while a sort of shaft or sheet of light went out from there to that black bottom point. I hoped it was going to lop off the dragon's heads, but I was not aware of any striking happenings.

### *Friday 2 September*

Another drab day and a drab start. In the oration I tried to throw light on the problem of how differently I take a snub from someone I love (leading to strong inferiority) and others (leading to wrath) and whether the difference is really basic or not. I was aware of having felt physically inferior for most of my life, and that is a possible motivation for my enthusiasm for vigorous exercise. In the case of weight training, there has been a positive solution value because, far from exaggerating the feeling to obsession, it has faded it—I had forgotten my earlier worries largely. But this is too obvious to be really important—for a lot of my feeling of inferiority was not concerned with size or strength, but with an envy of the way in which other people's minds and bodies seemed well matched in a happy partnership which made for physical coordination skill and quick decision making. Whereas I was awkward and twisted and unharmonious. And my pleasure with physical exertion is as much in the activity as in the results.

Visitors a.m. so I was a bit late and decided to meditate with oration. Really crummy, boring, and uninspired oration. The tedium was so awful I wept tears all down my front. God is awful. If he's so bloody omnipotent why can't he just send a real old "bad taste" angel in a nightie and gold wings to give me a pep talk. With a boost like that this last month would be a pushover.

In meditation I just hung on to nothing and achieved—wait for it kids—NOTHING! It's sale time at God's bargain store.

The weather is foul. All I want is food and a crazy afternoon with Adolf Hitler—in bed I think for it is too cold to stay downstairs.

Read Adolf all afternoon and again on going to bed. Felt very fed up; a lousy evenmed simply thinking about motorcycles for a short while. I did not learn any more from Adolf's book and was merely fascinated and distracted. Didn't finish reading till midnight.

## Saturday 3 September

Clear and sunny but foully cold. Slept till 6.30 and was not out till nearly 7.15. Short oration and meditation. Pretty hopeless, but I had a sort of gentle persistence. I left off reading about pre-war Germany for the time being. Although I would like to see if I can trace my last incarnation (which I'm almost certain was linked with it), the book was overriding all other activities.

After a high protein supper last night I do not feel too bad this morning. Of course, the blue sky is beginning to cloud before the ground has received any warmth at all. I'm fed up with this Abramelin retirement, but I must try to keep the tatters of my vow.

Quite a nice day. Some clear sky brought roses to my cheeks. Decided to walk across the common to combat sedentary life. Lovely stroll.

## Sunday 4 September

Dozed and had lustful and avaricious phantasies. Bitterly cold in the oratory—what am I in for this month?

Yesterday my "voice" made it clear that although I stopped physical fidgeting, and become one-pointed, I had overlooked a sort of mental fidgeting. Although holding my attention on one thing, I had still continued the internal equivalent of changing my viewpoint (i.e. when point of consciousness moves) and even more subtly of "changing my focus" internally. So I held frightfully still today and it seemed good.

Wrote a letter after break. It is lovely being on my own (N is away for a fortnight). I hope I don't get scared.

Rest of morning at K's so I was late back and decided to meditate with oration. Read over an hour of *Lieh Tzu* when there was surprise visit by Rs. Had tea, a walk, a drink, and by the time they left it was late supper, then a phone call from home made for a late oration.

The advice about holding my focus is like a revival of "watching the watcher". It makes for very pure, rather intense meditations where more time moves slowly. So my last few have been rather short.

## *Monday 5 September*

Noon meditation was only forty-five minutes. I set the alarm for fifty minutes but flaked out with the concentration five minutes early. This morning I drafted two distracting letters which have been on my mind for months. I hope they will distract less when realised.

Sharp bellyache as I sunbathed today and yesterday.

More imaginative orations today. Evenmed was intense but I found myself thinking as well as concentrating and was not long at it.

Read Hitler till 10 pm.

After six months of alchemy, Bible and other heavies, Austin Spare's *Book of Pleasure* reads like Enid Blyton.

## *Tuesday 6 September*

Nice dreams: one was the old favourite of a small branch line (private) which went up the Painswick valley to Cranham. It had occurred to me what an interesting business it would be to run a restaurant car as a serious gastronomic project; people would make the trip (and return) as an evening out and would have a superb meal with the bonus of moving scenery.

The other dream was of walking through a small country town (named "Stroud", but no resemblance) and an old man pointed out to me that I tended in my mind's eye to reduce ordinary little towns to boring sameness because I looked too much at the shop windows (which were universal) and did not raise my eyes to the higher stories where the original architecture survived.

Woke fresh and in good time. I was out before sunrise. Realising that the focus of my eyes recommended of late amounted to a staring (with closed eyes) out of the window, I consciously adopted that attitude. Rather a lot of invading ideas, and I was caught up at times, though attention held.

The phantom fleas are all over me. I wonder if it is the start of eczema or something. I've never known invisible fleas before. They have survived baths and hair washes and changes of clothes—but fleas can of course.

Crummy day—it tried to get me down and did not really succeed: (a) dry cleaning bovver about my curtain rings—OK, I did them in the coin machine and saved lots of money, (b) when I got change for £1 at the bank they wanted my name! (c) after buying fab cheap tomatoes (10p a lb) I was short-changed so they in fact cost 30p a lb. Most irksome was that I was puzzled by the change at the time but persuaded myself out of it, (d) struggled back with awkward load because of having done dry cleaning as well as laundry, (e) took all morning because of dry cleaning, (f) reading was interrupted twice by Mrs. Smith in a silly flap, (g) also by long phone calls, so that took all afternoon, (h) having made supper for Mrs. Smith she never turned up and I got wet and stung as I looked for her three times, (i) cutting my losses I gladly started eating on my own and then she turned up so all was late, (j) she did not enjoy supper a lot for flapping and apologizing, (k) plus sundry little clumsinesses during the day.

Noon meditation poor; I decided to think less of God and more of trying to see what happens—answer: more thoughts. Oration rather unconventional after. Also in evening. For evenmed I decided to go for the big one; I approached nothingness by philosophical stages (sort of neither-neither). I liked the result, time passed, my body did not hurt, no boredom or thoughts. Nice one.

### Wednesday 7 September

Last night I stayed awake too long thinking about *Thundersqueak*, and this morning I woke too early and dozed so I got up late with that "boiled head" feeling.

Again I did the nothingness bit and it was gratifying. "Voice" does not seem keen, I do not know why. One idea is that the "big one" consists of undoing the whole creation—i.e. an Abraxas trip and so not recommended by *Seven Sermons*, whereas the smaller one (just considering "me" if I had never been born and so on) is more akin to the "inner star" of *Seven Sermons*. Alternatively the objection could be that I should not think, I should not "try". But why then does this produce such a better state? A state where I no longer have to "try".

Same at lunch meditation (after oration). After lunch I read Austin Osman Spare and then a long stint of Hitler. I realised that there is a revolutionary, close behind me, who cheers on Adolf in his struggle against boredom, bureaucracy, and conformity and shares his delight in the swift, clean, "simple" solution. Ahriman I suppose.

At evenmed I only started with the elimination bit, with eyes open to set the tone. Then I closed my eyes and held focus. The result was just about best. At the end my eyes opened and I was told to watch. I did so till tears ran, but could not see the point. I was released at my request. One interesting extra this time was that, when well and truly fixed, I recalled the "distinguishing" bit and so withdrew consciousness. I meandered around doing a few checks then quickly settled, leaving the rest fixed. This seems good because (a) I was "distinguished from" or "not considering", (b) busybody consciousness retired, leaving the rest "Godbathing" and, I hope, being transformed free from conscious meddling, (c) also seemed to fit the alchemical separation bit somehow.

Indeed, recent meditations have been so much better that an old recurring idea appears once more: surely this is the starting point in *The Secret of the Golden Flower*; oh woe that there is no longer "one hundred days to go".

In the oration I pressed the case again for a complete transmutation in view of my reading of Hitler. I don't want dithering old me to come to power, I want "super-me'".

In these evenings alone in the house I feel the old "fear of the dark" bit is lurking, trying to persuade myself to scare myself. Apart from "walking a little faster" I have not succumbed.

I note that today is the day that "blue" and "green" biorhythms fall below. "Red" goes down on Saturday. Fortunately all are up for my week of summoning.

### Thursday 8 September

Last night I was too full of Hitler and did not sleep till very late. I woke late and was useless, so very late oration.

Noon oration was late too, after St. Albans. Meditation after. Achieved an immense, vast stillness and gentle return. Gratifying. It was like a mountain summit.

At about 5.30 I zoomed to Berkhamsted for clothes and to deliver a gift to S. She was looking her best in excellent white dress. Slight feelings of jealousy and nostalgia seeing their lives—Ivan was there. Curious thing nostalgia—I had a funny feeling that I would not be seeing them again. Perhaps it is "I" who will not see them again.

### Friday 9 September

Late start. Not a very good beginning to the last fortnight. Lunchtime meditation was an hour of thoughtful boredom, at least an hour goes a little quicker now. But basically it was microcosm of my life; I was waiting, in pain.

SA appeared around tea time. He wanted me to help him on Monday. Likeably, or kindly, I said "yes". I can be back for midday meditation, but will have to drop the reading that day. It turns out he "does" (or "is") Subud and he enthused. I wonder if I should try it. It is high time I lost myself in a movement.

After lawn cutting, supper was late, and oration was very late. Also short and crummy as my gut was bulging and I felt like going to bed. I still do. (9.30 pm.)

### Saturday 10 September

Very late, worst ever, and quite without excuse.

Excited by the signs of preparation for the Church End Elizabethan Fayre—like a child? (Perhaps I'll get into the kingdom of heaven!) Relieved that the weather has cheered up, though the wind shrieks. Not a bad lunchtime meditation, despite excitement.

I was sorely tempted to invite people along for a drink and it would have strained my routine a little. But I met Mrs. Lochner, so invited her back and gave her a hot drink instead. She said that Ron was a "great admirer" of what I was doing and I was very moved. I felt all the more determined that I should come out of this a better person. Oh, how I adore Grape-Nuts.

### Sunday 11 September

Woke ridiculously early, about 3 or so. Had sex phantasies until it was time to get up.

A curious thing I noted was that it was not altogether true to say I was "plagued" by sex phantasies because in fact I usually invited them back as if afraid to lose them. I would "awake" from some phantasy, tell myself off and say "enough of that", and then I would start reconsidering the phantasy quite objectively—as a librarian might: "Now then, how big were her tits? How many times did I want to screw her before breakfast?" But then the dream would again come to life and I'd be lost in it.

In the oration I asked why I seemed afraid to lose my phantasies and felt obliged to store them. The answer seemed to be because I misunderstood the nature of attainment. My ideal was to be a consistent human, not wracked by internal strife, and therefore effective and harmonious. So if, in October, I were to suddenly be quite devoid of interest in material possessions, it would be satisfactory because I would have no worries about either those I had, or those I lacked. If I was completely uninterested in sex it would be satisfactory because I would not worry about its absence. If I was to be completely and utterly evil it would be satisfactory because I would have no conscience to upset me. If I was no longer interested in motorcycles it would not matter … and so on. But in all those cases my present self feels that this operation would be a cheat if that was what was meant by attainment. This is surely not the stage of Magister Templi where even my God must desert me? Surely my ideals will survive this work? But does that mean I'm still going to be worrying about money and sex and being good? I hope not. What is wanted is *freedom* from all those things and so freedom to choose those which I still consider to be best. This is where the Taoist "non-attachment", Spare's "not desiring", Gurdjieff's "not considering" and *Seven Sermons* "distinguishing oneself from" come in. Earlier I was upset by the Gnostic descripttion of "God's athletes" who let their bodies waste away as they fasted and did penance, and I was anxious not to join them. To me they seemed deluded and unhealthy. But now I think that I misunderstood them. They are in fact perfectly free and, never having much interest in being healthy and being keen to do penance, they choose to act as they do. So I would in fact like to be like them, free. But because I have a higher regard for the flesh than for penance, I would choose to eat well (and that has never meant, for me, that I choose to eat badly) and take exercise. So I would simply look different from them but would, like them, be applying myself to what I considered good, without being a slave to it.

Noon meditation was crummy and thoughtful, so I continued for a while after oration and the ✡︎(crunch) thing happened.

In evenmed I ignored the "voice's" advice to concentrate with force and made a point of relaxing. The result was very good and quiet meditation, but lacking exciting events.

Visited S on a vegetable swap for bread and laundry. She kept making sex hints (e.g. "And something else happened, but I'd better not tell you about that until this is over"). She has no need to stimulate my jealousy like that. It perhaps put me even more on my guard.

## Monday 12 September

Late three times—it's unusual for me to be late at midday. Firstly, I forgot the alarm, but did not oversleep when I had a job to do ... but I did. In the oration I caught myself saying "today of all days" then realised that doing a job was *not* more important. Actually, the job was even more "divine" than I thought, as a whole church was completed and there we were building an organ (and discussing Subud). But I was late back and it was really hard to go out after all that exertion. Evening was just one of those "do I eat now or later" fiascos.

Whatever happened to the "dark night of the soul"? I anticipated times would be worse than anything I've ever known. They have been pretty bad. Now, for instance, when it seems too late for me to hope for any achievement and all is dry and useless. I defy the "voice" and it makes no difference and the "voice" crumbles. Diamond Sutra reminds me of non-existence of the ego, but being that non-existence puts me in so-whatsville.

Yet it is not as bad as a miserable love affair. Why? Or a dismal job. Why? Because I know it will be over soon (but if I achieved nothing, in what sense will it be over?) and that it is all my own choice. So I am less involved in this than I have been in my love affairs. That is not good enough for God. Or is it? Surely the depth of my involvement in those affairs was itself a big mistake and that "non-attachment" might have saved the day? If I was as wrapped up in this I would be guilty of "considering" it. Were it not for the vow I would have given up many times over.

### *Tuesday 13 September*

Good morning meditation. Very "neither-neither", very "Diamond Sutra".

Delightful trip to Hitchin in the sun, giving SA's assistant a lift as he was interested in Bloaters. No mention of any payment: this makes my job even more divine, especially as I must have used nearly two gallons of petrol doing the journeys.

Short and very late at noon. But again, very clean.

Annoying p.m. At 5.15 I finished reading and put on a quick tea before going to get butter. The phone rang and I did not think of ignoring it. Three quarters of an hour call from K and now the shops are shut, tea is cold and it's suppertime and no butter.

### *Wednesday 14 September*

Dream of the Susters. There was some slight embarrassment over a meal or something, then we went for a drive. I took them off the road onto a track (it was a sort of Sheepscombe Woods area). As I shut the gate we were waylaid by a gamekeeper. I was anxious, lest we were wrong in driving along this track. But no, he came to ask us to keep a look out; there were poachers from Russia in these woods and they were shooting rams illegally. They'd taken thirty-five (?) already and sold them for a fortune in France where there was a shortage. He was asking for the public's cooperation, which we agreed to give. We continued along the track, making for a pub. But we came to a corner that was clearly impassable for the car where the track narrowed. I was not even sure I could go on myself on foot, it was a scary corner. But somehow we made it and there was the pub, with B and M outside. We joined them. G was expected and yet B stood up and said we must hurry as it was time to go.

Unless the poachers from Russia, who were after the rams, were a warning to lay off my Gurdjieff reading (Sun in Aries) I cannot see the significance of the dream.

Horribly cold morning. I'm tempted to try a heater under the oratory. But a gorgeous day followed. Did some letters and shopping in Redbourn a.m. On my way back, the world again had that magic reality of a new place, a holiday, or a childhood memory. I associated it with the dissolving ego somehow.

In the morning meditation I dissolved and so did the world into a uniform grey mist and stayed that way with the occasional lump forming and needing to be re-dissolved. It was similar at noon, but I was in the sun, so it was a warm vapour.

Gorgeous day! I was able to sunbathe as I read after lunch. I invited Mrs. Smith to supper and it was better this time; I'm sure she enjoyed it. I tried the paraffin heater under the oratory—it was very promising, but alas the smell was distracting so I sadly removed it to the greenhouse for the night.

In the oration at noon and in the evening I found that my concentration on devotion positively *hurt*. There was a big pressure in my head, especially on the bridge of my nose. In the evening the dissolving was hindered by the smell from the stove, but I noticed an interesting effect. Having dissolved almost completely, and being aware of how thoughts make me quickly re-crystallize, I wondered why I should not crystallize *elsewhere* now that all was equal. So I did so, a few feet in front of my body. There was a whoosh of precipitating stuff and it was condensing *outside* me, and it was very droll, very slightly alarming in its dynamism. So I made an effort to re-disperse it again, then did the trick into my belly with the idea of getting the consciousness there. That brought me round, but the snag was that the "voice" did not like it. He'd been quiet of late, so I was a shade peeved at his spoiling my fun, so I demanded an explanation. I gathered that I should finish with it up again, so I pulled it up a bit before stopping. I removed the heater to the greenhouse; pity, as I would have loved to see what it was like a.m.

### *Thursday 15 September*

Mild morning. Dream of being asked to attend a woman's gym as an instructor for two mornings. Of talking to RLG who, it turned out, had an old motorcycle. I suggested a holiday together. We were then at the field above Man's Court, I had bought it to build a house. We went into the church which had a superb red and gold flag for St. James' day with a big L (for the fiftieth St. James Church). RLG said he liked it, to my surprise and was glad when a service started around us. Later we stayed and were sleeping in a dormitory.

Mild meditation, a bit thoughtful, less painful.

Noon meditation in the sun. I made it to the mountain, but was aware that the coming and going of the sun kept me from full take-off. Again it was the eyes which held the key; at times I needed all my concentration and perseverance not to shift focus, let alone move eyes. So tears flowed, but not in vain.

Neighbour Lynn said that last night there were thumps, and the elder tree between us was leaning and waving. But the ivy is thick and was not disturbed, and I could not wave the tree. It is near the oratory, and elders traditionally ward off evil spirits so perhaps Belial was having a punch up. Certainly I got the shivers as I came past in the dark after evenmed. Had to remind myself that the universe did not exist, let alone evil spirits.

Not a very good evenmed. Thoughts, heartthumps and ... (wait for it) too hot! Nice one, weather.

## Friday 16 September

Morning meditation not brilliant—ended up thinking about motorcycles.

Now 9.50 and I will look back over my *I Ching* advice for this period.

Ho ho! I've found further significance in the final hexagram 61 for the two moons! It concerns the right way to deal with "pigs and fishes" and I recall that this applies to N and S (who are most prominent in my life at present, apart from K) who astrologically are referred to fish and pig respectively. I don't understand the "strength in my toes" of hexagram 34.

Noon meditation disturbed mentally by arrival of S, knocking on the door, and conversations in the garden. But I managed reasonably.

Ate lunch outside; exquisite avocado mayonnaise, lentil roast with kohl rabi, served with baby new potatoes and mangetouts with butter and mint, rum and Barbados pancakes and a bittermint, all with the last of the elderflower champagne.

Evening routine shattered by the arrival of Biker John with returned motorcycle mags and a bottle of very fine Alex Corton which he insisted that we polish off. So I was late and tight. Had my other macaroni cheese with French beans with lemon and butter, then a rum and grated chocolate omelette to fill me up.

Being tight made it physically a bit easier; held my fixed gaze faultlessly. But I had to make an effort to remind myself before I started that I was not being "wicked", so that I was in fact testing to see if it was any better. It was not, because the heaviness in my head never evaporated; but it might have done had I not been so late.

## Saturday 17 September

Fast was fairly miserable-making. I felt how little progress I'd made and how little control I had. Very cold day indoors and out did not help. It was not till I had turned on all heat and lit the fire in the house, and had done some gardening in woollies, overcoat, scarf, and gloves that I managed some internal warmth.

Floperoo, time-doing noon meditation. In evenmed I used the little star of light as a concentration point. It was good in that it distanced me so I vanished, but it was not conclusive to an immediate awareness of local "reality". It was in fact a bit escapist and I'm not sure if that is correct or not.

## Sunday 18 September

Dream of trying to net fish in a garden pond. They seemed to disappear as I tried harder.

In morning meditation I again concentrated on the star. I felt that the star should be "in the zenith" as in *Seven Sermons* and *One Star in Sight*. This presented practical problems because I could not look straight up. But I managed pretty well. The complication made for a rather less effective meditation.

Same technique again at noon and p.m. Again poor results, but in each case it was promisingly poor, as though I was being deliberately distracted because getting somewhere, like the used car salesman who speaks faster as he sees you kneeling to inspect the chassis for rust. So I'll try again.

N's return is causing delays and some distraction. But I'm glad to note my malice is not bothering me yet. I've cheerfully ignored open doors, heaters left on, soap left soaking and so on! Fab.

## Monday 19 September

Dream of a woman like MF's mother who lived in a big house in Cheltenham full of wonderful things. I walked through and absent-mindedly picked up a hat stand and only just remembered to put it down as I went out. Hoped this had not been noticed. Rest of Cheltenham full of crazy old women, one was ranting and in a room lit only by fluorescent paints. At the foyer were shelves of elegantly bottled sex aids—aphrodisiacs, etc.—and I looked at them. Either before or after I was back at the woman's house and she was ranting because I'd left muddy footprints and had not put things in their right place. My marks would not come off the white marble steps. Anxious to placate her, I took sand and rubbed the steps clean very conscientiously. But disaster! She looked and said I had worn away the surface finish. Now she lectured me on the right way of hanging her trophies. I was holding an "assegai"; it was a weighted human skull fixed by a thin springy stem to a long stick.

Guests for morning coffee. The Wissendens are visiting Redbourn and I saw Ruby to my surprise yesterday. Lovely occasion, but I was such a gas-bag. Because everyone was so interested in the cottage, and what I was doing, all the stock patter gushed out. I was lecturing.

"Why did I leave HSA?" What do people expect? A one word answer? The reasons are so involved that I have to give my standard lecture. I do not bore, amazingly. This is only because I'm a good lecturer and plan my talks well, not because I am awake to their response at the time. In fact, I'm *sleep talking*. After an hour of crummy meditation, in my oration it occurred to me that this was why the excitement of the visitors has such lasting repercussions; as in dream material which comes in fragments and later needs to be ordered by the logical mind (according to recent theory) so the unreality of these wonderful occasions demands that they be constantly re-lived afterwards in order to link them to my "real life". It is only in the replay that I am spectator to my own brilliance.

Another lesson! God pulls it off again! Out of the chaos came forth sweetness. But it did not hit me at the time as I wailed and craved a miracle to save me. I "death postured" not inconsiderably and so became detached enough to survive oration.

Recently I have craved variation in my oration. It has been a real pain in the world-arse. For that very reason I have refused to alter the wording apart from minor embellishment. Why? Well, first the formula is really not at all bad. Second, it is too late to initiate and perfect any really new formula. Third, such wild cravings in my last few weeks I consider very suspect. Why should a bare half hour of slow prayer hurt so? It can only be old perfidious up to his tricks. So I banish "inspiration"!

Reading was a joy. *Why Lazarus Laughed*.[13] Although I've had this for a long time, I'd not read it. After six moons of mostly re-reading, I noted it as a willing virgin on the shelves. In its exposition of the Advaita philosophy, one passage threw light on one aspect of Spare's doctrine which had not satisfied me. There was also a relevant passage on "lecturing" which linked to my revelation at noon.

After delicious, but late, supper, I went to evenmed without my ego. Yeah, real onesville. Talk about non-attachment, man, it made my non-stick pan look like Dunlop Red Arrows on a good dry road. After noon, this was the called-for miracle. It also made the oration easier. As I had been approaching this state with my Austin Osman Spare and Diamond Sutra diet, the oration had grown distasteful not only for its near physical pain described above, but also because the format laid down of prayers, of confession and begging for blessing, ill fitted the nothingness scene. So I had to face an attack from two sides and had to include in my confession the confession that I was only confessing because I had been foolish enough to let myself in for a vow. Without it I would have chosen to cast off the past and so on.

But tonight the feeling of ego loss was so much more vivid, and less intellectual (in proportion) that it was easier to play out my role—like a spectator checking that karma was properly acted out—and I felt no pain or pressure.

And motorcycles, holidays, never crossed my mind.

Crikey. One week to go to blast off … the day I find I have not well used my six moons. I knew that by May.

### *Tuesday 20 September*

Read about the wolf children who, having been brought up as wolves, were not easily converted into humans. I have been brought up as Lionel Snell and cannot expect to be easily cured of it. I considered my handful of earliest memories, i.e. those of when I was at Paradise which we left

---

[13] *Why Lazarus Laughed: The Essential Doctrine Zen—Advaita—Tantra* by Wei Wu Wei.

before I was four and so memories of there were definitely dated, but of course I cannot order them. (1) Being taken in my pushchair on Beacon by mother, R (and Daniel?) were running beside us. R pushed back to look at a black thing by the path. He returned and said it was a "witch's hat". (2) On the lawn in front of the house with the family when the postman came with a parcel for me, a toy fire engine. It must have been a birthday (my third?). The present was from an aunt (?) I was a bit overwhelmed by the fact that it was for me and that I was the centre of attention. (3) I picked up R's jackdaw and washed it in the rain water butt. It was later found drowned. (4) Walked to Mr Johnstone on my own. (Brave) He was peeling shrimps or prawns in front of his house. He gave me one. It was the most delicious thing I'd ever tasted. (5) I was told off for drawing on the wall in the corridor, as R had done it too this seemed unkind. (6) Coming downstairs to breakfast, Daddy was angry. I was sent out puzzled. Later M came and cheered me. (7) I walked with R in the wood. He made a little trap—a hole covered with twigs and leaves. The next day we went to see if it was broken. (8) There was a little vase "Cornish Violets" which R found behind Mr Johnstone's outhouse. (One point of possible order; I think this was before no. 4.) I think I coveted it, or wished I'd found it, or something.

And from those ingredients is constructed "me" (!): (1) intrigued by magic, second hand experience; (2) the collector, awaiting gifts from God; (3) the bungling alchemist (washing a jackdaw when I should have been albifying a crow); (4) the epicure; (5) the artist (misunderstood of course); (6) watching and admiring R's creations; (7) *l'étranger*; (8) the collector again.

Evenmed very difficult because of arrival of PH, and we were going to dine together afterwards. In a triumph of will, I had carefully made preparation so that the meal involved no last-minute decisions or panics and I could give full concentration to the oration. But P had arrived in a Bristol, one car I'd really love a lift in. And I heard them leave the cottage, look at it, and go out in it. In view of the strong distraction I felt I really managed quite well, such an *obvious* pain—like my idea of the brimstone demons—almost did as much good as a reminder of the work as it did bad as a distractor.

And I felt the tip of "woe to the left-out one" trying to insinuate and this was revealing. This was a strong influence in the formation of my inferiority feeling (coming from No. 6, above). As the youngest by five years, it was often only me who could not join in family parties, or the trip to see *The Third Man*. And being fairly mature, it is not altogether true to say that they would have been wasted on me. I remember on Belvoir[14] lying awake in the fo'csle hearing jollity in the main cabin. The feeling of being left out at school age always hurt me disproportionately. Sex carried a lot of the burden because by its nature it tends to make a clear line between those having it and those not (uncoupled). So a lot of pressure of my worry about P and R going out in the Bristol was because I was "left out". But here my present appreciation of the oneness of reality was liberating, for how could I be left out of anything unless I made my own barrier? Far from being "left out" of their pub trip I was the essential part of it: because, if I was not at home to make the supper and set the table, N would have to have done it and they could not have gone out.

Anyway, I'll get my ride in the Bristol tomorrow.

## Wednesday 21 September

Slept light, a mass of dreams. Morning meditation not very good, but hung on reasonably.

After extended break PH took me to Chequers in the Bristol and I walked back. Gorgeous walk. The magic Bristol broke the chain of normality so the return walk was from a heaven and so was clear and new. Savouring the experience, I diverted across the fields and joyed on. The only temptation was to plan my winter lecture, otherwise I kept open. Except for one section where I shrivelled before the decision whether to greet two oncoming walkers or not. That was bad enough to cause me to retrace my steps in order to relive that section. To keep up the novelty I knocked on my own door before entering!

Short meditation before oration, forty minutes. I held my vision to the star again. This was a deliberate step backward as I could be complacent in my progress and, sure enough, I was not so good at holding on as I had been at my best.

Oration seemed very good. I pray to angels with my eyes open, so they are less visions of beings in white robes, or even moving lights, and more of the movements of nature, etc. (wind, sun, and so on).

It is now 5 pm and I will ask *I Ching* if there should be any final preparation or advice for this last week (Friday onwards).

---

[14]Recollection of a favourite family holiday on the Norfolk Broads in a sailing cruiser named "Belvoir", pronounced "Beaver".

Question: is there any final preparation, change or advice necessary for the week of completion?

| 5-4-4 5-8-8 | 5-4-4 5-8-8 | 5-8-4 5-8-4 |
|---|---|---|
| *Received* | *First* | *Second* |
| —— —— | —— —— | —— —— |
| —— —— | —— —— | —— —— |
| ——o—— | ———— | —— —— |
| ———— | ———— | ———— |
| ——o—— | ———— | —— —— |
|  | 34 | 40 |
|  | Power of the Great | Release |

Power of the Great again is, I suppose, welcome with its suggestion of breakthrough and success. But, alas, to have the misunderstood first change repeated; what on earth is the strength in my toes? The low down power? Certainly it is not physical strength, or sensual rage of emotion—i.e. is not "low down" on the physical to the spiritual scale.

If I had raised kundalini, or developed clairvoyance, or become powerful in some lower psychic faculty then I would understand. Is it the ego that is powerful? True, I would love to boast about being able to do spells, but that does not fit the power in the toes making one want to rush ahead.

The third line is relevant to my *obtaining* power, and is so much more understandable. Shame, it suggests that I should refrain from using it openly. Something I understand well and just wish I could forget! I'd love to outdo Uri Geller and his opponents, but just know what a disastrous waste of time it would probably be.

The change to Release seems relevant to my time after the operation. Return to "normal conditions", but in a sense my time after this will be abnormal. But perhaps not? Let us hope so, for I would like my life to continue on these lines (holidays and travel).

Again, I'm a bit perplexed by suggestions of not doing things too soon[15]: surely the timing is laid down unalterably, unless it means my "moons" are too short, but all other omens support the choice I made.

---

[15]Interesting in view of the timing question discussed in the Introductory Notes.

Could it refer to a temptation to do spells too soon? I was aware that I have no present desire to do so; my priorities are first the knowledge and conversation of the Holy Guardian Angel and then an adjustment to the new life. I had felt a bit cautious about spells. Certainly I cannot see this answer as suggesting any great omission to be cleared up before Friday.

Good evenmed. Started by gazing up at the lamp till tears flowed. One and a half hours.

## Thursday 22 September

Dream of K living here and we snogged and looked forward to the end of this work so we could screw properly. Dream of very sexy young girl in St. Albans, of the sort of tomboy type. Other forgotten dreams—oh yes, I was sweeping out a gymnasium as though it was a regular task—of a style that could have been very haunting and nostalgic, and yet they did not have that effect (with the possible exception of the tomboy girl).

Morning meditation attacked by thoughts, but with a huge effort I held them off.

Long noon oration and meditation together (as I was late back). Two revelations: one was that "self pity" was the devil which had done most of the damage (Moon in Cancer square Neptune?) and the other was that duality's illusory manifestations came from the fact that we could not hold two different ideas at once, and so they were necessarily separated (by space or by time). This was because of language which is one-dimensional when written, i.e. is a thread and so gives an idea of time. Language gives birth to time, an idea is not transmitted in one but as a *sequence*. In extreme form, i.e. the written alphabetic (rather than ideographic) languages like English, even a word is a sequence.

A test at last: time was running short on my last day and I still had much to do. As I read, postponing the rush, who should arrive but ML, hoping to visit and stay on Monday. Now she is staying this night and evenmed was dedicated to calming myself and accepting further delay to completion.

*PHASE FOUR*

# Consecration

On completing the six moons of preparation, it is time for the day of consecration:

> When first ye shall enter into the Oratory, leave your shoes without, and having opened the window, ye shall place the lighted coals in the Censer which you shall have brought with you, you shall light the Lamp, and take from the Cupboard of the Altar your two Vestments, the Crown, the Girdle and the Wand, placing them upon the Altar. Then take the Sacred Oil in your left hand, cast some of the Perfume upon the Fire, and place yourself upon your knees, praying unto the Lord with fervour.

The Orison:

> Having finished your Orison, rise from your knees, and anoint the centre of your forehead with a little of the Sacred Oil; after this dip your finger into the same Oil, and anoint therewith the four upper corners of the Altar. Touch also with this Holy Oil the Vestments, the Girdle, the Crown, and the Wand, on both sides. You shall also touch the Doors and the Windows of the Oratory. Then with your

finger dipped in the Oil you shall write upon the four sides of the Altar these words, so that they may be perfectly clearly written on each side:–

"In whatever place it may be wherein Commemoration of My Name shall be made, I will come unto you and I will bless you."

This being done the Consecration is finished, and then ye shall put the White Tunic and all the other things into the Cupboard of the Altar. Then kneel down and make your ordinary prayer, as is laid down in the Third Chapter; and be well ware to take no consecrated thing out of the Oratory; and during the whole of the ensuing period ye shall enter the Oratory and celebrate the Office with naked feet.

## *Friday 23 September*

DAY OF CONSECRATION. Up at 5.45 (BST so one up on Chevalier!) because I wanted to (had to) make notes before the consecration—something I was not able to do last night because of surprise visit. Had eggs for breakfast and was out 7–9.10.

Joined ML for morning tea and played her some records. During this work I have hardly used the gramophone, and then only with some intent (e.g. playing Gregorian chant for Easter, and so on). I was amazed by my emotional reaction to the songs, as intense as nostalgia. Was this the hidden (quiescent) "strength in the toes" being revealed to me before it was too late? I encouraged the emotion, as it was beautiful, but made an effort to keep it separate from "me" and not to identify or wallow. The effect was to sweeten and intensify the feeling and was very worthwhile. Definitely a thing to work on. Striking alchemical analogues are near my mind.

Poor, late oration. After a big thanks, I just made mantra of "God's Will be done" bearing in mind the *I Ching* caution lest I forget to ask for the right things.

God's will, it seems, has been to cause ML's car to break down. For on my return she was here again. As a result, lunch took longer and I must take her in search of spares. So much for routine! A very rattling situation. Just to emphasize possibilities, Biker John appeared, his return to college has been postponed indefinitely and he is now at a loose end. He meant to leave today.

Obviously I must not rattle. After all, I have it on the best authority, I don't exist.

ML left around 6. I read a little. Felt anxious. *Why Lazarus Laughed* describes verbal being; no subject or object, only the action (verb, not noun, i.e. only acting). I find I can think that way to quite an extent.

Oration was silent. This seemed a very smartyboots and OK thing to do in the circumstances. But so much so that I did consider whether I ought to defy all my intuition (for fear of deceit) and instead go for a totally unoriginal "same old formula" oration. Aloud, I asked the question "Should I speak?" and my voice was drowned by angry chatter of a bird. I took that as authoritative "no" because I had made an effort to attain my wit's end so as to lay myself in higher hands and I felt my Holy Guardian Angel could surely not permit that final deceit at my present stage of spiritual evolution.

Big, powerful feelings of sorrow, end of the line, nostalgia-powered agony potential. Why? A humble (insufficient) reason was fleeting visit of ML was over. Being insufficient justification I assume it was just the trigger to set off something aimed for the attacking. "I" am dying. That was a better reason. So I accepted Wei Wu Wei's Buddhistic advice (and Gurdjieff's) and detached myself from sorrow.

To save being overwhelmed by sorrow I could consider the joy of the rebirth or in my meditation focus my awareness on the star in the zenith away from the rotting corpse.

But to do so was to put a little bit of me up there. To think of rebirth was to produce danger of reincarnating at this rebirth. So a rather scary idea emerged. Should I not forget the Holy Guardian Angel's stars and rebirths and plunge fully into my old self for how else could I ensure that nothing of it escapes the judgement? The less there is of the "old me" in the ark of connecting awareness, the less limited will be the rebirth. But who has ever said that I should stop detaching myself just before the trump sounds?

So finally I just "observed", and a frantic jumble of images buzzed around.

One worry concerns the "robe of mourning". In circumstances I had interpreted as my worst old throwaway clothes—torn corduroy trousers and ragged black pullover—because the "not washing" instruction fitted middle eastern tearing hair idea of mourning more than my western idea of my black suit and clean shirt. But now I realize I really will be in mourning. So should I not wear my mourning suit. Answer, "no". Really not practical (just as I allowed the manifold convenience of this final timing to be a sign that I had interpreted the word "moon" correctly on this occasion[1]). But all the same, should I not wear my worst (but not torn) black trousers with that in mind? (The allotted cords were buff.) I think I will because the symbolism of two days in black, one in white, and three in red and gold over the white seems to fit my alchemical reading.

Heavy heartthumps today. Every fourth beat jumps and noted before evenmed. I have the sort of "livery" feeling as though I'd eaten too richly. (Could it be my unusual eggs for breakfast? Surely not.) Another thing, a lump on the joint (bottom) of my right thumb.[2] It has been there all summer; it grew large and then waned in the last two moons. But this week it again flared to full size (about like a petit pois) and today it has shrunk to its smallest yet. Some people will do anything to get rattled.

---

[1] Reference to my dilemma about whether a "moon" should mark the time it takes to return to its position in the zodiac, or the time to repeat its cycle of phases.
[2] Curiously, this lump re-appeared 40 years later as I edited this diary for publication. I have also suffered from invisible fleas for the first time since then.

*PHASE FIVE*

# Culmination

> We are now arrived at the term, wherefore the following morning[1] rise betimes, neither wash yourselves at all nor dress yourselves at all in your ordinary clothes; but take a Robe of Mourning; enter the Oratory with bare feet; go unto the side of the Censer, take the ashes therefrom and place them upon your head; light the Lamp; and put the hot coals into the Censer; and having opened the windows, return unto the door. There prostrate yourself with your face against the ground, and order the Child to put the Perfume upon the Censer, after which he is to place himself upon his knees before the Altar …

There was no child, other than my Inner Child.

> Humiliate yourself before God and His Celestial Court, and commence your Prayer with fervour, for then it is that you will begin to enflame yourself in praying, and you will see appear an extraordinary and supernatural Splendour which will fill the whole apartment, and will surround you with an inexpressible odour, and this alone will console you and comfort your heart so that you shall call

---

[1] That was Saturday.

> for ever happy the Day of the Lord. Also the Child will experience an admirable feeling of contentment in the presence of the Angel …
>
> … and shall pray the Holy Angel that he may deign to Sign, and write upon a small square plate of silver … another Sign if you shall have need of it in order to see him; and everything which you are to do. As soon as the Angel shall have made the Sign …, he will disappear, but the splendour will remain. The which the Child having observed, and made the sign thereof unto you, you shall command him to bring you quickly the little plate of silver, and that which you find written thereon you shall at once copy, and order the Child to replace it upon the Altar. Then you shall go forth from the Oratory and leave the Window open, and the Lamp alight, and during this whole day you shall not enter into the Oratory; but shall make preparation for the day following; and during the day you shall speak to none, nor make answer, even were it your own wife or children or servants; except to the Child whom you can send away … In the evening when the Sun shall be set, you shall eat but soberly; and then you shall go to rest alone; and you shall live separated from your wife during these days.

Curiously, a picture did appear misted on the lamen, but it was one that seemed to support the *I Ching* in contradicting Abramelin's instructions.

> Now the second morning after,[2] you are to be prepared to follow the counsel which the Angel will have given you. You will go early unto the Oratory, you will place the lighted charcoal and perfumes in the Censer, you are to relight the Lamp if it be (by that time) extinguished; and wearing the same Robe of Mourning as of the day before, prostrate with your face towards the ground, you shall humbly pray unto and supplicate the Lord that He may have pity on you, and that He may deign to fulfil your prayer; that He will grant unto you the vision of His Holy Angels, and that the Elect Spirits may deign to grant unto you their familiar converse … Then quit the Oratory, returning thither at midday for another hour, and equally again in the evening; then you shall eat after the manner

---

[2] That was Sunday.

aforesaid, and go to rest. Understand also that the odour and the splendour will in nowise quit the Oratory ...

The third day being now arrived,[3] you shall act thus. The evening (before) you shall wash your whole body thoroughly; and in the morning, being dressed in your ordinary garments, you shall enter into the Oratory, but with naked feet. Having placed the Fire and the Perfumes in the Censer, and lighted the Lamp, you shall put on the White Vestment, and place yourself on your knees before the Altar, to render thanks to God for all His benefits, and firstly for having granted unto you a Treasure so great and so precious. You shall render thanks also unto the Holy Guardian Angels, praying unto them ...

And then shall you first be able to put to the test whether you shall have well employed the period of your Six Moons, and how well and worthily you shall have laboured in the quest of the Wisdom of the Lord; since you shall see your Guardian Angel appear unto you in unequalled beauty; who also will converse with you, and speak in words so full of affection and of goodness, and with such sweetness, that no human tongue could express the same.

I stop there, because it did not happen as described.

## Saturday 24 September

Lovely dream: after some meeting with MY[4] I was involved with William Rushton and Eleanor Bron in an absurd parody of a trendy "ideal home" where nothing was quite right—e.g., opening bathroom door with a flourish pushed the fluffy bathroom mat into the sunken bath. I awoke chuckling and laughed all the way to the lavatory.

Not sure how wicked it was, I was up at 6.15 to have a boiled egg and tea before going back and getting up at 7.05.

Still in a dither about mourning clothes. I eventually went for black and scruffy look though they were terribly clean. In order not to break the thing about "do not dress *at all* in your ordinary clothes", I put on the trousers and under jersey inside out.

---

[3]That was Monday.
[4]An old school friend.

Bungled on in oratory splashing oil lamp. Opened side windows for the first time. Was out till 9.15. I tried to be prostrate as long as possible to train for tomorrow. My usual prostrate kneeling position is agony after about three quarters of an hour and so will not do. If I push the altar to the far east I can manage lying with lower legs up, I might try that. But only a short break, rising to kneeling position, enabled me to recover for more torture.

The "enflaming with prayer" was difficult, because I saw the present moment as one of the death of the past (and present) which more naturally expressed itself as a chilling descent to silence, and any "enflaming" was hard to dissociate from a re-inflation. But contemplation and wracking brought tears and sobs. I was not very eloquent in my grief.

After rising (keeping head bowed) and returning there was an appreciation of magnificence. It did make joy felt but again I did not want to embrace that joy. I cringed from it rather. As far as "supernatural splendours" go, it was not exactly cinerama, technicolour, sensurround—however I was relieved to consider its departure as time to go.

No symbol on the lamen. Shame. But when I turned it over it was marked in a misty way with a sort of folded cloth mark which I could not understand but decided to copy it in case it meant anything to me on reflection. When I had copied it I noticed for the first time a dot which to one's mind often suggests an eye. Suddenly the picture showed as a goat (black and white piebald, black stripe around the neck and patch around the eye) butting against a hedge. It was my *I Ching* change for the week! So was I wrong to struggle? Despite what Abramelin says? Am I now out of his care, and in the care of the Holy Guardian Angel?

I wish I could wash. 10 am.

5 pm and I'm in danger of feeling normal[5] again. Lay in bed, sometimes reading *Seven Sermons* and *Abramelin* and keeping high. N left about 2.30 and around 3 I was sitting reading. Made my incense. Activity made flashes of normal thinking return. After a period of willed resistance I eventually looked at my post. Money returned from Thompson and Morgan with apologising letter. That tended to set thoughts running. Now it rains and I'm cooking my tea.

Yes, I've been feeling rather normal. So I did a brief half hour meditation at sunset just to stop me being too humdrum.

---

[5] It did not seem right to be feeling "normal" at such a climactic point in the operation.

By bedtime I was back to planning magic spells, just.

### Sunday 25 September

What an ordeal, three hours of grovelling. I could not manage much longer than half an hour in my usual kneeling grovel. Any extension to three quarters of an hour would result in roaring pain in my haunches. So I alternated with as much flat out as possible.

I never solved the dilemma of fire and ice. I started gently, trying to let the enflaming take the form of one-pointedness rather than attachment. That was the dilemma, how can I enflame without becoming attached? After about three quarters of an hour or more I had to shift, lay out with jersey pulled over my head. I could not speak in that position, so I silently yearned. A "white" condition took place, near to sleep. Because it seemed to be strong in unattachment and ego freedom, I let it be for a half hour or so before returning to my kneeling grovel. At another time to balance this bliss I concentrated all my crud into a huge lump and died with it. There was also some real live enflaming and shuddering.

But I ask you, three hours of grovel and no satori, no visions, no nervous breakdowns, I must be made of steel. What would third degree interrogation get out of me I wonder? Through all three hours there was the repeated occurrence of Linda Ronstadt singing "Desperado". How can anything capable of enduring such an onslaught not be real?

Last night's dream. Saw neighbour's garden (we were in a row of cottages), it was much neater than mine so I was keen to show them how big my garden was at the other side of the house. It had bridges over a small stream, through trees, out into parkland. They were in a hurry to get back for lunch but I wanted to show all, because there was a lovely old sunken garden copse in the park with a folly. But they went back, and only the three children stayed with me. We went up a slippery slope and down the other side. For once I was not the fearful one, I encouraged them. (I blessed this operation for having overcome my fears). We made for the glade with the folly, and then I awoke.

Tried reading some of the huge Krishna book. It rather disgusted me with lurid accounts of demons being smashed. I gave up, but it fell open at a good account of a follower who, in a rage of materialism, did not recognize God and fought with him. The God playfully wrestled for twenty-eight days till he was exhausted. The man recognized who it must be and surrendered. Perhaps the struggle is a struggle with the God, and should continue till exhausted in order to surrender fully.

Midday oration was not very fiery, but very intense and thorough and clear. But it finished after only about forty minutes. So I de-agonised and resumed. This time I was fiery and enflamed.

I left the lamp burning and the window open today. Abramelin is not clear but it seems to fit the spirit of it and the "voice" seemed to approve.

I am not fasting by day, the garden has just presented the most wonderful sweet corn. True, it would be an even worthier sacrifice to the Highest to waste this work by refusing to fast (anyway, Abramelin is not explicit).

I was not very cosmic this afternoon. Hell! Here's N. I must rush.

Last grim oration of this second day of mourning. What could I say or do? Further prayers for my soul seemed obscene. To hell with it all! Afternoon reading: Gurdjieff seemed clumsy and *The Book of the Law* was too full of references for a scripture. So all I said for over an hour was "God's Will Be Done" over and over again like a machine. After forty minutes I hurt, so I lay out to unbend and for agony jabs to pass, still muttering and face to the boards.

Few thoughts managed to intrude that barrier of muttering, but as I faced the unbending agony, an exultant little thought came, "If only work had been like this!" Pain with a purpose? I don't know, but it all seemed huge fun.[6] The mantra had sometimes lost meaning and, as sound, appeared to say other things, e.g. "God swill me down" ("be" = "me", as when one has a cold, or blocked nose from pressing it to the floor), "God's Wilby. Done!", even "God's a banana" and "'Cos will be done". Anyway, it made a lovely rhythm and begat joy. Suddenly it all seemed fun and I looked forward to tomorrow whatever happened. It poured with rain. Perhaps this was what the goat was butting the hedge about? It was not the effort, the struggle and the fight that was wrong, but the fact I was not *enjoying* it? Certainly that goat had the least suggestion of a smile, and I had a great big one as my forehead butted the floor in time, "God's will be done because it's fun."

---

[6]Whereas I had left a mind-numbingly boring job, I was now doing something orders of magnitude more boring and repetitive than even the worst that work had to offer, and yet something about the fact that I had committed to it myself, with an overall sense of purpose (however mistaken that might turn out to be) meant that the agony somehow became a challenge, fun, even meaningful.

And I did one and a quarter hours! So I was not just saying that I enjoyed it.

### Monday 26 September

A Saturn-spirit delayed me for about twenty minutes in the morning. He was tall and bony and sooty and drove a coal lorry and delivered at 7 in the morning. I suppose it must be expected with Jupiter conjunct natal Saturn and trined by Venus, Sun, and Moon square natal Saturn, Saturn trine natal Sun. (Actually the Sun/Moon bit is tomorrow morning; that is when I expect the full Saturn works.)

Floperoo! Wearying morning praying, being cold, reading prayers and psalms and passing time in the oratory. Another great demon, Vanity, is winkled out, but the Holy Guardian Angel is hiding. I've had a break of one and a half hours to have mu tea, artichoke vinaigrette, avocado mayonnaise, blackberries, coffee, and chocolate. Also to pick some broccoli. Oh dear! Back we go.

Don't say the words "Abramelin", "God", or "Angel" to me. I'm stiff and tired and hungry and I've stupidly said I'll fast tonight just in case my Holy Guardian Angel is so cissy that he can't even penetrate a boiled egg and three slices of toast. After all, tomorrow is an astrological bombshell so I'll try again.

After that, God'll not see me for dust. But if he should want me, then my address will be c/o Mammon.

### Tuesday 27 September

Nothing happened (2.15). Well at least I *tried*. Yesterday I was rather "into" goats not butting hedges so I took it gently (well, comparatively) in order to keep up the spirit of cautious optimism. Today I really went for it. Real old fast (interestingly, it was less painful than those awful Saturday one-dayers). All morning I refrained from any extended thoughts. In order to help this I chanted "God's will be done" solidly for four hours. It was coming out of my ears, that must be about 12,000 repetitions. Anyway, I stuck it out from 7.10 till 2.15 and am still in the oratory cringing in the corner.

There was a good bit when I was muttering and prostrate when one by one my vices suddenly attacked me, e.g. a burst of self pity. I picture the angel Michael there waiting and grabbing them and yanking them out of me. I could really feel the wrench and I yelped. It was interesting to note which vices came out bigger than others—self pity beat vanity hands down. Love of money was surprisingly big. It was very refreshing and exhausting. Alas the angel was only internally vivid. He did not stick around to chat, so I do not consider I've made it.

Now what? Lovely sun outside. To stay in here is to invite insanity, a maniac phobia about incense, lamps, altars, robes, charcoal, angels, etc., etc.

Can I really take it that I've had it? Now vanity is slain, I can! If I go now and re-read *I Ching*'s advice for this week about quick return to normal life (I recall how that puzzled me, as it seemed to be more relevant to next week) and I will be easily persuaded to have a meal. Rejoice. I'll probably look in at sunset. If the Holy Guardian Angel still wants to see me from now it is he who will make the appointment.

Yes, 2.30, over and out.

Oh bliss! Extravagant joy! How could any mystical experience rival the glass of orange juice which I sipped in the warm sun (summer has come at last) or excel the artichoke which descended on wings of fire and vinaigrette with attendant host of avocado mayonnaise. A gastronomic symphony rising to the almost unbearable climax of a bowl of Grape-Nuts.

I felt dizzy. Walked slowly across the common to buy chocolate biscuits and weigh myself. Also bought more Grape-Nuts (the last packet at the old price) and came back with a lovely purple suitcase by Mappin and Webb.

On return, ML was here, cursing her car and fumbling in the works. I helped a bit after tea with blackberries and chocolate biscuits.

As she was unable to get it going I suggested she stayed and we ate out. Poor, short meditation after oration of thanksgiving. I flooded with sweat. Felt even odder after. Thought I might faint at suppertime, but the thought of a meal not cooked by me was wonderful, and of the companionship of eating out—something I've not done for over six months. Oh, it was wonderful, an egg pilau with mixed vegetable curry. And Indian ice cream. We were relaxed and at ease; N wasn't behaving as oddly as he sometimes does in ML's company. I made a few attempts at getting MF to join us, but he was out. Felt better after meal.

## Wednesday 28 September

Slept badly, awaking before 4 on a blustery night and tossing and turning. Mind racing. I tried to keep it in leash, eventually clobbering it with my mantra. But I awoke late, 8am, and feeling faint again. Short oration and meditation from 8.40.

There is a tendency for thoughts to swarm in. An obvious reason is that now I have time, a couple of days more than planned, and so the possibilities to plan are legion. But it is more than this I feel; it is also the clamouring of the hordes of potential squatters outside my newly vacated head, and I feel that I want to be very diligent to make sure I get a "nice English family, m'dear" as tenants, and not the old mob back again. But *I Ching* had said that "we ought to make our way back to ordinary conditions as soon as possible", so I am planning to be out and about and reasonably indulgent. But despite this morning, I would at least hope the dawn meditation and, for now, the evening one will remain part of "ordinary life".

The form of oration has been "thanks, you were great" (not said with irony, for this has been a most rewarding summer) "but please give me extra strength to adjust to my new life without losing and forgetting what you've given me. And when they are reasonably consolidated, have taken root, may they blossom and bear fruit to repay all family and friends who have supported, or simply not hindered, me by trusting me in this work."

(A test of "detachment" has come already: a letter from NGT rocketing me about letting the publishing slide. On a previous occasion, such a letter begat gloom. Now I felt a wrench, but it did not hurt much. I hope this is not just because of other joys, I need to work on it.)

I see the consolidating period as extending at least as long as heavy Saturn aspects continue. The next day of climax is Monday. But owing to Saturn's later retrogradation there will be some repeat echoes in later months.

Good example of crumminess unconquered this evening. ML left her fish in the fridge despite my reminders. As N was intending to cook the fish, and his own was frozen and was guaranteed for one week in the freezer compartment, I suggested he used it, and offered to join him to help him eat it (assuming she'd brought a double portion) as a "break in" to communal eating. But it became clear later that N was reluctant, talking of "its unknown history" and so on. This irritated me more than it should.

In the oration I saw this was a bad habit, shared by B, from my mother; we so hate waste that we tend to burden others with gifts which would otherwise be wasted. Now this can upset plans (I know this from being victim to B's efforts) and instead of sympathizing we are offended that a gift is taken reluctantly. Worse still we are actually right, because N should have made a little effort in order to help out a situation, but of course not right enough to merit the ensuing pain.

Anyway, in the oration I had to fight this anger and also to fight off over-clever "solutions", e.g. once N has resigned himself to cooking the fish, to cheerfully announce that I had persuaded the neighbours to take it, and so on. Self pity came in on it—I really feel sorry for those fish and their wasted death. So it was a riot of "detachment" to make sure they did not take me with them in their death.

I made it, just. Also I survived Nigel's letter thanks to a quick reply to get it off my mind and to help detachment. But all the same this is BAD. One interesting point is that this morning I circulated light for the first time for ages. "Voice" said "no!" and I said "shut up". I wondered if the circulation had stirred something up, and whether the "voice" had a point. So this evening I did his thing thoroughly.

### Thursday 29 September

Another lousy night's sleep. Could not get to sleep till after 1. Thinking, thinking, thinking. Out about 7.30–8.30 and again my meditation took a while to calm down.

N has rebelled over the fish! Not only did he make the problem worse by saying he would cut it up for the cats and then not so doing (and now it's another night older), but he has left all the food out, the door open, the soap in the water. Fortunately after the meditation I had not had time to get screwed up, so I swallowed my pride and Abramelin's injunction about touching dead creatures "of any description whatsoever" and cut it up for the cats. It's all a question of whether the operation in considered to be finished or not. Recently I've seen two dead squirrels on the road and wondered about moving them.

Shopping in St Albans very slight, but huge bills like tax disc and electricity and suitcase to pay. At 12 I went to St Michael's Church, it was his day. Alas they were locking up, but I had time to look at John Bressie's grave, the one who left this life "ano Domine 1691 on 1st April at age 38". Found a mound with a seat in the churchyard where I sat and attained peace. Children were playing in the school yard and the only clear voice I could hear was always calling out "Michael, Michael!" On my return (I waited till 1 pm) I played Graham Bond's "My Archangel Mikael". He speaks of no. 8 for Mikael because eighth Tarot trump is of Strength. I'd been haunted by "8" symbolism at church. I had intended to go back for the evening service (at 8) but N suggested a film—a sudden and curious decision of his. We saw a Bond film.

The rest of the afternoon was poorly planned. I'd not expected the Occultique to be shut and for me to cancel the Northampton trip. But I did the lawn edges thoroughly before supper. Fixed to visit R and C this weekend.

## Friday 30 September

Another lousy night, tossing and turning till nearly 3. Was woken by N's movements at 8. Felt very pickled and had idea of meditating in bed.[7] Surprisingly I worked very well so I continued it 6.10–8.50 and now I feel better. I have a clear state which, by a slow adjustment, I'm trying to carry into the day.

Last night I finished Nott's Gurdjieff book. Anxious moment, because it ends on an account of his supreme effort and persistence which broke him through a barrier. This made me wonder if I should have kept up my all-day orations till the angel appeared. I had to think back carefully. There did seem to be a difference, but was I kidding myself and making excuses? The big difference was this: Nott had an open-ended problem, without a time limit, and depending on his trust of Gurdjieff. Mine was to a timetable, really Monday was *the* day and I only continued to Tuesday because of Saturn's "climax" on that day (and the day of the coal man was like an omen saying Saturn = delay). But that was a definite decision of mine to make an extension. Surely a similar argument would demand an extension till next Monday, or even till the final Saturn transit months ahead? Perhaps, but the difference is that such later dates go way out of the Abramelin time, whereas my one extra day lay within the time it would have been if successful.[8] So, to have persisted day after day would not so much have been analogous to waiting in Southampton for the QE2 to arrive with a friend, and when friend is not among the passengers, to continue waiting at the dock.

---

[7]The book does permit orating in the chamber in case of sickness, but this choice was more to do with a running down of the operation.
[8]Many years later the George Dehn edition of *Abramelin* was published, the version that describes an eighteen-month operation, and it made a lot of sense of this feeling that I needed longer.

The image that helped to cause the anxiety was that Nott was digging for a spring, and for me the *I Ching* said it was the year for digging a *well*. So I identified the two incidents. But in fact, Hawker Siddeley was the better analogy with his situation, because there I was in a hopeless situation, was utterly glum and all the colour had left my life; and there I was aware that I ought not to just leave and get another similar job, but rather slog on and try to find gold, or adjust to it. And then came the breakthrough in the form of this work, that was the finding of this work, that was the finding of the spring which has been sustaining me since and inspiring me.

When I got up today I checked the *I Ching* wording which had made me decide to stop. It was as I thought, it definitely said it was wrong to continue, and references to rapid return to normality were unequivocal.

## Tuesday 4 October[9]

Was out from 7.40–8.40 today. Meditation and oration were weak and unreal-seeming. Invasion of thoughts, none serious, but distracting through multiplicity. I realise the importance of retirement to meditation. I'm sure that had I continued for a while, the calm would have been totally regained. But the experiences and activities of the weekend are too numerous to have been assimilated. So I must make a point of cleaning this up before I lose the thread.

I passed the weekend at Brighton, staying with R and family. I went down on Friday so I could go by Eton and get traveller's cheques, and returned on Monday to give me a second chance to get to Brighton shops. On the way back I visited Forbes at long last and saw film.

The routine was shattered. The tendency to be woken by little children reduced me to slight meditation in bed. As I was sleeping on sitting-room floor, late nights were unavoidable.

The noise of the children could put me way on edge, my residual calm helped and I was able to sneak away for snatches of re-centering. On Sunday I had that familiar feeling when visiting R, or the Mill, of rootlessness—"I hope I'm not asked to do anything new". I'd travelled light and not taken old clothes. Again self-remembering helped to ease the build-up.

---

[9]The operation was meant to be finished, yet felt unfinished. So I did maintain some of the practices while adjusting to normal life, but this was the first time I had skipped a weekend.

Another ordeal was that spare crash helmet (so I could take R out on Bloaters) and a big bag of vegetables (for C) were stolen from Bloaters. I was more sorry for the vegetables—my own grown lovely French beans and tomatoes—and hoping the thief would cook them and not bung them away. This anxiety made me prone to negative emotions, but I managed to defuse them.

Another danger was buying suitcases! (The confessions of an addict.) A nice practical one in Eton was only £3, so that was not too bad, but in Brighton there were two expensive crocodile cases and I had them on my mind over the weekend. In the end I realised that it is better to buy, for one is less haunted after.

Finally, there was the book-selling ordeal. Non-attachment helped a lot. I had nice chats and sold a few, though the university were not buying.[10]

In all cases I was much better for my inner calm but the old anxieties were all around and I still need to waste too much effort in defence. It was necessary to take time off to meditate. I was not able to snap clear in "real time", "online", etc.

Saw the film "Pumping Iron" about Arnold Schwarzenegger and his pals. He gave a very good example of non-attachment. So far I've enjoyed films, but not been swept away. This is partly because I've not seen anything really stirring, but all the same it was unusual not to have been terrifically involved.

Big write-up this morning after break. I'm keeping up my other diary day by day, but I'll not bother to keep this one every day because it is too much to take two diaries on my travels.

Yesterday (Monday) had Sun conjunct radical MC, Moon almost conjunct radical Moon (and so sextile radical Sun), Mars trine radical Mars and sextile radical Jupiter, Jupiter opposition radical Saturn, Saturn trine radical Sun (and so sextile both Moon and radical Moon) and Uranus semi-sextile Sun.[11]

I would hope for a bombshell, but no. I bought a nice case, sold books to a new shop (Solstice) and was welcomed. Met Forbes for the first time. Perhaps something amazing will grow from it all.

---

[10] I was probably trying to flog copies of *SSOTBME*.
[11] Quite a dramatic confluence of astrological aspects, so I had noted it as potentially a significant day for the operation, but nothing much happened. The only error was in the MC: about fifteen years later I discovered that my time of birth was wrong by a few hours.

## Thursday 6 October

Tuesday was a horrid lesson about the meaning of a return to the real world: I went to the bank to get money, then had a haircut, bought fish and steak to experiment, filled up with petrol and took K out in the evening for a very ordinary pub supper and must have spent over £11 in the one day, i.e. more than a week's allowance.

Also had first screws for two months and they were excellent and I noted the tentative confirmation (which still needs the test of time) that Abramelin improves one's sex life.

But, as so often happens with me, Wednesday brought an £11.50 cheque! (Just as when I was telling myself that expensive crocodile cases in Brighton were out of the question, R said that someone wanted to buy my VTR monitor!).

Apart from that, I was under attack on Wednesday. I took the laundry over and was surprised by a queue, and it was such a lousy drying day that I gave up and returned.

Morning was filled with cooking, etc. I picked shaggy caps and put them to stew, dug potatoes because N "did not know where to dig", gathered apples, and cooked Algerian mackerel (also picking tomatoes and fennel for that). D came and I spent a long time cutting bits off fallen and bruised apples to stew them, because I knew N would only leave them to rot. I also split up a marrow bone with an axe.

Then we went out to the pub and on our return I picked broccoli and we had the mackerel with white wine, then steak Bordelaise with D's red, with new potatoes, broccoli, and shaggy caps, then spiced the stewed apple, then coffee and mint chocolates. During chat, D spoke of muscular stiffness so I suggested we went to Berkhamsted and he was massaged. That was a break for me, for on return there was a mountain of washing up and as D had brought two bottles of wine, not much hope of eating out. So I made *frijoles con queso*, with French beans and the rest of the potatoes. Both N and I forgot the bread so I made chapattis, which takes time. All that washing up, plus cooking could well have got me flustered, as I'm always tense cooking for others. But I found I was "awake" and was enjoying the experience of working at full efficiency, planning as I worked. Despite the fact that my carnivore transition was not going well and I was suffering diarrhoea and indigestion.

The next blow came when I rang CM late. *New Scientist* had not shewn any interest in my book and his "rationalist" press tutor had torn it to shreds. I was quite happy with that, hoping he would write a critical review; but C said he would not, as he was "so negative about it". So I went to bed with the "fighting spirit" trying to invade my post-Abramelin calm.

But Belial was too transparent, he'd overdone it. He'd given me the news at the end of a rather tiring and exploited day (a new mound of washing up awaits me). First, CM asked me to return his alchemy book straightaway, which was irritating as I'd just missed a chance after two Berkhamsted visits, and the expense of posting books was unwelcome now. Then he said he *sent* the book to the reviews editor and had not heard from him. This was a pity because I could have sent it, and was full of ideas for a covering letter; and I thought the idea was that, being in the same building, C was going to *deliver* it and so have more "impact". At first I was glad to hear of Prof. Rationalist's attack because I'd expected it and had looked forward with interest to a sharp criticism which was also informative (for so far reviewers have only been in favour of the book). Apparently he wrote at great length about it. Yet C says he thought there was a lot to answer to in the book, and if that was so, why should he not criticise it publicly in his magazine? It gave me the impression that he was reacting in fear, a torrent of abuse in private and a public covering up.[12] And of course there is no chance of finding out till I get back from my holiday. So thanks to the angel for de-fusing my anxiety.

But the enemy did perhaps have a minor victory, sleepless and indigested, I had a strong urge to masturbate. It was first class. The first for months, the first ordinary me for half a year!

*Here ended my official Abramelin diary.*

---

[12]This could have been a great disappointment. *SSOTBME* had had one or two good mentions in the occult community, but I really wanted to see how others might react to it. I really was looking for some sharp criticism of the basic ideas, so I could learn and improve them. All I got was these pages of defensive jibes of the sort that an academic might share with friends against a rival, but would have the good sense never to publish.

*POSTSCRIPT ONE*

# Introduction

What is the reader to make of a six-month spiritual retreat that seemed to fizzle out with a whimper rather than end with a bang?

A sceptical rationalist would find that hilarious: proof enough that the whole exercise was a waste of time. They might even encourage people to read my diary—as a lesson for people still stupid enough to put so much trust in the superstitious religious fantasies of our ignorant ancestors.

If I now say that the ending was for me perplexing, uncertain, but by no means meaningless; that I have never at any time then or since felt that my six months was a waste of time; that even forty years later I still consider it to have been the most significant six months of my life—does that simply confirm my status as a gullible fool?

I have in the past tried to explain what happened in these terms: "what I seem to have achieved was the knowledge of, but not the conversation with, my Holy Guardian Angel". Apart from a sense of silent presence, stillness, and peace, and an experience of heightened reality, my strongest memory was a feeling that the operation had ended but was not finished: that it somehow needed more time. This was especially interesting to me many years later when I read the Georg Dehn edition and learned that there is another tradition that says the operation should take eighteen months, rather than six.

More recently I have been reading about Tenzin Palmo who spent twelve years alone in a cave in the Himalayas.[1] For the final three years of strict retirement, she passed her nights in a three-foot square meditation box and never even lay down to sleep. I would never wish to compare my humble six months with her achievement, except to say that her description of the result of her retirement is not essentially different from mine. Her retirement was interrupted, while mine was not, but we both had a sense of something not finished and yet a sense of nothing or emptiness that was meaningful. She was not expecting miracles, or to achieve full enlightenment, because in her system it would take even longer than twelve years: it would be the work of several lifetimes. So one could argue that it would have been asking a lot for me to turn into an enlightened and fully fledged master wizard in just half a year.

Like Tenzin, I had restrained my childlike expectations and was aiming for silence and emptiness rather than visualising a desired outcome. But I did not have her comparatively well-defined Buddhist tradition and clear sense of what to do next. At the time that I finished I was simply puzzled. The *I Ching* had been an important guide, and it appeared to insist on a return to "normal conditions" and refraining from the open use of power—power that I was not aware of having achieved.

Jumping forward to my next visit to Gerald Yorke at Forthampton Court: I shared with him my sense of puzzlement and non-completion. He said I had actually done well because "most people simply gain the knowledge and conversation of their ego on the first attempt". He explained that, in his and Israel Regardie's opinion, that had been Crowley's true error: not admitting that Aiwass was a personification of his own enormous ego, a mistake that reduced the quality of all Crowley's later work. At the time I was more astonished at his hint that one might perform this operation more than once: how would I ever be able afford the time and arrange circumstances for another six-month retreat?

As I drove home I reflected that it would have been a lot more fun to have met my ego. When people speak of an "ego-trip" they usually mean some great inflation of boastful pride—so what would my own

---

[1] As described in *Cave in the Snow* by Vicki Mackenzie.

ego be like? Would I have emerged as some charismatic, pumped-up Thelemic Master in florid robes and the darling of trendy London society? I stopped the car by the side of the road, as I suddenly realised that failure was my ego!

I was born the youngest child by five years, so was a little brat to my elder siblings. I was born at an inconvenient time: just as my family were moving from Hertfordshire to a new life in Gloucestershire that would mean years of living in a building site while a ruined water mill was being converted into a family dwelling. So it was very easy for me to feel that I was a burden, and being in the deep country I had no-one around younger than me that I could lord it over or humiliate in compensation. The very lowest in the hierarchy was my ingrained state of being. The fact that I was later singled out for a scholarship to an English "public" (i.e. private) school, had most of my education paid for by a loving government, that I consistently achieved distinctions in exams, went on to win a scholarship to Cambridge University and a teaching job at the world's most famous school—all that did nothing to shake my secure non-belief in myself. When I finally failed my Diploma of Education exam, I actually felt huge relief, rather than shame: because I had for the first time achieved an exam result that was worse than I thought I deserved.

So my sense of failure and insignificance was not some priceless jewel of spiritual humility, it was simply the backdrop of my life, against which every achievement or award needed to be "explained away".

Thus the absence of a visible Holy Guardian Angel to lead me into a week of congress with demons could be interpreted as my "ego-trip". That understanding shifted a few of my blocks, but not in itself enough to make real sense of the operation.

So it is now time to answer two questions that are most likely to arise in readers' minds. The first is "what happened following the operation?"—because Abramelin has a reputation for turning its aspirants' lives upside down, if not actually ruining them. The second question is: "with the benefit of forty years of hindsight, did Abramelin change my life?" or in other words: "was it ultimately worth doing?"

POSTSCRIPT TWO

# What happened after Abramelin

The combination of being told to return to "normal conditions" without delay while feeling that the work was not finished was paradoxical. Was it really time for me to enact Zarathustra's down-going?

To soften the descent, I did continue for some weeks to meditate when possible, but without the full ceremony, and for shorter times—in fact I revisited some of the meditations for years to come. You might not think so from reading the diary, but I had cut myself off from much social contact during the operation, especially the last two months, and so I decided to catch up with some visiting and explain myself to friends with whom I had been out of contact. These included an old friend of my parents who had retired to Malta and had been complaining of neglect. I decided to visit him and some others along the way.

Although I had been out of work for seven months, I had been required to sign on for unemployment pay. If I had not signed on, I would have been forced to pay National Insurance without having any income to cover it. Because of my simple life, vegetarian diet, and growing my own vegetables, I had actually saved enough in those six months to pay for a trip across the channel with my motorbike and to ride down through France, Italy and Sicily to take another ferry across to Malta.

That was 1977: I do not think today's social security would ever provide enough money for a trip like that!

What was meant by "normal conditions"? My normal conditions for the last few years had been dominated by the tedium of dead-end nine to five office work. It is not easy to quantify tedium, so I give one example: in months previous to making the decision to retire I had taken to ignoring the usual urge to empty my bowels upon getting up, in order to leave me with something to look forward to, some brief daily relief from the tedium of sitting for hours at my desk, wasting time in a large open-plan office.

In such terms, my journey back to the ordinary world turned out to be very far from normal. After taking the ferry to France I diverted towards the south of Paris to call upon an acquaintance that I had not seen for years. I planned to spend my first night there, but stayed for five extraordinary days, sleeping in the studio of the French artist Nikki de St Phalle surrounded by the fairy-tale set for a movie she was making for French television. The bed was huge, covered with nothing but black satin sheets and a huge wolf-skin rug. I found myself in a milieu that then seemed impossibly glamorous: mixing with film-makers, artists and actors, calling on Paris fashion designers, being shown round the Swiss artist Yves Tinguely's massive "head" sculpture under construction in the Forest of Fontainbleu, and ending upon the last day in a French television "blue room", dressed in a lurid St Phalle bodystocking for a sequence in her sado-masochistic fairy tale movie.

It was time to head south. Time was running out, so I rode my motorcycle for up to ten hours a day and was surprised by the welcome I received everywhere. In Britain a lone traveller on a motorcycle would be a second-class citizen, but here I was treated like royalty in the cheap hotels and guest houses where I happened to stop.

Someone told me later that I had emerged from my retirement with a certain serene charisma that people found immensely attractive. Unfortunately this seemed to afflict the man I stayed with in Malta. I might describe him as an elderly uncle figure, who had introduced my family to Ted Bryant (an ex-disciple of Crowley and friend of Frieda Lady Harris), and to Dr Joyce Martin (who was then engaged in the study of LSD as a psycholytic aid to therapy). But now he suddenly decided that he had fallen head over heels in love with me. He had grown immensely fat and decrepit, and his expressions of romantic love required me to do such things as wank into his whiskey, so I was less than happy.

What was worse was that he was also convinced that I had also fallen deeply in love with him, but that I was too reserved to admit it even to myself. Fortunately he had a sexologist friend, a major figure in the 60s sexual revolution, whom he invited to dinner in order to help me to "see the light". I was able to take the man aside and explain my predicament, and he was most understanding. But the encounter resulted in the sexologist also falling in love with me on the spot, wanting me to kiss him, and later sending me love letters.

While my voyage south had been an idyll of the most lovely coastal and scenic routes, my money was now almost gone. I had to get back quickly, taking the most direct route I could see on my small scale, single A3 page map of Europe. What I had not considered was that my chosen route would entail crossing the Alps via the St. Bernard pass. It was the end of November and I found myself in a total white-out of horizontal driven snow and shrieking winds, like something from a Scott of Antarctica movie, with only a row of posts to indicate the edge of the highway. When I reached the tunnel between Italy and Switzerland, night was falling and the border guard was incredulous: how had I got there? They had not seen another motorcycle for weeks.

The fact was that my motorcycle, a MotoGuzzi V-1000 iConvert, was absolutely brilliant at going up icy slopes, because it had a fluid flywheel drive that delivered smooth thrust with no clutching or gear changes that might cause wheel-spin on any other touring bike. But for going down a slippery slope it was disastrous, because the very same feature meant there was no engine braking except at high speed, and MotoGuzzi's clever linked braking technology meant there was no way to apply a touch of brake to the rear wheel alone. For hours I was dicing with death, continually cadence braking the front wheel with my agonised right arm, while trying to make out the route ahead through swirling snow and misted goggles. I saw not one single vehicle going up or going down, until I reached the bottom and found somewhere to stay the night.

After that I got back to England and fell hopelessly in love.

## *A gradual awakening*

I have my everyday diary outlining the events of the following years, so I could now give a step by step description of everything that happened to turn my life upside down. But reading that would be as tedious and chaotic as I experienced it at the time.

On the other hand I could spare the reader all these personal details. I could spare my blushes and simply say that although a lot of bad things happened, I never really lost that sense that it was all somehow meaningful and necessary. Without consciously taking it, I was effectively learning the oath taken by Crowley "that I will interpret every phenomenon as a particular dealing of God with my soul".

A third approach would be to exploit the benefit of forty years' hindsight and pick out just a few examples of how everyday life turned out to be an initiatory journey. In the late 80s someone asked me how it was that I was so wise. I replied that it had been my privilege to spend many years at the feet of the world's greatest teacher—"her name is Failure".

Although the following examples might seem pretty pathetic or trivial, they will give some readers a feel for the way that a spiritual journey can provide a sort of thread of meaning that links together life's jumble and thereby transforms what would otherwise be a chaos of unconnected beads into a wearable necklace.

The first realisation that something was going on began when I was teaching a class of unruly school children. My first job on returning to "normality" had been to take a job teaching mathematics at a Waldorf School. (It happened to be the same school where my brother and sister had started their education before we moved to Gloucestershire.) I was still at the stage where I felt obliged to take any job offered to me, regardless of my feelings or aptitude.

I had never liked school as a child, having been plucked from a quiet Cotswold country life into the horrors of a big city public school at a tender age. So, as I walked up the hill to the school on my first day, I felt a leaden lump of dread in my stomach. The job had been a tough choice, because Waldorf schools take pride in never turning down a pupil—at times this tendency felt to me like: "he may be a crazed psychopathic chainsaw murderer, but I'm sure that we can help him". So my large class included some pupils that government schools would not accept. It was in any case a very difficult time to be teaching—at the birth of the radical punk era, and Pink Floyd's "Another Brick in the Wall", with its refrain: "we don't need no education". Some of my pupils were wild.

I remember one time getting into a fight with two or three of them in class, forced down on the floor with my shirt ripped. Funnily enough, I quite enjoyed that. Many years later I discovered that I am what is now known as an "empath"—someone who tends to soak up others' feelings and so either identifies completely or reacts against those around. When teaching rebellious children I began to feel like a rebel myself. It was a part of me that I had named "Angerford" (see below). It often meant that I was useless as a disciplinarian. The same had been true when I taught at Eton; but there I had earned some respect because I was also recognised as someone with an unusual ability to empathise with teenage rebels, and communicate where other teachers and parents were failing.

When I was called into other teachers' classes and told that "my" class was misbehaving, I had to find some way to exert a measure of control. One day I silenced a noisy class by striking my desk with a ruler. It worked, and I suddenly recalled Abraham the Jew's instruction on handling wilful spirits: "If ... they should appear with tumult and insolence, fear nothing ... Only show them the Consecrated Wand, and if they continue to make a disturbance, smite upon the Altar twice or thrice therewith, and all will be still."

That night I re-read the chapter on handling the spirits and it was a pretty good summary of the sort of behaviour and tricks being meted out by my pupils! That opened my eyes and I began to see how the apparently endless tribulations and trials I was suffering might be revisited as a working out of the final week of the operation. I was being encouraged to "interpret every phenomenon as a particular dealing of the HGA with my soul" while learning how to cope with my demons, not in the oratory but in everyday life. What should have happened in seven days eventually spun out over seven years.

For a laid-back bachelor, life can have few more significant and vexing initiations than the discovery that you have impregnated the one you love, that she wants to keep the child, and that you will soon be responsible for feeding three mouths instead of one. That happened in the same year that I started teaching. I was paid very little, because it was assumed that a Waldorf teacher would become part of a community, largely sustained by the school's own communal facilities. This created a huge tension between my life as a teacher and my private life, because it was seen that I was spending long hours with "other people's children" instead of my own family—while having little financial support to offer in compensation. The transition from free bachelor to responsible father is one of life's greatest initiations—all the more so when struggling to make ends meet.

The partnership was passionate, and explosive. It eventually blew up and we separated on non-speaking terms. I later re-interpreted this this as another lesson about life's demons.

We had both started life as children of middle-class couples who met in radical reforming movements. My parents met in the Kibbo Kift, John Hargrave's curious woodcraft-cum-folklore-cum-ritualistic-cum political/economic movement. Her parents met in John G. Bennet's Gurdjieff and Subud inspired movement. Both of us were singled out at an early age for our intelligence and were sponsored as poor pupils to expensive schools, and we both found ourselves floundering way out of our depths.

Then the difference emerged. Her school was in her home town, so she knew the area well and was able to escape. She ran away, played truant, went to live in a caravan site and rebelled against her posh upper-middle classmates. But my school was in a big unknown city where I, a country boy, saw no-where to flee to. So I learned to survive, to keep my head down and avoid conflict, to work hard and beat the system.

When I met her, what I saw was someone who was everything I was not: a courageous rebel who had had the will and strength to break out and forge her own streetwise way of life among petty criminals, druggies, and drop outs. She had survived and triumphed where I had simply meekly knuckled under and done what I was told. What I could not understand then, but now believe possible, was that deep down she saw me quite differently: as someone who had had the guts not to run away but to apply my brain to beat the system and rise to the top with a scholarship to Cambridge and then teaching at Eton—while she had simply chickened out and run away.

That is a very simple outline of a very emotionally charged split: basically we each experienced in the other the part of ourselves that had been repressed and unexpressed. I thought she was utterly wonderful and could not understand why something like a self-deprecating ironic remark about my supposed "poshness" should whip her into silent fury, nor could she understand why I felt utterly boring and worthless when meeting what she saw as her "low-life" associates. When, for example, I acted untypically and made arrangements for a supply of cocaine for her friends, instead of welcoming me into the fold she hit the roof!

It was a ridiculous scenario, I later realised, but a dramatic playing out of the way that a demon arises from a split in unity, where one thing becomes a polarised, mutually antagonistic and yet fascinating pair—as I later described in my *Little Book of Demons*.

Although I did not understand as much at the time, it was also resolving a problem that I described as "my snobbery" at the very start of the operation. When I was given a scholarship that would take me from village school into the British public school system, I later learned that my father was not happy about it, because he was a class rebel who despised that sort of thing and did not want me to be taught to call people "sir". So I saw myself as aloof from all that class nonsense, and yet was in my own way afflicted with a sort of inverted class snobbery. I found that tendency hideously magnified in the form of my beloved. It was like pus bursting from a wound.

Another aspect of the snobbery was explained in Chapter Four: it was my reaction to the change taking place in society as the Thatcher mentality encouraged the notion that people out of work were useless, parasitic scroungers. Whereas the dole in 1977 was more than sufficient to allow me to be both a supportive citizen and to practice a spiritual retreat, by 1980 the Department of Whatever were turning extremely unpleasant. After my unsuccessful teaching experience I found myself each week queuing for hours only to be told by a surly and unhelpful bureaucrat that I was in the wrong queue and would have to start all over again. After weeks of being treated like dirt I decided to take action.

The next week I took with me a large shopping bag. It contained a gallon can of petrol and matches as well as my documentation. The transparent screen separating the plebs from the bureaucracy was of bulletproof plastic, but it would not stop me from tipping the petrol through the document slot and chucking a match after it. However, an inner voice, as I had sometimes experienced during the operation, suggested that this *auto-da-fé* would only be valid if I gave the Department one final chance. According to those instructions, when I reached the head of the queue I handed over my papers and stared hard at that week's surly official. He took my papers and promptly and courteously dealt with my submission, even handing back the material with a kindly smile. So I walked away with my explosive burden unused.

This was another example of a demonic split within me finding some sort of resolution in action—but what was the source of this split?

## *Angerford and Lea*

After my first term teaching at the Waldorf school and before the discovery that my partner was pregnant, I was able to take the summer holiday as an opportunity to write *Thundersqueak*—the follow-up to my first published book *SSOTBME. Thundersqueak* was a sort of loose dialogue between two parts of my being that I had called Angerford and Lea.

Angerford was a sultry teenage rebel and Lea an avuncular eccentric who loved peace and quiet and growing vegetables. In *Thundersqueak* I found ways to indirectly express some of the things that had happened during my Abramelin retirement. In particular I described the peeling away, like the layers of an onion, the many labels given by society with which we have come to identify ourselves, until one was left with a relatively featureless and yet utterly warm and universal sense of common humanity. Even more apposite was the chapter where I describe a sort of implosion into nothingness, a sort of abyss where there is no rudder or means of control, but where one can at least take aim before jumping.

So who were Angerford and Lea? I had in the 1970s identified them in terms of the opposition in my natal horoscope between my two ruling planets Mars and Jupiter. Meanwhile an elderly cousin had died and named my brother as her executor. Her estate included several boxes of notebooks containing her astrological researches during the pre-war years, and I was asked to find out if they had any value. At the time Charles Harvey was head of the Astrological Association and he said that they would love to add the material to their library "provided that I first documented and classified the material". It was not a lot to ask, but those boxes hung around for many more years before eventually, in the early 90s, I decided to clear them out.

As I took out the very first notebook, a postcard fluttered to the floor. The handwriting was familiar. My long deceased father had written on the day I was born saying that an unnamed child had been born at 3.45 am. That meant that I had what Charles Harvey told me was a "chart transplant": a couple of hours difference meant that my ascendant was not Sagittarius but Capricorn, and my ruling planet was not Jupiter but Saturn.

This struck me as a major disappointment—who could want to give up Sagittarius for boring old Capricorn? But a lot fell into place as I adjusted to the fact. For a start: how had I accepted a Jupiter ruler and identified with Sagittarius for nearly fifty years? The answer was that my true ascendant was very closely trine to Jupiter, allowing a strong identification. More importantly, the Mars and Saturn rulers amounted to a sharp split in my character between a passionate Aries desire to fight and make a big impact versus Capricornian reserve and careful planning.

Returning to my Abramelin years: I recall a conversation with Vaughan Purvis who was running a short-lived occult bookshop in London on behalf of Jimmy Page. Purvis commented that among the occultists of the day, no-one was "living a truly Thelemic lifestyle" and I remember how the statement tore me in two. One half of me felt shame that I was so boring: why had I never dropped out in full hippy style, thrown all my worldly goods away, made a penniless trek to the Himalayas and sacrificed all for enlightenment? The other half of me remembered something I had told my pupils at Eton when I was among the pioneers teaching the "New Maths" syllabus, designed to make mathematics seem exciting and relevant for a modern world. I told them to forget that nonsense: "Our next topic is actually extremely boring, and that is all the more reason to tackle it—because boredom, not outer space, is our civilisation's final frontier. This week will really separate the boys from the men."

Another earlier example of the split was manifest when I had written my first book and failed to get it published. I was working for Hawker Siddeley Aviation at the time and so had easy access to flying lessons. I realised that I was ideally placed to learn and qualify for a flying licence and could gain access to a Jet Provost. I could fill its tanks with fuel and dive at full thrust from a great height into the Houses of Parliament, confident that the combination of unspent fuel and huge kinetic energy would totally destroy the building and all within. After such an act, publishers would fight like wild beasts to publish my book—even if it were utter crap.

This looked like a winning strategy, except that the other voice pointed out that I had completed a reasonably interesting book before I was thirty years old and asked whether that had completely exhausted my potential? Was it not possible that I might have other ideas for some future, even better book? In which case it would be a stupid waste to blow my whole life just to promote this current *oeuvre de jeunesse*.

I was to learn that this battle between the Big Gesture versus Careful Attention to Detail was for me a very serious demon that emerged in many forms. One of those forms had been my falling madly in love with what I perceived to be a Big Gesture rebel girl, while despising my own steadfast Capricornian endurance. It also resolved that "mama's boy" feeling that ignited my lament dated 30 August in the diary: I was identifying with my Saturnian caution while projecting my Martial wildness onto others.

## A pattern of lives

Among the many other lessons there was one that was a lot more interesting in terms of its actual magical content. I had been earning a bit of extra money editing the work of a well-known astrologer, and it included her description of what she called the "Uranus Half Return" when, typically, a man has his mid-life crisis, falls absurdly in love with someone half his age, and makes an utter fool of himself in his early 40s.

Tut! Tut! I noted that my Uranus opposition was starting that year at age thirty-eight.[1] Thanks for the warning: I would be on the lookout for that sort of nonsense and make dead sure that I did not fall for anything so blatantly stupid!

Meanwhile I was back in that miserable frame of mind that told me I had hit rock bottom. After my glory days of Cambridge and Eton I had failed to find a career, I had descended into poverty and a failed relationship, failed as a magician, failed as a teacher, fooled a few people into believing I had some wisdom to offer, and had been on the brink of being sent to prison for an anti-government arson attack. Then a letter from my old college somehow reached me, inviting me to an anniversary celebration of an exclusive Essay Club that I had once been elected to. Apart from being an unexpected honour for an un-cultured and un-literary mathematician, this club had in a very significant manner launched me on my path to writing about magic. Still, I could not see any point, but I might as well go to meet one or two old friends.

The evening began with current members of the Essay Club on stage, reading extracts by past members. Since my time, the college had begun admitting female students, and one of the speakers was a young woman with a soft American accent with whom I felt an overwhelming sense of familiarity and belonging. What would my time at Cambridge have been like if she had been there then? It was not a sexual attraction but a sense of profound friendship. During the interval my friends had

---

[1] This was younger than the average, because Uranus had long been retrograde by the time I was born.

spoken to her and said that we must meet, because she was herself an ex-mathematician who had turned to anthropology and was preparing a thesis on "something like witchcraft in England".

Wow! At any time in the past I would have been wildly excited to discover that a Cambridge academic had any awareness of modern witchcraft, let alone be interested enough to be actively researching it. But in my present abject condition there was simply no point in meeting her. I would probably just appear as a fool. All I had to do was walk over and introduce myself, but I simply ignored the invitation.

That sense of friendship was so intense and vivid, and yet I did not at the time recall an identical feeling that I had experienced some months earlier. An acquaintance had decided to cheer me up and provide an outlet for my Uranus opposition by inviting me to join a panel at some New Age festival. As I sat on stage watching the audience trickling in I felt out of place, an unknown and insignificant non-entity dropped amongst the great and good of the New Age occult scene. One of the people entering caught my eye: not because she was a woman, nor because she was in any way striking in her plain clothing and rainproof coat, but because I felt such a sense of instant empathy. If this had been a party, that would be the one person I might choose to spend time with. But what would be the point?

Then there was a third experience, as utterly unconnected as the experiences in Cambridge and at the London festival. A friend invited me to join a private dream group in his house in North London. I arrived early and was drinking tea when a voice said: "Haven't I seen you before?" It was the same American academic that I had seen on stage and ignored at Cambridge. And I later discovered that she was the very same person that had seen me on stage at the festival. She had already read my book *SSOTBME* and was looking forward to discussing ideas with me.

There followed a most remarkable eruption of spontaneous memories of past lives on my behalf, and further remarkable coincidences of the sort already described. But I was intensely embarrassed, and desperate to hide my inappropriate feelings. If there was one bit of advice I would have given to an attractive young woman starting an investigation into the occult underground, it would have been this: "Should you meet a man twice your age who starts claiming to have met you in past lives, run for it!" Despite the warning and my resolution never to allow it, I had fallen heart first into a classic Uranus opposition drama.

I will not divert the reader with further details now, except to say that the ensuing connections and coincidences were dramatic enough to furnish an entire occult novel. The only thing that saved me was the very process of detached self-observation that had played such a major role in my retirement.

The word processor was a novelty at the time, and I had the idea of writing a "word processor novel" where the narrative would at a certain point split into two parallel columns. The first column would continue as an accurate description of my subjective experiences of discovering bit by bit the pattern of past lives that had brought us together and provided such a vivid explanation of my current circumstances and our relationship—a strongly healing yet disturbing experience. The second column would then begin to describe and "explain" the very same experiences from the point of view of an observing analyst along such lines as: "Then the subject rationalised his anima projection by experiencing a vision that …" As I slowly managed to restrain my demons and come to terms with the experience, there would appear a third column in which I started to write the same events through the eyes of an author who had decided to record the experience holistically, striving for an integrated account that maintained a balance between the actual subjective experience and society's acceptable objective explanations.

During the time that I was living out this drama we were initiated together into the same magical order. Or should I say "magical group" because this was not a formal order claiming ancient lineage but rather a collection of innovative magicians building our own system in the experimental spirit of the chaos magic current, but without being directly affiliated to it. Our group performed a number of rituals both in its own basement temple and in some of Britain's sacred sites. Magically it was highly rewarding, at a time when I was in danger of going off the rails.

My job prospects were improving, as I had started working as a technical writer and was earning enough to buy a car on hire purchase. One morning as I was speeding to work—late as usual—I crashed headlong into a vehicle coming out of a side turning. My car was a write off. As people pulled me out of the wreckage they said, "The main thing is that you are alive."

I was shocked, but undamaged. I was taken somewhere and given hot tea. I pondered why they had thought that my being alive, when the car was wrecked, was "the main thing". Surely the car was blameless, and yet it had taken the punishment when it should have been me that was wrecked. I was taken back to my lodgings where I lay on the bed and wept. The "voice" that I had experienced at times told me that I needed to thank my guardian angel for saving my life. So I mumbled something along these lines: "Thank you, my Holy Guardian Angel, for saving my life. This suggests that, for you at least, it was a life worth saving."

I had spoken these words in the grudging manner of a silly boy who has been forced by his parents to apologise to teacher for being rude in class. I decided to repeat the same words again, trying for greater feeling. It was as if I almost meant it. I said the same words one more time, loudly and distinctly, and found that I really did mean it. There followed a profound sense of peace.

This was another turning point in my life. Since about seven years old I had from time to time considered whether I should commit suicide and put an end to all this stuff called "Life". But now I had at last made a proper connection to a part of me that really wanted to live. Since that day, I have never again ever seriously considered committing suicide.

Looking back at these lessons I see a theme that began seven years earlier when I first wrote about an "inner democracy". With the growing recognition of my many parts or "demons"—including Angerford and Lea—the question arises as to how to manage them. Traditional demonology encourages us to separate good spirits from bad and to bind the bad spirits with threats, but I evolved a more twentieth-century approach by giving them all the vote.

Instead of an inner dictatorship, or even an inner theocracy, I saw my being as a democracy. This still seems to be unusual. When some atrocity has been committed it is still normal for media talking heads to describe the act as "unthinkable", even though it could not have happened if it had not been thought up and, what's more, thanks to media hype it is now being thought about by millions of people.

Even the sweetest person is quite capable of thinking awful things so, instead of denying it, and casting the demon into outer darkness, they should have the courage to acknowledge the demon and give it the vote. This takes some courage, and it does require trust that one's inner majority is actually wholesome—so it helps to love one's self.

My experience—illustrated in the petrol can and the air crash examples—is that in a healthy inner democracy bad tendencies tend to lose the vote, but at least feel acknowledged.

If only more people adopted this inner democratic approach, then outer democracy might start working better.

## A resolution

Soon after the crash, I got my first really suitable and promising job. I would be working as one of a small communications team for a youngish, innovative British IT company.

Not only was I able at last to do interesting and often challenging work with a group of people that soon became good friends, but it also meant me moving to live in Winchester—a town with which I fell in love at first sight. I was at last earning enough in a steady job to get a mortgage to buy a small one-bedroom flat. It was utterly exquisite, with two floors and a bedroom that had French windows onto a little patio roof garden with stunning views: over the sparkling clean waters of the river Itchen, towards the famous cathedral, and across water meadows to a sacred hill boasting its own ancient miz-maze. It was adjoining the cathedral precincts just outside the old city walls in a converted water mill. I was back to my earliest memories, living with the sound of water churning under a mill.

My new life began utterly bare of furniture—apart from a camp bed. It represented a whole fresh start for me. I then drove back to Hertfordshire and loaded up my car with books and possessions, including the Abramelin altar filled with the full regalia that had never been opened since the end of the operation. I arrived late and far too tired to take my stuff up to the flat, so decided to leave everything in the car overnight. Then it suddenly felt wrong to leave the altar like that, so I went down to collect it. As I carried it up the stairs I felt my scalp prickling and a scary feeling that I had not experienced since the very earliest days of the Abramelin operation. It then dawned on me that this was the eve of the very date, exactly seven years ago, when I should have completed the operation.

I placed the altar in my bare upper room and the next morning woke before sunrise to put on my linen robe and light the incense, kneel and perform one more time my old oration. I wish I could say that the room filled with effulgent light and rainbows and that I levitated out of the window—instead it was that same exquisite silence. But then my voice said: "Now you are a magician."

It was nice to hear that. But what could it mean to me? Was it time to unpack all those magic squares and start the big magic of causing armies to appear, to fly through the air, to know all secrets and so on? No, I was not interested and no longer believed all that sort of stuff had any place in my life. I did not feel I had earned any magic powers. All I had gained was a level of inner peace and a detachment that had helped me to survive seven difficult years, and that probably marked the level of spiritual advancement that I could expect to achieve in this lifetime. At that point I made a decision that I never formalised into words, and yet it has become clear over the ensuing decades.

What is it that draws people to magic, especially from a culture of sceptical rationalism or religious disapproval? For me it was the need for something more than "the inferno of the normal" mentioned in Austin Osman Spare's *Earth Inferno*. Why should my body remain imprisoned in the inertia of material existence while my spirit is free to fly to the furthest reaches of time and space, to envisage and populate multiple universes and countless other dimensions? Why be stuck believing in the truth of a mere physical body, when it could also be cloaked in a hierarchy of etheric, astral, mental, and spiritual forms? The world handed to me by my education and culture made me feel claustrophobic. The more it was explained, formalised and tied down with bureaucratic and economic restraints, the more cramped it felt. So I reckoned that many people turn to magic in order to find more glorious spaces to inhabit.

I recall at the nadir of my boring job, before I quit to do the Abramelin operation, one middle-aged man who sat at a desk behind me in the Stress Office. Like all of us he was under-worked in a business that was being run down in anticipation of nationalisation, and he spent months at his desk studying travel brochures and planning his annual January holiday. Then for months afterwards he would be showing people his photographs and souvenirs, regaling us with tales of his wonderful experience.

We younger office workers used to laugh behind his back at this simple-minded existence. Was that really all he lived for? Actually, I also admired and envied that man: because he had found a formula for surviving in a work environment that could drive me insane.

For many people magic plays just such a role. It provides another place to live and dream in. Whether it is Hogwarts, a faerie kingdom, other planets or dimensions, spirit realms or Great Old Ones outside the circles of time—there is a sense of another place, another greater realm whose existence makes all this stuff bearable.

So why did I not copy that man's solution? The answer is that it did not work for me. A holiday in France is magical, but it is a magic that makes my normal life seem even more boring by contrast. Other people possess the necessary imagination to escape, but "otherness" simply does not work for me.

What I needed was not a better alternative, but to find a way to bring magic into my normal life: to feel the vividness and sense of meaning that I had glimpsed at times during the operation and very occasionally afterwards. My magic path was not one of glorious enchantments and physics-defying miracles, it was to transmute more of the lead of everyday existence into gold. My Capricorn ascendant had taken the reins from my Arien wildness.

Without making it a conscious decision, that would become the way that my ideas and my writing continued to evolve. For example: my *Little Book of Demons* does not start from sweeping statements about the hazards of the spirit realms. Instead, it begins with an observation about how natural it is to speak angrily to the office copier when it misbehaves. I argued that this was nothing to be ashamed of: on the contrary it was a natural reaction that opened a doorway to a process of viewing the whole world not as dead matter but as a complex community of intelligences. It was a way to discover how we humans possess innate yet despised abilities to address such complexity.

While my peers had been fighting reductionism, I had stepped right into it and discovered that reductionism has a reverse gear. For example: they resisted the idea that the conscious mind might be "no more than" a by-product of a complex information exchange, assuming that would amount to "proof" that soul and spirit did not exist. But for me it was a brilliant notion, because it freed spirit from substance and allowed it to dwell in any complex information exchange. It provided a model where I could reincarnate in other peoples' bodies; and the by-product of something as complex as a waterfall or the flow of wind through the leaves of a tree might itself emerge as a strange and alien consciousness, a sylph, dryad or landscape deva. I even argued that a universe created as a model to test some "theory of everything" would necessarily be a magical universe.

Instead of flying people to a holiday in a distant, exotic world, my magic would encourage them to explore their own mundane locality with new eyes and a fresh light. They could still get to those exotic places, but by walking rather than flying or tripping. Even if some people find this approach to magic less thrilling, I was certain that it provided a much needed complement to the then prevalent magic of escape.

## A work in progress

Those seven years were an ordeal, and they were followed by seven years in Winchester that I consider to have been among the happiest in my life. I played a role in the revival of the OTO in Britain, had some wonderful experiences as a guest and member of the IOT, and attended and contributed to occult essay clubs organised by Gerald Suster, Christopher McIntosh, Nicholas Goodrich-Clark, and other names in the UK magic scene. Apart from these more formal organisations I also enjoyed experimental work with a group of friends, visiting or staying at sacred sites and devising and performing rituals arising from the experience of the sites themselves. In other words "working with" the sites and the spirits of the place rather than arriving and imposing rituals that had been conceived elsewhere.

Although the Abramelin experience happened forty years ago, it has left its mark. The lessons it taught continue to help me, and I am still learning and growing in a way that can be in some part traced back to those times.

In the book about Tenzin Palmo, it mentions several times the way that commitment to a spiritual path can throw up uncanny challenges in everyday life. Who, for example, could have expected that Tenzin Palmo's isolated meditation at over thirty thousand feet in the Himalayas would be interrupted by a policeman ordering her to leave the country next week? Nothing quite as dramatic happened to me after those seven trying years, but what some call "the curse of Abramelin" still shows its traces. Not that I believed that nonsense could impact my humble efforts.

About thirty years after the operation my publisher took my Abramelin diary to be transcribed into digital form with a view to later publication. When this was completed, the transcriber had a breakdown and was institutionalised for some months. At the start of 2017, forty years on, I decided to go ahead with this project once I had published *My Years of Magical Thinking*. I told the publisher that I should be able to complete editing by April and it is now August—because so many obstacles have kept me from the project. In the past two months I have twice had to erase and rebuild the software on my Apple Mac system—after about twenty trouble-free years. A week after I got the system up and running, and was working again on the project, my office was burgled and only one thing was taken: it was the Apple computer system that I was using to edit the diary. My work last week was held up by a medical intervention that caused a septic wound, and yesterday it was diagnosed as cancer. I have four days to complete this edit before the operation.

Last week, as I was in an aeroplane coming in to land, I wondered why the "powers that be" had not simply killed me if they did not want my diary to be published. It would have been a doddle as I slithered down the slope from the St. Bernard Pass in November 1977. Then it occurred to me that this could be evidence in support of reincarnation: kill me, or Tenzin Palmo, and we would simply reincarnate somewhere else and continue our spiritual journey. Instead our demons decide to act like mafia thugs: trash the workplace and leave the guy alive with a warning "we know where you and your family live". Something tells me, they obviously care about us.

*POSTSCRIPT THREE*

# Is it now worth it?

By now the reader should agree that, at least for me, the Abramelin operation was undoubtedly significant. It taught me lessons that might seem trivial, but it has left me better able to cope with circumstances and mental states that seem to shatter other people. I see people looking to religion, science or magic in search of solutions to life's problems while, for me, magic is increasingly a means to celebrate life, as well as life's problems. I find it hard to believe, but others sometimes assure me that I am a "good presence" that can provide calm or healing.

I have taken to sharing some of my thoughts on a YouTube channel and am rewarded by people's expressions of interest and signs that they like what I say. But I feel embarrassed when they see that as evidence that I am very wise. It is surely a simple matter of courtesy? If people are to spend precious time listening to me, I owe it to them to try my best. Occasionally I make a start then realise I am rambling, so I stop and re-record a better version. If they saw me during the rest of my day, doing stupid things like singing nonsense to my cats, they would think me an idiot—or at best disarmingly childlike—rather than wise.

So, Abramelin was worth it for me, but has it any greater value for humanity other than being a short course for sorting out one troubled soul?

Having read my diary and account of what happened, are you, the reader now feeling excited and curious to explore Abramelin further? Or has my account simply confirmed that Abramelin from a bygone age is no longer relevant and no longer works?

## The full monty

The question is about expectations. At the time I was hoping for a visible manifestation, an angel I could see and hear. Instead there was a sense of presence, nothing visual or auditory. This was disappointing because, forty years ago, we placed much greater value on visual manifestation. For many magicians the measure of a successful evocation was how clearly people could see the spirit presence, and how far they could agree on its appearance.

Auditory experience was not rated very highly in the 1970s because decades of telephone familiarity had made it so commonplace. If I had only heard the angel speaking and not seen it, then I might have dismissed the experience as "hearing voices", some sort of schizophrenic hallucination.

Even though nearly every home back then had a colour television as well as a phone, visual presence was still highly valued. The videophone was something people talked about, but the technology did not take off until the arrival of the smartphone many years later. Nowadays, however, visual manifestation is too commonplace to be exciting, because we can conjure the real-time visual image of friends and relatives all around the world via the internet. This is still interesting, but I am aware of the beginning of a backlash: that a growing number of people are finding this visual and auditory contact unsatisfactory. They long for a return to the more rounded feeling of being in the presence of the other and sharing physical space. This is something much closer to what I experienced at the end of the operation.

I can see the value of my experience better now, although for some people the real test of this type of operation would be whether it ends with a visible appearance of a tangible angel that, in the course of one week, introduces the practitioner to a hierarchy of spirits and teaches how to control them. Anything less would be a failure. Such a reader would be disappointed by the fact that I ended with a significant absence rather than a refulgent presence, and I subsequently addressed the demons as internal states over a longer period.

But my experience did permit me to retain some belief in the possibility of a tangible angel, because there were signs of how much more dramatic the operation could be if I had been able to withdraw completely from normal life. I did sense a powerful and awesome energy in the first days when I was on my own, and again when I moved into my uninhabited flat in Winchester.

There were plenty of remarkable occurrences of the sort that would convince a magical student, but not a scientist who could easily dismiss them as coincidence. In terms of coincidence, there were many things that happened during and after the operation that were eerie enough to make my scalp tingle, but I have not recorded them because I do not greatly value other people's lists of amazing coincidences. I see them as messages to the person who experiences them, messages that others may misinterpret, and they are often not understood by the recipient. Joel Biroco, author of *World of Dust, The Mandate of Heaven* and many Kaos pamphlets, likened them to footnote markers in the script of life, where no related footnote can be found.

There was only one physical manifestation that defied explanation, and that was the big tree that shook in the night before 15 September. But even that did not take place under laboratory conditions. For someone who wants to perform Abramelin for the sake of physical manifestations that could "prove science wrong", then ultimately the whole operation would have to take place under laboratory conditions—and I do not think such conditions would encourage spiritual progress. I have explained in my other writings that "laboratory conditions" means conditions developed in order to exclude anything paranormal.

So my advice to anyone who considers it vital to attain the full monty—angels, demons, bells, whistles, and nothing less—is as follows:

1. Do it in isolation, away from civilisation or any "normalising" conditions, and cut yourself off as completely as you can.
2. Instead of practicing towards silence and emptiness, as I did, you should focus on practices that build up the imagination and the body of light, and develop them to become as vivid and tangible as possible.
3. Note that Tenzin Palmo carried isolation to the extreme—a cave in the Himalayas—but she too came towards emptiness. So isolation

alone is not the whole answer, there must also be aspiration towards manifestation rather than emptiness.
4. However far you achieve isolation, the operation might still end prematurely. Even in a lonely cave, Tenzin Palmo was stopped by bureaucracy. So I recommend taking my precaution, of writing into the vow a condition that "overwhelming outside opposition will be interpreted as a message from the angel to cease". Then such a stoppage would not count as failure.

## Ground zero

Even if the reader is not planning to do this operation and is only reading out of curiosity, it is still possible that my conclusion might be a disappointment. It might be taken as confirmation that Abramelin "does not work". So it is necessary to say a little more about my aspiration towards the unmanifest, as opposed to manifestation. To what extent is this a cop-out?

Iamblichus, in his commentary on the mysteries, points out something surprising about the pagan religion. For all the wonder and richness of polytheism, there is a tradition that places a "higher" deity above all others, and the temple to that higher deity is a bare and silent space. So, as in eastern ideas about the ultimate nothingness, the Tao that cannot be described, or whatever, even the lush landscape of pagan tradition inclines towards the notion of an ineffable ultimate that lies beyond.

The cabalistic Tree of Life suggests three veils of the unmanifest beyond Kether, the first sephirah. Crowley himself claimed that "the highest shrines are empty" and there are many references from his Buddhist period that support the idea of an ultimate nothingness.

Ultimate nothingness, emptiness or the unmanifest is common to many religions and philosophies around the world. Zivorad Mihajlovic Slavinski, in his book *Aspectics,* writes: "Most systems of Oriental and Perennial philosophy talk about Emptiness or the Great Unmanifest as the pre-source of the whole manifested universe. But those teachings are always and without exception purely theoretical." He goes on to contrast that with his very practical approach to working with troublesome "aspects" of one's self—analogous to those I described as "personal demons" in my *Little Book of Demons.*

I will not attempt to describe his process in detail—it is very effective and should be read in full—but the essence of it is to dialogue with the aspect, asking what it is trying to achieve—i.e. its "goal". On receiving a response, you then ask it what is its "higher goal". For example: a demon that causes a person to stutter or be speechless in critical meetings might say that it wants to stop the victim speaking. Its higher goal might then be to silence the victim before he makes a fool of himself. This starts a chain of dialogue that, according to the author (and my experience) tends towards a point where there is no higher goal—i.e. towards nothingness. He then takes the aspect into a direct experience of that nothingness, before working back down the chain towards a healing or solution of the original problem.

So, after six months of aspiring to a state of silent emptiness, I might be expected to have welcomed that final non-manifestation with open arms. Instead I felt confused and not a little disappointed. For seven hours I was in the oratory first in silence and then for four hours drowning thoughts with a chant of "God's will be done" while under attack from a series of personal vices.

Forty years later, during the course of preparing this diary for publication, I read Jozef Karika's essay on Choronzon[1] and it brought back to me the significance of these associations. Karika suggests that the "Real HGA" (Holy Guardian Angel) should not be nice, but a "terrible entity—the nothingness in [the] human, his abyss" and he suggests that confrontation with Choronzon, the demon of the abyss, would be a sign of success in the operation. He quotes Crowley's words from *The Vision and the Voice*: "For Choronzon feareth of all things concentration and silence: he therefore who should command him should will in silence ..."

Am I to understand that Choronzon is an essential aspect in the move from the unmanifest into manifestation? Was this what was on my mind when I produced the cod-gnostic text *Liber Salpinctis Per Tenebras Sonantis*?[2] It went like this:

> NOTHING
> There is no beginning.
> There was no word.
> Beyond and throughout the Everbecoming standeth Vacuum.
> Behold the surface of the waters—is it water?
> Water it is not.
> Is it air?

---

[1]Jozef Karika: *Liber 767 vel Boeingus*, Megalithica Books, 2009.
[2]Published in *The Satanist's Diary*, Aquarian Arrow (No. 13), Spring 1982.

Air it is not.
Verily the surface is neither air, nor water, for it existeth not—excepting that there is some created being to conceive it.

NOTHING IS
It is not, yet we see in it a being. Yea, we see our very selves in reflection. This being, which is not, we name Vacuum.

NOTHING IS NOT
And when this Nothingness seeketh to explore his Nothingness then doth the surface move, curl and seek its own reflection. It reacheth to embrace itself.

CREATION
The wave breaks, Nothingness is divided against itself, the surface becomes a frenzy of foam.
Created Being.

UNDERSTANDING
Oh the eternal agony of Vacuum.
The endless quest to perceive its Nothingness begetteth an endless accident of Creation.
Created Being standeth apart from Vacuum—yet is all-pervaded by Vacuum. So also is the foam not the surface, yet an endless division of that surface.
Oh the eternal agony of Vacuum—the agony of impotence ever-mocked by the virulent seethings of Created Being.

WISDOM
Vacuum is old and bitter, Created Being is young and lusty.
Vacuum is uncertain in his Nothingness, Created Being is arrogant in her Existence.

When writing that, I had this impression of a transition from emptiness to manifestation that demanded an explosive effort, a rage for manifestation that shattered a featureless surface non-membrane into a frenzy of foam. Might this be the essence of Choronzon? Crowley said "Choronzon is dispersion", not in the sense of something that disperses into nothingness but a splitting into manyness.

In those last days I had achieved a level of silent emptiness that I had never known before or since and yet, looking back after all this time, I realised that there was still part of me that wanted something to happen. I was divided. Choronzon may have been commanded by my silence, but it would not go away.

Last week I watched the movie *A Dark Song*. It is about someone performing a retirement inspired by Abramelin—although for cinematic purposes the process had been embellished with a lot of extra symbolism and ritual that makes Abramelin seem a bit tame in comparison. (It made me want to try their version.) Someone behind this production knows their magic—unlike most occult movies. I could not help identifying with the frustrated heroine who kept asking why nothing was happening!

If I live another lifetime that allows me to attempt this operation another time, I hope I first make up my mind what I will be aiming for. Will I aspire to manifestation or the void?

As I write these final words in my seventy-fourth year, it feels that we live in complex and chaotic times. Thoughts of silence, peace and a sense of completion are far more attractive to me now than any ability to make more things happen.

www.ingramcontent.com/pod-product-compliance
Ingram Content Group UK Ltd.
Pitfield, Milton Keynes, MK11 3LW, UK
UKHW021613220126
467229UK00012B/311